The End of the Charter Revolution

THE END
OF THE
CHARTER
REVOLUTION

Looking Back
from the
New Normal

Peter J. McCormick

UNIVERSITY OF TORONTO PRESS

Library and Archives Canada Cataloguing in Publication

McCormick, Peter J., author
    The end of the Charter revolution : looking back from the new normal /
Peter J. McCormick.

Includes bibliographical references and index.
Issued in print and electronic formats.
ISBN 978-1-4426-0833-7 (bound).—ISBN 978-1-4426-0639-5 (pbk.).—
ISBN 978-1-4426-0640-1 (pdf).—ISBN 978-1-4426-0641-8 (epub)

    1. Canada. Canadian Charter of Rights and Freedoms. 2. Canada. Canadian Charter of
Rights and Freedoms—Cases. I. Title.

KE4381.5.M395 2014   342.7108′5   C2014-902301-4
KF4483.C519M395 2014   C2014-902302-2

We welcome comments and suggestions regarding any aspect of our publications—please
feel free to contact us at news@utphighereducation.com or visit our Internet site at www
.utppublishing.com.

North America
5201 Dufferin Street
North York, Ontario, Canada, M3H 5T8

2250 Military Road
Tonawanda, New York, USA, 14150

ORDERS PHONE: 1-800-565-9523
ORDERS FAX: 1-800-221-9985
ORDERS E-MAIL: utpbooks@utpress.utoronto.ca

UK, Ireland, and continental Europe
NBN International
Estover Road, Plymouth, PL6 7PY, UK
ORDERS PHONE: 44 (0) 1752 202301
ORDERS FAX: 44 (0) 1752 202333
ORDERS E-MAIL:
enquiries@nbninternational.com

Every effort has been made to contact copyright holders; in the event of an error or
omission, please notify the publisher.

The University of Toronto Press acknowledges the financial support for its publishing
activities of the Government of Canada through the Canada Book Fund.

Printed in the United States of America.

For Lorraine,
Who puts the music in my life.

CONTENTS

ILLUSTRATIONS

FIGURES

TABLES

ACKNOWLEDGEMENTS

I should like to thank four people for their help.

The first is Michael Harrison, from the University of Toronto Press, who sat in my office one day a couple of years ago and casually asked how my courses were going. His reward for such politeness was an extended grumble about how much harder it was to teach Charter law now that the novelty has worn off, the big questions are all answered, and the news headlines no longer remind students how exciting and current things are—at the end of which Michael simply said, "That sounds like a book to me." Quite so, and I had a formal proposal in his email inbox by the time he got back to Toronto, but I am not sure the grumble would have become a book without the nudge.

The second is Rainer Knopff of the University of Calgary, who was supposed to be an anonymous assessor who would briefly say whether or not the manuscript was publishable, but who switched instead into pen-in-hand professor on the hunt for things that were not quite right, of which he found a fair number; and he voluntarily relinquished his anonymity to allow me the chance to argue back. Some were just "oops" mistakes, some were unclear ideas that needed tightening, some were points on which we still disagree but I gained from knowing how to focus my argument. This book is much the better for Rainer's generosity, which is not to say that the arguments won't resume next time we meet.

The third is Beth McAuley and her assistant Melissa MacAulay at The Editing Company, who patiently went through every line to accommodate the style guide that I had completely ignored. They also tried (not the first people to do so) to curb my strange notion that longer and more complex sentences are always better than short direct ones, that semi-colons are an endangered species that need our help, and that no page is complete without several sets of brackets. They are also ferocious folks with strict ideas about deadlines, which professors tend to forget or ignore.

Lastly, although of course I really mean especially, is my wife Lorraine, a.k.a. "The Duchess." She is actually a musician (voice, guitar, piano, handbells, harp, recorder) who nonetheless listens patiently to endless drafts of articles and chapters about courts and judges, from time to time subjecting me to that most devastating of criticisms, "I didn't understand that." I am endlessly grateful for her patience and her support.

For the errors and infelicities that remain, I take full responsibility. Unless I can somehow blame Rainer.

INTRODUCTION

The Canadian Charter of Rights and Freedoms became an entrenched part of the Canadian constitution on April 17, 1982. It was, to put it mildly, a game-changer of the first order. Canadian politics has never been the same. The Supreme Court has never been the same—anyone who tried to call it a "quiet court" today (and this was once the serious non-tongue-in-cheek title of a law journal article)[1] would be laughed out of the room. Any government that thought the story was over once they had passed a law or introduced a new policy would be making a potentially serious mistake. The Supreme Court is now a national institution of the first order, and it is the Charter that put it there.

The Charter has carried the courts, and the Supreme Court in particular, into the heart of many of the biggest controversies and the hottest issues in Canadian politics. The biggest surprise has been the way the courts rose to the challenge. Given the strength of English-rather-than-American traditions, given the Court's unimaginative-to-the-point-of-invisibility timidity with the 1960 Diefenbaker Bill of Rights, given its

---

1 Ronald I. Cheffins, "The Supreme Court of Canada: The Quiet Court in an Unquiet Country," *Osgoode Hall Law Journal* 4 (1966): 259.

failure to strike a boldly Canadian jurisprudence after the end of appeals to the Judicial Committee—given all these things, one might have expected at best a slow start, and at worst barely a start at all, to the remarkable challenge of an entrenched Charter of Rights. Quite the contrary; the Dickson Court tackled it with a real will, not only striking down federal and provincial legislation right out of the gate, not only setting aside as irrelevant even recent pre-Charter precedent, not only tackling the hottest and most socially divisive issues like abortion, but doing so in a way that laid down the foundations while deliberately leaving things open for continuing judicial action in the future.

The Lamer Court followed up with genuine panache, repeatedly using the Charter to change the parameters of government action on a bewildering variety of issues; if abortion was the seize-the-nettle moment for the Dickson Court, gay rights was the comparable headline-grabber for the Lamer Court. The Supreme Court has long been theoretically one of the major institutions of Canadian national government; in a dramatic way, the Lamer Court seized the opportunity to make it unambiguously so, in fact. "Negotiating in the shadow of law" has been a way of understanding how courts influence private disputes even when those disputes do not actually go in front of a judge; "legislating in the shadow of the Supreme Court's charter" is clearly the world that governments discovered they were living in during the 1990s. The Charter was not the only vehicle for the Court's assumption of centre stage—Aboriginal rights were of major significance as well—but it was certainly a very large part of the story. Canadians are more aware of the Supreme Court than ever before; and concerns about the extent of that power and the implications of how the Court has used it have emerged in the academic literature and in election campaigns.

No Canadian who followed the news could have failed to take note of this new institutional development, and this new constitutional factor. The Court had its critics as well as its fans, but it did a remarkably effective job of husbanding and augmenting its stock of what Gibson et al. have referred to as "diffuse support."[2] There were, arguably, only a handful of occasions when it came close to dividing its normal supporters

---

2 James L. Gibson, Gregory Caldeira, and Vanessa Baird, "On the Legitimacy of National High Courts," *American Political Science Review* 86 (1997): 343.

and squandering the carefully accumulated reservoirs of good will; the list would include *Seaboyer*[3] (the rape shield case), *Sharpe*[4] (the kiddie-porn case), *Daviault*[5] (the drunkenness defence case), and possibly *Chaoulli*[6] (which compromised the medicare debate by mandating private health insurance). That is a remarkable record for a Court that was facing such a complex string of challenges, in a country that was more intrigued by the idea of an entrenched Charter than really familiar with what that would look like in practice. That is in itself a tribute to the Court's explanatory and persuasive educational role, aided of course by a generally supportive political elite, mass media, and academy. And of course every successful boundary-shifting decision, every decision from which governments backed down, every suggestion which governments meekly accommodated, simply added to the diffuse support that the Court was accumulating. It was a remarkable and steadily building drama, amazing to watch.

I followed these developments particularly closely, because my teaching duties included a senior level political science course on constitutional law—which actually became two separate courses once the Charter decisions became so numerous that they could no longer be squeezed into the classes that were left after the federalism cases. Of the two, the Charter course was by far the most exciting to teach and drew the higher enrollments. Every year, I would introduce the Court by saying, "We are following the cutting edge of Canadian politics, not studying dusty old decisions engaging judges and political leaders you have never heard of, but playing off today's news headlines. Make sure you keep up with current events, because the Supreme Court is often part of those events, and the planned lecture schedule is always subject to disruption if the Court does something to make last year's or last month's lecture notes obsolete." For many years, the Supreme Court lived up to this billing, giving me the headline decisions that kept me scrambling to stay up with the latest developments in Charter law, bringing the students into class anxious to discuss the decision that had been handed down the previous Thursday.

---

3 *R. v. Seaboyer; R. v. Gayme*, [1991] 2 S.C.R. 577.

4 *R. v. Sharpe*, [2001] 1 S.C.R. 45; 2001 SCC 2.

5 *R. v. Daviault*, [1994] 3 S.C.R. 63.

6 *Chaoulli v. Quebec (Attorney General)*, [2005] 1 S.C.R. 791; 2005 SCC 35.

The Supreme Court was the best show in town; the Charter presented it with its marquee events; and I was like the movie critic during that time of year when the major studios release their summer blockbusters.

But for several years, this opening spiel has been ringing hollow. There have been whole semesters where the Charter course lecture schedule remains largely undented by current events, when last year's lecture notes and PowerPoints will do just fine. My list of cases for the "summarize and explain a recent Supreme Court decision" assignment has to compromise currency by reaching further back for a list of reasonable length, like a water well chasing a shrinking water table. When there are Supreme Court decisions on the Charter, they tend to be detail-shufflers rather than groundbreakers, interesting to the initiated but eye-glazing to those who are still getting up to speed. I have also been surprised how often this dwindling number of interesting cases involved slightly (and sometimes not-so-slightly) surprising setbacks for the rights claimants. And of course the rhetoric of "changed Canadian politics forever" rings hollow when this all happened years before any of the current crop of students were even born; they have never known a time when there was not a Charter in place, never known a time when the major iconic Charter decisions were not an established part of the political and legislative background. My course is no longer the current hit parade; it is the golden oldies show, a trip down memory lane for those who weren't paying attention when those songs were hits.

As far as the Charter is concerned, it would seem that the heroic age is over; the pedestrian age is upon us.

On reflection, though, why should we be surprised? Go to the bookstore, buy a new book by your favourite author, and start to read—and one day, even if you have rationed the chapters and circled back to read the best parts a second time, you will find yourself turning the last page. Move to a new city, and after a few years there are no longer surprises lying around corners you never noticed before, no new artsy neighbourhoods you haven't investigated, no intriguing music clubs you absolutely have to check out, no museums or art galleries you haven't explored. Similarly, get yourself a new entrenched Charter of Rights, and after a while all the big issues have collected an elaborate conceptual and procedural gloss, and the possible collisions and conflicts between different pairs or combinations of rights have been addressed, and even those increasingly secondary issues that have not been directly answered are surrounded by doctrinal neighbourhoods that already provide a good part of the answer. Revisit *this* to clear up some emerging confusion; reconsider *that* because you may have gotten off on the wrong foot—but sooner or later you reach a point where the mystery has been exhausted, where the once-exotic has become the now-routine. For a time, we used to say: the Court hasn't really addressed the question of freedom of religion; this last decade, they did. Then we said, freedom of association still remains a bit of a question mark; but during the same decade, this has become travelled ground. Year by year, the Supreme Court has put check marks in all the big boxes, and most of the middle-sized boxes as well; and even if precedent does not hold the iron grip that it once did (at least in theory), it nonetheless constitutes a significant constraint on the Court's future range of motion.

This is of course a little too simple, too reductionist; there will always be little islands of uncertainty, or points of difference between the judges that adroit lawyers can turn to their advantage, or modest rethinking by particular set of judges that results in some degree of circling back for a self-described clarification that is actually a minor adjustment, but this is no longer the high drama of the early days, and the surprises are small, few and far between. On the one hand, the law aims at certainty, at making sure that as many questions about legal obligations and restrictions as possible have obvious and objective (if not always easy) answers; on the other hand, this clearing away of genuine uncertainty and questions without definite answers simply opens the space for new controversies and questions to arise—pushing the border of uncertainty out can never be the same thing as making it go away altogether, and the complexity of issues that can arise as legal ideas impact an evolving complex society defies smooth generalization. But the basic point remains: the courts work steadily to reduce genuine uncertainty about major legal issues, working down some notional checklist to provide the answers around which people and governments can organize their activities with some real predictability. The really big questions are gradually answered, and then there are fewer big questions remaining.

This thought is hardly new. Chief Justice Beverley McLachlin has said as much on several occasions. When she was first appointed, she talked about the fact that the "heavy lifting" on the Charter had already been done; and, interviewed 10 years later, she repeated the thought that "most of the major battles have already been fought" leaving the Court to deal with "subtle interpretations." "In [the Charter's] early years, the court did a huge amount of very good work laying down the basis," she said. "We are just building on that. To my surprise, there are new Charter issues that come once in a while—but not to the same extent."[7]

Similarly, Justice Moldaver (then of the Ontario Court of Appeal, more recently of the Supreme Court of Canada) suggested in a speech in 2005 that with respect to criminal law:

> Most of the Charter issues that you are likely to encounter on a day-to-day basis have been thoroughly litigated, all the way to the Supreme Court of Canada. By and large, the governing principles are now firmly established.
> And where that is so, the time for experimentation is over.
> It's finished.
> It's done.[8]

This book is therefore an extended gloss on these same ideas: the "heavy lifting" is over, the major battles have been fought, the governing principles are clearly established, the concern now is with subtle details, and it will be a bit of a surprise when something new and significant arises for the Court to deal with. The Charter has changed many things in Canadian politics and Canadian law; but when we say this, we speak primarily about yesterday and we do so in the past tense. Speaking in the present tense for today, and in the future tense for tomorrow, there will be much less to say about change and transformation—not "nothing," to be sure, but most definitely "less."

In this book, I will tell a story about the Charter, about the big ripples that have gradually but steadily died away such that the surface of the pond is now almost smooth. I will take this story through the three Chief Justiceships that have created the waves, and then (I will suggest) let them damp out. This will involve selecting a small number of cases

---

7 "10 Years as CJ for McLachlin," *Globe and Mail*, January 7, 2010, A1.

8 Cited in James Stribopolous, "Has Everything Been Decided? Certainty, the Charter and Criminal Justice," *Supreme Court Law Review* 34 (2nd series) (2006): 381. I should add that the Stribopolous article is a vigorous rebuttal of the idea.

from the much larger caseload, and I acknowledge that they will be cases that demonstrate my point rather than a completely conscientious cross-section, but I do not believe that I am distorting the story or misrepresenting the trend.

The Charter represents a very large change in our constitutional order, and the story of its impact on Canadian law and society is a complex one. As when the blind men encountered the elephant, there are a number of true (or at least not-false) stories to be told, depending on whether the particular blind man has found the trunk, or the ear, or the leg; since I am arguing for the end of the Charter revolution, I guess I have the tail. But just as we can learn something real and objective and beyond question about the elephant by putting it on a truck scale, so we can establish solid and objective things about the Supreme Court and the Charter era by drawing on empirical data, and this is what I will be doing in Chapter 6. Some of the possible stories will hold up better than others in the light of that empirical evidence, and I will be trying to persuade readers that mine holds up very well indeed, that the empirical data supports my story of a trajectory of Charter interpretation and application that has now reached a different and much less dramatic phase.

CHAPTER ONE

TOWARDS THE CHARTER

The year 1949 marked an important date in the history of the Supreme Court of Canada—it was the end of appeals beyond the Supreme Court itself to a "higher court" in the form of the Judicial Committee of the United Kingdom of Great Britain and Northern Ireland, which had, until that point, been the "real" Supreme Court for Canada. (Parliament marked the occasion by increasing the size of the Supreme Court itself from seven judges to nine, with one new appointment from Quebec and one from Ontario—Fauteux and Cartwright, respectively, both of whom subsequently served as Chief Justice.) The "end of appeals" had been actively promoted by the legal profession and the academic legal community as a "coming of age" for Canada and its judiciary, but the first decade of this new era was a profound disappointment. The Supreme Court repeatedly declined the opportunity to pronounce itself free of Judicial Committee precedents and generally followed the same style, and the same willing acceptance of English authority, as before. Then professor (later, Supreme Court Justice and Chief Justice) Bora Laskin famously deplored this as the English captivity.[1]

---

1 See Bora Laskin, "The Supreme Court of Canada: A Final Court of and for Canadians," *Canada Bar Review* 29 (1951): 1038. This famous comment explains the

FALSE DAWN: THE SUPREME COURT IN THE 1950S

The apparent exception to this refusal to chart a new course was a string of decisions regarding civil rights that seemed to mark the dawning of a new era. There were five cases in this string, nicely spread out through the decade so as to occupy the odd-numbered years, all arising from Quebec, and all but one involving the Jehovah's Witnesses. The Court signalled the importance of this string in a highly visible way—all were heard by the Full Court of nine judges. This was unusual for a Court that heard almost all of its cases in panels of five or seven judges (and, even more attention-getting, one of the string started as a seven-judge panel and was then re-argued before the full nine). All five involved a challenge of government legislation or action on the grounds that individual rights had been violated; in all five cases, the challengers were generally success-ful,[2] although only one was unanimous.

Today, if we were talking about a string of cases building towards some substantive new principle of law, we would take a number of things for granted. First, we would assume that there were a block of judges on the Court supporting the development, possibly over coherent and persisting opposition, and that this block was growing by winning over individual opponents or by recruiting new appointees. Second, we would expect that each case in the string explicitly built upon the ideas in the earlier cases, such that the new doctrine was clearer and quite possibly more extensive at the end of the string. However, as I signalled by starting this paragraph with the word "today," this is an anachronistic expectation for the pre-Laskin Court, which operated rather differently, and it is simultaneously an overreading of the alleged "string." As the "False Dawn" title of this section implies, the sun wasn't really coming up after all.

---

title of Ian Bushnell's major history of the body, *The Captive Court: A Study of the Supreme Court of Canada* (Kingston: McGill-Queen's University Press, 1992). Fittingly, it was Bora Laskin as Chief Justice who later declared that Judicial Committee deci-sions were no longer binding precedent on the Supreme Court in *Re: Agricultural Marketing Act*, [1978] 2 S.C.R. 1198.

2 Although the *Saumur* case did not end all that well—the legislature promptly repassed the offending legislation, and Saumur's challenge of the new legislation was rejected by the Supreme Court in 1964 on procedural grounds. See *Saumur et al. v. Procureur général du Québec*, [1964] S.C.R. 252.

The first now-surprising feature of these decisions is that all but one of them were *seriatim* decisions. This describes a practice in which each judge on the panel wrote up complete and separate reasons, these being combined as votes to generate an outcome with the result that some of the sets of reasons (the outvoted ones) became dissents—except that when they were being written there was not a judgement of the Court to which they were responding, and they did not know they were dissents. By the same token, there was no unified voice for the majority whose votes drive an outcome; the modern emphasis on a clearly designated judgement of the Court around which minority reasons organize themselves emerged only later.[3] Instead, each judge had written his own somewhat parallel but often idiosyncratic reasons. This made it more difficult than we would expect today to work out the core precedent-generating reasons on which doctrine could build.[4]

The second surprising feature about all five decisions is the way that they managed, on the face of it, not to be decisions about "rights" in any direct sense: three were decisions about the federal/provincial division of legislative jurisdiction; one was about the correct textual interpretation of a federal statute; and the last invoked a principle that has been part of English common law since the thirteenth century. This is summarized in Table 1.1. To be sure, when the constitution does not have an entrenched set of rights, a Court with some rights-consciousness may be obliged to achieve desirable outcomes in oblique ways; it is also possible, however, that the camouflage goes right through, such that there is no deeper level at all.[5]

The third surprise would be the absence of a citation trail. In the modern style, we expect later cases in a sequence to build on the earlier ones, and to do so in an explicit way by citing them. Citation does not necessarily indicate mere ditto marks, and later cases may expand or refine (or retreat from) the ideas in the earlier ones, but this process creates a

---

3 My best guess of the year is 1969, which means that we owe the innovation in decision-presentation and report to Chief Justice Cartwright.

4 See Claire L'Heureux-Dubé, "The Length and Plurality of Supreme Court of Canada Decisions," *Alberta Law Review* 28 (1989–90): 581.

5 The casual unanimous dismissal of what we would today see as "*Saumur 2*" is completely consistent with this.

TABLE 1.1 Issues and Grounds of the Major Rights Cases of the 1950s

CASE AND CITATION	ISSUE	GROUNDS
Boucher v. The King [1951] S.C.R. 265	Seditious libel in pamphlets	Interpretation of federal statute
Saumur v. City of Quebec [1953] 2 S.C.R. 299	Distributing pamphlets w/o police permission	Federal/provincial division of legislative authority
Birks v. City of Montreal [1955] S.C.R. 799	Closing of stores on holidays	Federal/provincial division of legislative authority
Switzman v. Elbing [1957] S.C.R. 285	"Padlock law" re communism	Federal/provincial division of legislative authority
Roncarelli v. Duplessis [1959] S.C.R. 121	Premier revoking liquor license	English common law principles/officials need clear authority to act

TABLE 1.2 Citation String for the Major Rights Cases of the 1950s

	SAUMUR	BIRKS	SWITZMAN	RONCARELLI	TOTAL
Boucher	0/7	0/3	0/8	3/7	3/25
Saumur	–	1/3	1/8	0/7	2/18
Birks		–	0/8	0/7	0/15
Switzman			–	0/7	0/7
TOTAL	0/7	1/6	1/24	3/28	5/65

"thick meaning" of precedent whereby initial suggestions are firmed up and early hints are clarified. There is no such precedential trail, however, through the alleged block of rights cases in the 1950s. Table 1.2 indicates the number of sets of reasons in each of the cases, and the number of these different sets of reasons that cited each of the earlier cases that were available for citation. (Being the first in the string, *Boucher*, of course, had no earlier cases to cite; and, being at the end of the string, *Roncarelli* had no later cases that could cite it.) Had every set of reasons in every later case cited every available earlier case, the total count would have been 65; the actual total is five. As citation pyramids go, this is unimpressive.

This just makes the point that I will cash in later: this was not the Court, nor did it have the organized decision-making style, or the disciplined citation practice, to generate a rights revolution. The next section, on the fate of the Diefenbaker Bill of Rights, will be a sustained demonstration of this. It is not that courts that are so-minded cannot generate rights from rather unpromising material—the High Court of Australia during the 1990s showed that they can—but simply that this particular Court was not so-minded. Creating an appropriate Court was as important as entrenchment itself to generate the Charter revolution.

FALSE START: THE BILL OF RIGHTS

STEPPING STONE OR CUL-DE-SAC?

On the face of it, we seem to have a simple logical progression: a rights-conscious Supreme Court blazing the trail in the 1950s, a statutory bill of rights in the 1960s, and an entrenched Charter of Rights in the 1980s—a simple one-two-three, with each step building on what went before. On the face of it, this seems a perfectly plausible account that fits well with Canada's evolutionary-not-revolutionary pattern of constitutional development. But I have already discounted the myth of the judicial explorations of the 1950s; I will now defend my serious reservations about the "Charter on the cheap" or "Charter in embryo" vision of the Diefenbaker Bill of Rights of the 1960s.[6]

This is one of those stories that is hard not to tell backwards. We are a bit like somebody who is reading a murder mystery but has already looked at the last page; the story has been made more fun by an intermediate chapter that (for the conventional "one chapter at a time" types) has gently steered us off track. We know that the outcome is going to be a strong Charter, entrenched in the constitution, robustly enforced and expanded by a solidly "on-side" Court, intending to render offending legislation null

---

6 Perhaps the book that comes closest is Christopher Maclennan's *Toward the Charter: Canadians and the Demand for a National Bill of Rights 1929–1960* (Kingston: McGill-Queen's University Press, 2004)—but notice that even the title surrenders to what I have just said we need not to do, which is to allow the Bill of Rights to vanish under the shadow of the Charter. The book itself is curiously ambivalent, sometimes examining the Bill and its emergence on its own terms, sometimes presenting it as an introductory transition to the Charter.

and void; we are anxious to get on with it, and frustrated that Diefenbaker gave us such a small piece of this highly attractive pie. But we forget that the menu in the 1950s and 1960s was rather different and that politicians and the public had a different sense of what counted as attractive (or even as feasible). Even the American model that we now think of ourselves as following, the "Warren Court" that has so strongly directed everyone's vision and expectations (or fears) about activist national high courts, was really just emerging in the 1960s, and was not in any simple sense "there" to be copied or emulated for a prime minister whose majority victory dated to 1958. In any event, Diefenbaker's preferred models were English, not American—this was, after all, the prime minister who issued a stirring invocation of the Commonwealth in an attempt to persuade the United Kingdom not to enter the European Community in 1963. We should not be thinking "Canada's Warren Court" (this is more plausible for Trudeau), but rather "twentieth-century Magna Carta."

John Diefenbaker was an unlikely prime minister; even now, his name stands out as the only prime minister who was clearly neither British nor French. "Renegade in Power"—the title of Peter Newman's celebrated biography of Diefenbaker in office—nicely catches not just Diefenbaker's background but his style and his impact.[7] After a narrow minority win in 1957, he won one of the greatest landslides in Canadian history,[8] although his record in office never lived up to these initial expectations. His slogan of "unhyphenated Canadianism" and his deep love of English political and legal traditions made him an unfortunate choice to deal with the emergence of the Quiet Revolution in Quebec, and his stand on nuclear weapons not only led to a major cabinet revolt but seriously disrupted Canada–US relations. From minority to landslide to minority to opposition in barely six years, his was a truly meteoric career, and his remarkable effectiveness as a campaigner denied the Liberals a majority for several more elections. His legacy included the redrawing of the political map of Canada; the propensity of Western Canada (and especially

---

7 Peter C. Newman, *Renegade in Power: The Diefenbaker Years* (Toronto: McClelland and Stewart, 1963).

8 Although political scientists continue to argue about whether his was slightly larger or slightly smaller than Brian Mulroney's 1984 landslide, a close call that depends on exactly how you define your criteria.

the Prairies) to vote Conservative was very much his doing, as was, less fortunately, the lasting Conservative weakness in Quebec. He also left us the Diefenbaker Bill of Rights, something to which he turned his attention from the very beginning of his period in office.

In terms of modern expectations, there are two serious flaws to the Diefenbaker Bill of Rights, both following from the fact that it took the form of a normal piece of federal legislation. First, the Bill only affected federal legislation and federal government action; anything to do with the provincial governments was completely untouched, even though the 1950s string of cases had all involved provincial government actions. Second, it gave the Bill an ambivalent status vis-à-vis other federal legislation, especially later legislation—the general principle is that Parliament has a right to change its mind, so that newer legislation generally prevails over older legislation if the two directly conflict.[9] Further, there is no clear procedure for bringing measures before the Court on a declaratory basis; if, for example, you objected to a new statute or a new section of an old one, you could only challenge it by finding a police officer who would charge you for violating it.[10] By contrast, under the Charter, one can make an application for a declaration of invalidity without the inconvenience of being charged or the risk of suffering that penalty for an unsuccessful challenge—the recent case of *Bedford*,[11] which struck down several of the Criminal Code sections on prostitution, was initiated by just such an application, not by criminal charges. Finally, there are no enforcement provisions—that is, no clear statement of what happens— should legislation violate these rights, and certainly no indication that the normal and reasonably automatic consequence is for the legislation to be rendered null and void. Under the Bill of Rights, the courts are only directed to "construe and apply" federal legislation so as not to violate the indicated rights, and even that obstacle could be bypassed should

9 The rule is actually not quite that simple, because there are other factors that can be brought to bear—for example, more specific or focused legislation generally prevails over more general legislation—but "newer overrides older" is one of the stronger presumptions.

10 When Alberta passed its seatbelt legislation, for example, I remember news stories about people driving around Calgary with their seatbelts deliberately dragging on the ground in the hopes of attracting a traffic violation ticket.

11 *Canada (Attorney General) v. Bedford* 2013 SCC 72.

Parliament invoke an early version of the "notwithstanding" clause that appears in section 2 of the Bill.[12]

One feature of the Bill of Rights that did imply more direct action, and that has not been carried on into the newer Charter of Rights, was the requirement that the minister of justice "flag" every piece of new government legislation that infringed upon the protected rights. This is the sort of thing that, at first glance, seems a pre-emptively good idea, but does not really survive closer scrutiny. I will try to dismantle it now, the more so because the basic idea, if not the specific operationalization, survives in the Charter's "notwithstanding" provision.

What these measures presuppose is what we might call the "big obvious rights" approach. It encourages us to think of rights as things that carry highly visible labels for all to see, buzzing loudly if some government action bumps into them. It follows, then, that a government could never infringe upon these rights accidentally or innocently, but only deliberately. This in turn means that it is not really difficult to know ahead of time that a piece of legislation is going to be problematic (although governments that are up to no good might pretend that it is). Under the Bill of Rights, we want the minister of justice to stand up in the House of Commons as the legislation is introduced and say, "We know we are violating rights but we think it is important to pass this legislation anyway." In the override provision in the Charter of Rights, we want governments to admit within legislation as it is being drafted that it needs to be shielded from Charter scrutiny (and even expect them to know which Charter right is involved), which can only mean that they know full well they are violating a right.

But protected rights do not work this way. For one thing, their boundaries are necessarily fuzzy, set out in constitutional poetry rather than quasi-statutory detail. Even more importantly, once rights become potent assets to deploy in constraining governmental activity, a wide variety of actors have a powerful incentive to find ways to present their interests or demands in terms of rights, to find novel ways of bringing their claims under a rights umbrella. Governments can be genuinely surprised at the uses to which some rights can sometimes be put. Taking this provision

---

12 According to Hogg, this exemption clause was invoked only once, in connection with the FLQ "October crisis" in Quebec in 1970. See Peter Hogg, *Constitutional Law of Canada. 2012 Student Edition* (Toronto: Carswell, 2012), section 35.3a note 15.

seriously would mean that governments would be introducing almost every single piece of legislation with the proviso "this may (or may not) generate Court challenges in the future under the Bill/Charter of Rights, and those challenges may (or may not) be successful." If they did so, however, this would mean either that the government is voluntarily tarnishing its reputation or that the Bill/Charter is becoming routinized and trivialized.

Rights, whether legislated under the Bill of Rights (and whether the Bill of Rights has merely statutory or quasi-constitutional status) or entrenched in the Charter, usually have a "big obvious" core, as well as a not-at-all-obvious penumbra that will be explored (from the one side) by parties seeking to promote their interests through these devices and (from the other side) by governments who have regulatory and policy goals to advance. This will also be explored by judges who want to deal with these problems in a way that provides a stable basis for future expectations. Now, 30 years into the Charter era, we have a solid idea of what those boundaries look like,[13] but this was not true when the Bill was first passed or when the Charter was first entrenched.

The Supreme Court's performance with cases arising under the Bill of Rights was, to put it mildly, a major disappointment, and indicated clearly that the rights cases of the 1950s were not an emerging sign of anything. The Bill guaranteed freedom of religion, but the Supreme Court found in *Robertson and Rosetanni*[14] that the Sunday closing rules in the Lord's Day Act did not violate this freedom because people observing a different day of worship were not prevented from voluntarily closing on that day as well. The Bill recognized a right to counsel on criminal matters, but the Supreme Court held in *Chromiak*[15] that a demand by police for a breath sample did not constitute "detention," and that therefore the right to counsel was not applicable. The Bill mentioned a presumption of innocence, but the Court said in *Appleby*[16] and *Shelley*[17] that a "reverse

---

13 And therefore, ironically, my objection has less rigour if the Charter revolution is truly over, and the rights in the Charter have now acquired the hard-shelled meaning they lacked at the outset.

14 *Robertson and Rosetanni v. The Queen*, [1963] S.C.R. 651.

15 *Chromiak v. The Queen*, [1980] 1 S.C.R. 471.

16 *R. v. Appleby*, [1972] S.C.R. 303.

17 *R. v. Shelley*, [1981] 2 S.C.R. 196.

onus" clause (that is, a provision that once certain facts are established, the person is guilty unless they can prove their innocence) was acceptable so long as there was a rational connection between the fact and the presumption. And so on.

The Bill had a single moment of bright success[18] with the *Drybones* case,[19] where a person was charged under the Indian Act with being "intoxicated off a reserve." The trial judge held and the Supreme Court agreed that this offended the Bill by creating a crime that some people ("Indians") could commit but that others (non-"Indians") could not commit, no matter how they tried. Furthermore, they agreed that this clearly violated the "without discrimination with regard to race" principle proclaimed by the Bill. But this was not the signal for a major move against the treatment of Indians; the Court promptly returned to its earlier form by finding in *Lavell*[20] that there was no discrimination on the grounds of gender in the provision of the Indian Act whereby women who married non-Indians lost their status but men who did so did not. And in *Bliss*,[21] the decision that probably still arouses the most ire, the unanimous Court found no sexual discrimination in the provisions of the Unemployment Act that denied benefits to pregnant women—this was discrimination not on the grounds of gender (which would be problematic) but rather on the grounds of "being pregnant," a targeted distinction that was neither arbitrary nor irrelevant but "part of a valid scheme of legislation enacted by Parliament in discharge of its legislative authority under the *British North America Act.*"

I would venture to suggest that Diefenbaker did not contemplate a "real Charter" like Trudeau's only to simply lose his nerve in the execution; I think he had a clearer idea of what he wanted, and I think he gave it to us. Once our mental engines have adjusted to the high-octane nourishment of complete entrenchment, robustly enforced by an aggressive judiciary, the 1960 Bill looks disappointingly limpid. Put in the context of

---

18 More correctly: this was the only time that a section of a federal statute was set aside by invoking the Bill. There were a handful of other occasions when the invocation of the Bill had a more modest effect.

19 *R. v. Drybones*, [1970] S.C.R. 282.

20 *Attorney General of Canada v. Lavell*, [1974] S.C.R. 1349.

21 *Bliss v. Attorney General of Canada*, [1979] 1 S.C.R. 183.

the times, however, Diefenbaker's choices make much more sense. There is something to be said (which is not to say that I now expect you to be satisfied by the saying of it) for having a government publicly commit itself to a particular set of standards or expectations, thereby accepting the political costs of violating those standards or falling short of those expectations. For someone like Diefenbaker, steeped in the British traditions, a passionate believer in Parliament as a chamber for the vindication of rights, and an advocate of the capacity of voters to respond to real outrages, it is enough to make this commitment and, when necessary, to face up to the political costs. It is up to an opposition party, amplified by the public media, to make this case, and up to the voters to rally to the call and punish the government at the next election. If the opposition is not up to the challenge, or if the public does not care, that is, of course, its own problem, but in the 1960s the courts were not yet the obvious solution.

The same device of formally toothless commitment is still used today. Fixed election dates and balanced budget requirements have been legislated into effect in a number of Canadian jurisdictions, but not in ways that enable courts to call off elections mid-campaign or order the retroactive increase of tax rates. Since these just become part of the list of things around which a particular election campaign might organize itself, the results to date have been less than impressive. To say that something is not judicially enforceable is not to say that it is totally useless; it is to say that it is not useful in the same terms or under the same circumstances as it would be if it were judicially enforceable. Even if we wish to think of "pre-commitment plus neutral enforceability" as the complete package, formal pre-commitment on its own is considerably more than nothing.

It is unlikely that Diefenbaker intended to create a Charter of the sort we now have, or to invite then Chief Justice Taschereau to become a Chief-Justice-Lamer-before-his-time,[22] only to somehow lose his nerve or botch the drafting. Rather, he likely intended to give a largely traditional set of rights a higher profile than these ideas had ever before

---

22 If only because one first had to create the kind of Court of which Lamer could be the kind of Chief Justice which he would always be remembered as, and this is a point to which I will return below.

enjoyed in Canada,[23] and Diefenbaker committed his government in a way that no previous government had ever been willing to do, especially the Liberal government that he had just defeated and replaced. That is all that he wanted to do, and it was all that the Supreme Court, as it was then staffed and configured, was prepared to work with. In the next chapter, I will expand upon the ambiguous purposes of a Bill of Rights; for the moment, my point is to situate the Diefenbaker Bill at the bottom end of that broader continuum.

This can be discussed in terms of a specific historical development; Charles Epp[24] has suggested that it is a mistake to think that "rights revolutions" are the product of constitutional documents alone, or even of courts alone. Instead, even a Supreme Court can be fully effective only if there is a supportive structure of public interest groups that are directed towards rights promotion, and that act aggressively and strategically to impact public opinion and prepare the court cases that raise the rights issues in useful ways. The support structure, emerging public opinion, and judges within the Court are what generate an effective rights revolution. Epp's image is less of a Supreme Court acting majestically from above than of the Supreme Court working with elements within the wider public to create and expand a culture of rights; these extra-judicial support groups are crucial. He takes the recent history of both the United States and Canada to prove his point. On his account, this structure was not in place in Canada in the 1960s, but it emerged over the following decades.

Why did the Bill of Rights have so little effect on the Supreme Court? To be sure, there were a number of objective factors that limited the impact of the 1960 Bill: the lack of a specific remedy or enforcement section; the "interpretation squeeze" created between "have enjoyed and shall continue to enjoy" (or, the lack of change to any pre-1960 status quo); the supremacy of Parliament (such that no Parliament can absolutely limit future Parliaments); and its status as an ordinary piece of federal legislation that did not constrain the provinces.

---

23 Therefore the dramatic gesture of printing up thousands of copies of the Bill to be posted on the walls of school classrooms across the country had a substantive as well as a melodramatic element to it.

24 Charles R. Epp, *The Rights Revolution: Lawyers, Activists, and Supreme Courts in Comparative Perspective* (Chicago: University of Chicago Press, 1998).

THE BILL OF RIGHTS AS FUMBLED OPPORTUNITY

But the problem wasn't the Bill of Rights—or at least not only the Bill of Rights. It was the judges.

Judges bring rather more to the job than a dictionary and a knowledge of English grammar. They bring their training, their experience, their awareness of a tradition, as well as their sense of an evolved and shared concept of the judicial role in a democratic society—more specifically, their own society. These constrained any enthusiasm on the part of the Supreme Court in the 1960s for the aggressive role we now criticize them for not having embraced. Their training and tradition were, of course, English and not American—the Canadian legal profession at the time was not just indifferent to American ideas and practice, but was, in many respects, positively hostile to it. At any rate, as I will discuss below, the American "tradition" of aggressive rights-protecting judicial activism was in the process of being created during the 1960s; it belonged to current events rather than to history. It was therefore neither an obvious model nor a logical starting point for senior Canadian judges at the time.

Let me illustrate this by taking a closer look at *Singh*.[25] Normally, this case is discussed as one of the early significant Charter decisions, with Wilson declaring both that the appeal provisions for refugee claimants do not meet Charter standards, and (famously) that "mere administrative convenience" is not enough to constitute "reasonable limits" under section 1 of the Charter. The case, however, is more complicated than that. It was decided by six judges—the seven-judge panel was reduced to six when Justice Ritchie retired from the Court after oral argument, before the decision was handed down. Three judges (Wilson writing, and Dickson and Lamer signing on) handled the case as described above. The other three (Beetz writing, with Estey and McIntyre) agreed on the outcome, although by a completely different route; they chose to decide the appeal under the terms of the Bill of Rights, even though it had not been argued that way before the Court and the lawyers had to be called back to make supplementary arguments. Wilson said nothing about the Bill of Rights; Beetz explicitly "refrains from expressing any views" about the

---

25 *Singh v. Minister of Employment and Immigration*, [1985] 1 S.C.R. 177.

Charter except to say that, for the situation at issue, the Bill of Rights is better suited ("tailor-made") for application. This different route, however, ends in the same place—the existing procedures are an unacceptable violation of rights—and orders the same remedy—a declaration that section 7(1) of the Immigration Act has no application to the appellants.

Which of the two sets of reasons is the "real" judgement of the Court? In one sense, neither of them are, since neither represent the doctrinal position of a majority of the panel that heard and decided the appeal; in another sense, both of them are, because they have diverged in such a way that they do not directly disagree on anything. Since the Charter has become steadily more important, while the Bill of Rights has more or less disappeared, it is Wilson's Charter-based reasons that draw the citations.

Beetz and his colleagues, however, follow the Bill-of-Rights trail to the same rights-protecting, legislation-killing conclusion, which involves a truly major repudiation of official policy and procedures—it can be argued that our refugee and immigration process has never fully recovered. This raises an intriguing historical might-have-been: What if the Beetz interpretation route had emerged a dozen years earlier? What if the Laskin/Lamer ideas about the constitutional status of rights documents had become guiding doctrine?[26] If these things had happened,

---

26 In the pre-Charter case of *Hogan v. R.* ([1975] 2 S.C.R. 574, at 597), Laskin suggested that the Bill of Rights enjoyed a "quasi-constitutional" status—that is to say, it was less important than a formal constitutional provision, but more important than an ordinary statute, and this meant that conflicts between the Bill and ordinary statutes should be resolved in favour of the requirements of the Bill. In *Insurance Corporation of British Columbia v. Heerspink* ([1982] 2 S.C.R. 145, at 157), Lamer pushed the argument one step further: within any Canadian jurisdiction, he suggested, human rights legislation (in this case, the B.C. Human Rights Act) enjoyed a comparable quasi-constitutional status such that it should prevail in the case of any conflict with ordinary legislation. Both statements are in minority reasons—a dissent in *Hogan*, a separate concurrence in *Heerspink*—but ideas often make their way from minorities to majorities over time, such that a Diefenbaker Bill of Rights with judicial teeth is not beyond the realm of possibility. Interestingly, the recent American literature has also developed the notion of a "superstatute"—a statute that is so important, and so transformative of public expectations, that it should enjoy a special status above other statutes. See William N. Eskridge Jr. and John Ferejohn, "Superstatutes," *Duke Law*

would there have been the same political and public pressure to "fix" the "failure" of the Bill of Rights by entrenching a "real" Charter of Rights in the constitution?

Only half of the problem of the Bill of Rights, then, was the fact that it put the judges in a box, for both the "interpretation squeeze" and the lack of an explicit remedy. The other half of the problem was the fact that the judges of the day did not want to get out of the box. A different set of judges could have found a way out—Beetz belatedly did so, and some minority voices on the Court had been pointing to it all along. By the time of the Charter, we did have that different set of judges in place that was much less reluctant to embrace and develop the notion of judicially enforced constitutional rights protections. This part of the story is just as important as the formal act of entrenchment itself.

PREPARING THE REVOLUTION: TRANSFORMING THE COURT

Let me introduce you to one of the underexamined transformations of Canada: it is what might be called "the great Canadian judicial revolution," referring to the complete transformation, from top to bottom, of the Canadian judicial system during the "long decade" of the 1970s, between 1968 and 1982.[27] The broad scope of the changes is all the more impressive because every government, federal and provincial, was moving in a similar direction more or less simultaneously.

At the provincial level, the "section 92" courts,[28] the old "magistrates courts," were replaced with the modern provincial courts. The new court

---

Journal 50 (2011): 1215; Eskridge and Ferejohn, "Super Statutes: The New American Constitution," in Richard W. Bauman and Tsvi Kahana, eds., *The Least Examined Branch: The Role of Legislatures in the Constitutional State* (New York: Cambridge University Press, 2006); Eskridge and Ferejohn, *A Republic of Statutes: The New American Constitution* (New Haven, CT: Yale University Press, 2010).

27 Just as historians talk about the "long nineteenth century" that came to an end only with the outbreak of World War I in 1914, I am speaking in terms of a "long decade" that is slightly stretched at both ends.

28 So-called because they are established by the provincial legislature under the jurisdiction assigned in section 92.14 of the Constitutional Act, 1867 (formerly the British North America Act, renamed in 1982).

was staffed exclusively by lawyers in good standing (grandfathering only the best of the previously numerous lay magistrates) and was reconstituted as a formal court of record with an expanding jurisdiction, with its own Chief Judge as an administrative buffer between it and government, and with both judicial discipline and judicial appointment enhanced by new Judicial Councils for Provincial Judges.[29] The section 96 provincial superior courts also underwent change, as the long-standing separation of two section 96 trial courts (District or County Courts and Supreme Court Trial Divisions), which had prevailed in every province save Quebec, was replaced with a single superior trial court. At the same time, the number of provinces with stand-alone, full-time courts of appeal went up from 6 to 10.

At the federal level, the Exchequer Court of Canada, which had been created in 1875, was replaced in 1970 by the Federal Court of Canada with a Trial Division and an Appeal Division.[30] More was involved than simple renaming; the new court was given a major role in federal administrative law and dealt extensively with immigration and refugee issues. Its growing caseload demonstrated its success. The two-tier structure also helped to contain[31] what, at the time, was a steady and somewhat problematic burgeoning of the Supreme Court caseload.

The Supreme Court of Canada changed as well. One important change involved docket control, or the extent to which the Supreme Court decides for itself which cases come before it. Before the 1970s, there was a very low threshold for "appeal by right" cases—that is to say, those appeals that the Supreme Court was obliged to hear regardless of whether they raised a major legal or constitutional issue. These cases amounted to about 85 per cent of the Supreme Court caseload by the early 1970s. As of 1975, the Court was given much greater control over its docket, with most appeals requiring an application for leave from the Court (which is usually refused) before being considered by a full panel.

---

29 See Peter McCormick, "Judicial Councils for Provincial Judges in Canada," *Windsor Yearbook of Access to Justice* 6 (1986): 160.

30 Subsequently, the two have been formally separated, and as of 2003, the Federal Court of Appeal has been established as a completely separate body.

31 Because the Supreme Court was no longer the first appeal beyond the single-tier Exchequer Court.

(The shift was not complete—appeals by right still accounted for about one-third of the Lamer Court caseload in the 1990s, and even after a further narrowing in 1999, they make up about one-sixth of the McLachlin Court caseload. The change from before 1975, however, is dramatic and significant.) Docket control is important twice: first, because the Court can control its caseload (how many cases they consider each year, and therefore how much time they can invest in the typical case); and second, because it has some control over the timing of issues that it will decide. A court that controls its own docket is, or at least can be, a strategic court, as distinct from a purely reactive one.[32]

But most critically, the 1970s saw a change in the personnel of the Court—not only in the sense that, over a number of years, the Trudeau government gradually replaced every member of the Court save one,[33] but in the much more profound sense that they transformed the accepted profile of a Supreme Court appointee, completely and apparently permanently. What was favoured within a candidate's credentials was not as in previous decades partisan political service or connections but public service, such as Law Reform Commissions; not limited trial judge experience, or none at all but appellate experience, and usually for a fair period; not a "lawyer's lawyer" active in the trenches but an academic lawyer, who had spent at least some time (or, as with the several law school deans, a solid portion of his or her career) with a university faculty of law. Snell and Vaughan described the Trudeau appointees who constituted the Laskin Court as "the most learned and scholarly group of justices ever to join the Supreme Court."[34] What establishes this as transformation rather than aberration is that the same patterns have continued under subsequent prime ministers—appellate experience, trial experience, public service experience, and law school teaching experience dominate the ranks of the post-1970 Supreme Court.

---

32 Slightly earlier—apparently in the 1960s—the Supreme Court began the practice of regularly meeting in conference after hearing oral argument on an appeal, and also began moving toward the designation of a particular set of reasons as the judgement of the Court. It seems quite remarkable that this practice is so recent.

33 Only Ritchie outlasted Trudeau's two interrupted terms in office.

34 James G. Snell and Frederick Vaughan, *The Supreme Court of Canada: History of the Institution* (Toronto: University of Toronto Press, 1985), 236.

The point is not that these were necessarily "better" judges in some absolute sense, as if previous prime ministers and ministers of justice had somehow missed the point. What is being described is an important evolution in the nature of the judicial role, and therefore in the kind of experience that best qualifies someone for such service and best justifies their appointment. Different expectations yield different judges, and different judges yield different results. When we change our standards of what a well-qualified appeal court judge looks like, as well as what sorts of explanations we expect those judges to give us for their decisions, this has implications that go well beyond the particular set of judges that are sitting on the bench at any specific time (which is not to downplay the importance of this factor as well). To skim the volumes of the Supreme Court Report as it moved from the 1960s towards the Charter era of the 1980s demonstrates this changing role, from a frequently cryptic, closed conversation between legal professionals to an open explanation of its decision process in more accessible language, and in both official languages.[35]

Did Trudeau "stack" the Court before giving it the Charter to play with? Let us start with the awkward but obvious: there is no question but that a Canadian prime minister who served long enough[36] could stack the Court if he or she were so-minded, and, within very broad limits, this is as true today as it was 20, 30, or 40 years ago. Assume a law degree, assume an absence of actual notoriety, and a prime minister can appoint anyone he or she wishes. Being careful with my wording, I note that it would be irresponsible for a prime minister not to reflect on whether a potential appointee's values and views are appropriate to the position. It is quite remarkable how "stackable" our Supreme Court is—as Peter Russell, the guru of Canadian court-watching political scientists, has observed, no

---

35 I have discussed elsewhere the emergence of a distinctive and unusual decision format for Supreme Court decisions, emerging in the 1980s and fully formed in the 1990s; see Peter McCormick, "Structures of Judgment: How the Modern Supreme Court of Canada Organizes its Reasons," *Dalhousie Law Journal* 32 (2009): 35.

36 Over the last six or seven decades, the average Supreme Court justice has served for about 13 years, which means that prime ministers appoint justices, on average, once every 18 months; which means that it takes about eight years, on average, to replace a majority on the Court. Most recent prime ministers have served that long or longer.

other country in the world gives the leader of the national government such formally unfettered appointment powers.[37]

Trudeau (and his justice minister, John Turner) did indeed transform through appointment both the Supreme Court of Canada and the provincial courts of appeal that constituted an important part of that same hierarchy; they did so, however, more by creating a dramatically different set of terms for the legal conversation than by seeking ideological purity. The Trudeau appointees included both Charter enthusiasts and Charter skeptics, as well as (for that matter) judges with provincialist leanings and those with more centralizing views. This was not "stacking" but "rebuilding," in the sense of establishing the normalcy of a new set of judges with a new typical set of experiences and credentials—a set of judges who were considerably more ready to tackle the new challenge of the Charter in a new age, where judicial activism was starting to come into vogue.

ACCOMPLISHING THE REVOLUTION: ENTRENCHING THE CHARTER

It would have made a terrific television miniseries, but it doesn't really sound like a formula for a successful new constitution,[38] or a fresh start to a threatened country, or a way to bring about a major change in the way that politics is done in this peaceful country. In outline, the road to the Constitution Act, 1982 was as follows:

- a failure, followed by
- a deadly challenge, followed by
- a comeback, followed by

---

37 Professor Russell made this comment in his presentation to a Senate committee at a time when it was holding hearings on possible changes to the appointment procedure for Supreme Court judges; I was present waiting to make my own presentation. As I recall it, the two of us were the only two in a long string of witnesses to worry about the absence of any provincial role in such appointments.

38 As a professor, I must nitpickingly add: it is not really a "new constitution" because the "old" constitution is still there, almost entirely unchanged; it is rather a very large set of bells and whistles added to that old constitution. But it is so often described as our "new constitution" that it is fusty to insist otherwise.

- a triumph, followed by
- a bold initiative, followed by
- frustration, followed by
- political and constitutional deadlock, followed by
- a redemption tinged with betrayal, followed by
- a triumphant new beginning, tainted by
- a problematic aftermath.

All this was wrapped around an irreducible element of "bait and switch." It was quite the political drama for several frantic years. Nobody who lived through them will ever forget them.

The failure was Pierre Trudeau's first period as prime minister—from Trudeau-mania in 1968, through to the minority government of 1972–74, and then regaining his majority by campaigning furiously and effectively against wage and price controls only to impose such controls himself (without even alerting his own cabinet) shortly after the election. His initiatives on constitutional reform went nowhere—a tentative move towards a "house of the provinces" was rejected by the Supreme Court of Canada—and shortly after he announced that separatism was "dead," his own province of Quebec elected a Parti Québécois government committed to sovereignty-association. His 1979 defeat at the hands of Joe Clark culminated in his resignation as Liberal leader after which he (famously) headed off on a Yukon adventure, giving us wonderful pictures of a bearded Trudeau paddling a canoe.

The deadly challenge was the Quebec referendum, called by the PQ government to give them a mandate to negotiate sovereignty-association, which early public opinion polls suggested was headed for a fairly comfortable "yes" vote. Early on, this seemed like a very serious project indeed, the more so because the federal government it confronted was a Conservative minority headed by Albertan Joe Clark (dismissively referred to as "Joe Who?") without significant representation or leadership in Quebec. This was a definite handicap in a battle for the hearts and minds of Quebeckers, especially when matched up against the widely-popular Quebec premier René Lévesque.

The comeback was Trudeau's return to lead the Liberals into an election that was provoked by the fact that Joe Clark misjudged twice: first, in assuming that the small group of Ralliement créditiste MPs would stay onside for his budget (they abstained); and second, in assuming that his minority win in 1979 showed an electorate in the process of swinging away from the Liberals and towards his Conservatives. "A real change deserves a fair chance," was the Conservative's somewhat plaintive slogan, but they had really just thrown away the only chance that voters were prepared to give them—they lost 33 seats and returned to opposition as the Trudeau Liberals won a majority victory. Between the time that the referendum was called and the time that the vote was actually held, a Progressive Conservative minority federal government that was weak in Quebec had been replaced by a Liberal majority government that took every seat in the province save one—the political equivalent of the staple western movie plot where the cavalry arrives just before the bad guys attack the fort.

The triumph was Trudeau's passionate campaign against the sovereigntists, which ended in a solid defeat for Lévesque in the referendum (40 per cent yes, 60 per cent no), even after initial polling had suggested that the referendum would probably succeed. The campaign was very much a head-to-head between Trudeau and Lévesque[39]—the sort of personalized confrontation that television loves, with no love lost between them—and the outcome was very much a Trudeau triumph. A central feature of the campaign, however, had been a firm commitment that the "no" forces in Quebec were not voting for the status quo, but rather for a "new federalism" that would respond in a positive way to the recent changes in that province. This guaranteed that the drama was not over; there was more to come.

The bold initiative was the comprehensive package of constitutional proposals presented by the federal government, taken to the premiers in a series of First Ministers' meetings. Instead of focusing on the federal–provincial division of powers, as many of the premiers (and, I think it is fair to say, many of the Quebeckers who voted "no") had expected, the focus was on the proposed Canadian Charter of Rights and Freedoms, skilfully presented as the rights-seeking "people's package" versus the power-seeking "premiers' package." It was capped by a novel procedure in the form of publicly televised hearings of the joint Commons/Senate committee on the constitution, which lasted throughout the summer in

---

39 The National Film Board's superb three-part documentary series was entitled *The Champions.*

Ottawa. The hearings focused almost exclusively on the Charter issues,[40] both reinforcing the federal strategy ("people's package" versus "premiers' package") and contributing to a growing public support for the idea.

The frustration was the resistance of a broad front of provincial premiers, opposed for different reasons in different provinces but contributing to the formation of a "gang of eight" (all of the premiers except Ontario's Bill Davis and New Brunswick's Richard Hatfield) that developed its own set of counter-proposals to the federal initiatives.[41] Their strategy included a trio of court challenges that put the unilateral federal initiative under a constitutional cloud. This inevitably led to a reference to the Supreme Court, where a divided court gave an inconclusive result that threatened to send Canada's constitutional divisions overseas into the British Parliament. The unique drama of the moment was compromised by the mishandling of the Court's first great moment in the spotlight, when a microphone mix-up turned the nationally televised decision (from inside the Supreme Court courtroom itself, with the nine judges fully robed in their scarlet and ermine) into a barely audible mumble.

The deadlock was a dramatic, last-ditch First Ministers' conference, as the clock counted down to the gamble of a unilateral federal request to the UK Parliament, highlighted by passionate confrontations between Trudeau and Lévesque. Since neither side in the showdown was completely confident that they would prevail if the drama shifted to London, there was some incentive to compromise; neither side was quite sure that they would *not* prevail, however, and so major compromise was unlikely.

The dramatic redemption was the "night of the long knives,"[42] whereby a deal between Ottawa and the nine provinces other than Quebec saved the

---

40 Speaking as someone who appeared before the committee for a group whose major concern was the proposed amending formula, I can somewhat ruefully confirm that ours was very much the secondary sideshow.

41 At this time, territorial premiers—of which there were then two, Nunavut not yet having been carved out of the Northwest Territories—were not part of the First Ministers' processes leading to the constitutional package.

42 "Night of the long knives" is how it is known in Quebec. In English Canada, it is generally the blander label of the "kitchen accord," referring to the locus of a late-night meeting between federal justice minister Jean Chrétien and a number of provincial

constitutional package (albeit with some major compromises, including the notwithstanding clause and a different amending formula); this deal, however, came at the price of lasting resentment in Quebec. Lévesque always said that he had been betrayed by his English "gang of eight" allies; they retorted that his flirtation with a "battle of referendums" with Ottawa risked sidelining all of them.

The triumphant new beginning was the British Parliament's easy and now-routine passage of the Canada Act, which included the Constitution Act, 1982, which in turn included the Canadian Charter of Rights and Freedoms, as well as a new set of amending formulae for the Canadian constitution.[43] Critics might point out that the approval of the new constitution did not live up to the new amending formula that it had itself now entrenched, but this was just armchair-quarterbacking after the Supreme Court turned down Quebec's after-the-fact challenge to the loss of its assumed constitutional veto.[44]

The problematic aftermath of the new constitutional settlement was the festering political resentment in a Quebec that saw itself (and has ever since portrayed itself) as ignored, excluded, humiliated, and betrayed.[45] This led, on the one hand, to renewed attempts to pursue sovereignty, culminating (so far) in Canada's near-death experience of 1995, when a massive turnout defeated the second Quebec sovereignty referendum in something as close to a tie as one could imagine. On the other hand, this led to decades of federal politics preoccupied with national unity issues and with how any particular policy initiative might play out in the particularly heated politics of that province.

---

ministers. More recently, Newfoundland's Brian Peckford has challenged this version by insisting that he had put the package in play earlier in the meetings, and the midnight conference was only a minor feature of the unfolding story.

43 None one formula, but five of them—but this is another story.

44 *Re: Objection by Quebec to a Resolution to amend the Constitution*, [1982] 2 S.C.R. 793.

45 The most recent example is an allegation that Chief Justice Laskin was inappropriately consulting with the federal government and the British government before the decision in the *Patriation Reference*. See Fréderic Bastien, *La Bataille de Londres: Dessous, secrets, et coulisses du repatriement constitutionnel* (Montreal: Les Éditions du Boréal, 2013); see also the counterargument in Philip Girard, "A Tempest in a Transatlantic Teapot," *Osgoode Hall Law Journal* 51 (forthcoming 2014).

My "bait and switch" comment refers to the fact that the constitutional package that had been "sold" to Canadians as a sincere response to the concerns of Quebeckers, just as it had been "sold" to Quebeckers during the referendum that preceded patriation, actually did nothing whatsoever to address those concerns. Quebeckers had been looking for changes to the federal/provincial distribution of legislative authority, the "division of powers," to enhance the capacity of Canada's only francophone province to pursue the cultural and economic initiatives that would allow them to protect and promote this uniqueness. When the smoke and dust cleared away, the division of powers was unchanged, save for a new provision (section 92aA) that responded to the resource issue priorities of the Western provinces. Quebeckers had been looking for some recognition of their unique status within Canada—a "Canada à deux." They did not even get an amending formula based on a regional vision of Canada (Quebec, Ontario, Atlantic, and the West) of the sort that had dominated the mending formula debate for decades, that would have denied full quality but at least retained Quebec's veto on constitutional change—a "Canada à quatre," if you will. Instead, the final deal included an amending formula that responded to a notion of the equality of the provinces, an idea that was very much a late comer to the constitutional debate—a "Canada à dix" that completely ignored Quebec's new sense of its identity and its place. Adding injury to insult, the most pointed and detailed provisions of the new constitutional response to Quebec's demands gutted the highly popular legislation through which the province had sought to assign formal primacy to the French language (that is, the curiously called Bill 101, referred to as if it had still not been legislated into law). All this, bizarrely, had been marketed as a favour and a service to Quebec, a response to Quebec's concerns and demands; consequently, in many parts of Canada (including my own Western Canada) there was a tendency to think of the whole thing as "account closed" and of Quebeckers as whiners who would never be satisfied.

The price we paid for the new constitution, including the Charter that was part of the package, was a quarter-century of complete preoccupation with Quebec's frustration, now aggravated by a strong sense of betrayal, and predictably exploited by the sovereigntists. The pursuit of closure on the new constitution ultimately destroyed Brian Mulroney's majority

Conservative government (and arguably the Progressive Conservative Party itself) after the successive failures of the Meech Lake Accord and the even more ambitious Charlottetown referendum. "Triumphant conclusion" may therefore be a somewhat dubious label for this outcome, particularly after the PQ returned to government in Quebec in 2012.

CHAPTER TWO

INTERPRETING THE CHARTER

The Charter was now in force; all the Supreme Court had to do was interpret it and apply it.

My statement is deliberately mischievous—it treats interpretation and application[1] as if they were simple and straightforward, the easiest part of the process. But this is not remotely true. There may be a non-problematic core of meaning for any statutory or constitutional provision, but, necessarily, all legal terms either have contestable and therefore fuzzy boundaries, or embody conflicting principles that can sometimes play off each other in subtle ways. The Supreme Court's project is all the more difficult because judges do not simply find things constitutional or unconstitutional the way that baseball umpires call strikes and balls (as in United

---

[1] Strictly speaking, these are two different things with a distinct logical separation: *first* we decide (for example) what "freedom of expression" means in the context of the Charter; and *then* we decide what that general conceptual and definitional statement means with respect to someone stapling a poster about their rock band's performance to a telephone pole. The American scholar Keith Whittington has actually written two different textbooks, one on constitutional interpretation and the other on constitutional application, for which his preferred term is "construction"; but for present purposes, I will just fold these two ideas in together.

States Supreme (USSC) Court Chief Justice Roberts's unhelpful meta-phor),[2] they provide reasoned justification for often subtle judgement calls, such that the immediate position fits reasonably well in the context of prior judicial decisions and commits and constrains what the Court will do in future decisions. This is what makes the first set of Charter decisions particularly critical—precisely because they were less doctrinally con-strained than most cases by what went before (obviously, nothing defini-tive could have gone before for the Canadian novelty of an entrenched bill of rights).[3] At the same time, they will constrain all the more effectively everything that comes after, because those later decisions will build on, will follow or incorporate these early decisions that are, for a time, the entirety of the domestic procedural trial background.

Some of the sections of the Charter echoed the Bill of Rights, although they did so in a different frame; some drew heavily on the Criminal Code to entrench basic but already established ideas of criminal law, while some of the sections were deliberately new ideas. Even the ideas with some historic pedigree, though, were transformed by the stark clarity of sec-tion 52 of the Constitution Act, 1982, which states that the constitution is the supreme law of the land, and any legislation that conflicts with it is null and void. The Dickson Court had to walk a difficult tightrope—to decide clearly, while not unnecessarily foreclosing the learning that alone will flesh out the details—and, by and large, it did walk it very well.

---

2 Understandably, American legal academics have had a field day commenting—usually disapprovingly—on Roberts's metaphor. See, for example, Neil Siegel, "Umpires at Bat: On Interpreters and Legitimation," *Constitutional Commentary* 24 (2007): 701; Charles Fried, "Balls and Strikes," *Emory Law Journal* 61 (2012): 641; and Vaughn R. Walker, "Moving the Strike Zone: How Judges Sometimes Make Law," *University of Illinois Law Review* (2012): 1207. But the umpire metaphor falters on even more casual grounds—just ask any hockey fan whether referees do (or should) call penalties differently in the playoffs from the way they do during the regular season, or whether they are quicker to call penalties when a marquee player is on the receiving end. "Call it tight" or "let them play" is a continuum along which referees slide, depending on the occasion.

3 The Court made it explicit that pre-Charter decisions on similar questions would not be binding on the Court's early Charter decisions—as only one example, the early Charter case of *R. v. Therens*, [1985] 1 S.C.R. 613 explicitly and directly rejected the recent but pre-Charter precedent of *Chromiak v. The Queen*, [1980] 1 S.C.R. 471 regarding Breathalyzers.

I may not yet have persuaded readers that there is all that much to the interpretation business. As USSC Justice Black famously said of the US constitution's First Amendment, "I read 'no law . . . abridging' to mean no law abridging,"[4] with the glorious finality of "which part of 'no' don't you understand?" However dramatic and memorable, this is misleading because the harder part is defining the "freedom of speech" that is not to be abridged (what is "speech"? whose speech? with what possible content or purpose or context limitations?) and, for that matter, distinguishing between "abridgment" (which is bad) and other forms of limitation or regulation or restriction (which might be good, or not, depending on the context). All this must be done in a way that is consistent, that "makes sense" to the relevant publics ("publics" being a term which itself is capable of different meanings), that allows reasonable actors to anticipate what the court might do in specific circumstances, that is capable of evolving over time to meet changing expectations and conditions, and that has due respect for national security concerns in times of war or similar emergencies. To say that "'no law abridging' means 'no law abridging'" does not really help us all that much; what constitutional provisions really do is not so much provide us with clear answers to a lot of the questions, but rather provide us with the parameters and the language within which those clear answers must be developed, largely by the courts.

Our current Charter of Rights is considerably longer than the Canadian Bill of Rights mentioned in the first chapter—the Bill counts out at less than 1,000 words, whereas the Charter is just over 2,500— but considering how much ground it covers, this is still cryptically short, a constitutional haiku rather than a detailed prescription. We generally think of statutes as containing grinding, cover-all-the-details, say-everything-three-times specificity (although this expectation itself is somewhat dated, given that modern statutes tend to be very broad and general with the details left to subsidiary regulations).[5] Nevertheless, most constitutions, including our own, aim at no such detailed precision. Since our constitution is extremely hard to amend, this is just as well; this

---

4 Concurring opinion in *Smith v. California*, 361 U.S. 147 (1959).

5 See Roderick Macdonald, "The Fridge-Door Statute," *McGill Law Journal* 47 (2002): 11.

level of detail might create its own problems down the road.[6] Flexibility in the long run, however, involves a degree of vagueness and imprecision in the short run, and it is the Court's responsibility to bridge that gap as intelligibly and consistently as possible.

Judges should just follow what the constitution says—how hard can that be? The words are there in black and white, and words have discrete, discoverable meanings. If only. There will, to be sure, be many easy questions[7] whose answers are so obvious that it is impossible to imagine anybody investing the time, energy, and not-inconsiderable money that is necessary to bring them before the Court. Because the answers are so easy, and because it is so hard to imagine governments wanting to do these things in the first place, the questions themselves look silly: Can the government do away with jury trials, even in major criminal cases? Can Parliament pass a law prohibiting any inhabitant of Quebec from crossing the border into Ontario? Can a province fine people for not going to church on Sunday? On the other hand, there are quite a few words and phrases that do not unfold themselves in any particularly easy way—such as "reasonable limits" in section 1, or "cruel and unusual punishment" in section 12 (does it really have to be both cruel and unusual? Or would either one on its own be a violation?). There are a few phrases which, at the time of passage, were even more mysterious, such as the "principles of fundamental justice" in section 7, which really had no developed judicial background at all. Any new legal or constitutional document is a string of intellectual puzzles of varying degrees of complexity, giving rise to questions that may not have been anticipated by the drafters or the enactors, and that are to be applied through changing circumstances over a considerable period of time.

---

6 One less-than-critical example: the Constitution Act, 1867 provides that one cannot become a Senator unless one holds $4,000 of real property free of debt or encumbrance—this was once a very considerable amount of money (the average annual wage for production workers in 1900 was $375, for office workers and managers $865), but in any major city today it wouldn't buy the doghouse.

7 Frederick Schauer long ago wrote a fascinating article suggesting that we are too quick to dismiss these constitutional "easy cases" without stopping to think about what makes them easy and why this matters. See Frederick Schauer, "Easy Cases," *Southern California Law Review* 58 (1985): 399.

Solving those puzzles, and doing so in a coherent and consistent fashion, is the challenge. For a change as fundamental as an entrenched Charter, it was a major challenge.

MODES OF CONSTITUTIONAL INTERPRETATION

There are several "modes" of interpretation, that is, several different ways to frame the judicial enquiry according to what the words in black and white actually mean.[8]

The most obvious interpretive mode is the textual—just read the words, and do what they say. Presumably, the drafters of the document knew what they wanted to say, and knew how to use the English and French languages to say it, and all one has to do to channel their ideas is follow their words. If there are any mistakes, misstatements, or omissions, then the same people who drafted them (or their office-holding successors) can amend the document to correct this, making it unnecessary for the judges to guess and anticipate. This suggestion is not entirely fanciful—it has been suggested that the High Court of Australia has very much tended to a formalist and literal interpretation of that constitution—but it has not been the dominant style in Canada, either before or since the Charter.

The problem with the textual approach is that it tends towards a static formalism—static in the sense that it is based on the unchanging text, and formal in the sense that it employs technical rules for the extraction of meaning without being distracted by the human realities that might be involved. For example, given that the US constitution empowers Congress to create an army and a navy, but never mentions an air force, one could ask whether the United States Air Force is constitutional.[9]

---

8 I take my basic list from the American literature—specifically, Philip Bobbitt, *Constitutional Fate: Theory of the Constitution* (New York: Oxford University Press, 1984)—but a similar set of categories frames the discussion in other comparable countries as well.

9 See, for example, Samuel Issacharoff, "The Elusive Search for Constitutional Integrity," *Stanford Law Review* 57 (2014): 727. The originalists must get very tired of this argument, because their opponents bring it up constantly.

According to a purely formalist approach, perhaps not.[10] Another example (from the days when one had to lecture on the Charter even though there weren't many cases yet) arises in section 2 which mentions "freedom of conscience and religion"; is this one right or two? After all, it could have said "freedom of conscience, and of religion," which would clearly make it two rights, one of which is a "freedom of conscience" not directly or necessarily linked to religion. Perhaps, though, the absence of the comma binds these together as a single right, such that "freedom of conscience" only works if it is linked to religion. If you find yourself thinking "You've got to be kidding!" as you read this, you have some feeling for why the purely formalist and textual approach is not always satisfactory and why "formalism" tends to be a negative term in this discourse.

The second interpretive approach is the historical mode—if the constitution is a historical document, then it has to be understood in its historical context, and that context will give us real directions on how to interpret it. The purest form of this argument is originalism—currently and rather surprisingly the flavour-of-the-decade in the United States—which argues that the correct meaning of any word or phrase in the constitution is what the drafters meant when they used it, or perhaps (as originalism has a number of variants) what the average, reasonably informed contemporary to the drafters would have understood them to be saying. If words have migrated in their meaning in the meantime, then it is the earlier meaning and not the later one that matters—for example, "domestic disturbance" today means husband–wife violence, whereas 200 years ago it meant riots bordering on insurrection. If the drafters didn't think of something (perhaps because it didn't exist at all—the evolving technology problem—or didn't exist as a problem—such as global warming and environmental pollution) then the document is understandably silent on these issues and remains so unless and until we amend it. It would be easy to put this idea down, and until recently, the literature (especially the American literature) very much tended to do

---

10 Or a little less frivolously: on a strict reading of the US constitution, if you were to try to impeach the vice-president of the United States, the person who is required to preside over these hearings in the Senate is—the vice-president of the United States.

this; it has undergone a strong revival, however, especially in the United States.

Originalism is tempting at first look because the people who drafted the Charter were still around as the early Charter decisions were being handed down. The Australian High Court in the early years of the twentieth century went one better in this regard, in that several of the first set of judges on their high court had been key actors in drafting the constitutional document in the first place. But this can be a trap;[11] as the founding becomes more and more remote, the precise intentions of the drafters can become harder and harder to determine, and as society changes and evolves, these original intentions can become less and less helpful. Our Supreme Court put this interpretive option firmly to one side in *BC Motor Vehicle Reference*[12] in 1985 by explaining that what the drafters intended the words in a particular section to mean could not be the guiding principle of interpretation.

Even so, history can be used in a less mechanical fashion to inform constitutional interpretation. The Supreme Court decisions in the early 1980s on the extent of the federal government's "criminal power,"[13] especially with respect to who made the decision to prosecute, hinged heavily on historical arguments, as did the string of decisions in the 1980s on the scope of the jurisdiction of the provincial superior courts.[14] The problem is that judges are not skilled historians, but rather legal experts who make focused use of some selected history. In my first example, Laskin and Dickson (in what was surely a battle of the Canadian judicial heavyweights, if ever there was one) differed vigorously on what message this

---

11 Quite apart from the fact that sometimes the honest answer of the drafter would be "we had no idea that this issue would ever be raised in this way in relation to this provision"—at a much more mundane level, I discovered this the hard way when I served for several years on the bargaining team for my university's collective agreement.

12 *Re B.C. Motor Vehicle Act*, [1985] 2 S.C.R. 486.

13 The two most significant cases in this sequence were the companion cases of *A.G. (Can.) v. Can. Nat. Transportation, Ltd.*, [1983] 2 S.C.R. 206 and *R. v. Wetmore*, [1983] 2 S.C.R. 284.

14 Most importantly: *Re: Residential Tenancies Act, 1979*, [1981] 1 S.C.R. 714; *Attorney General of Quebec v. Grondin*, [1983] 2 S.C.R. 364; and *Sobeys Stores Ltd. v. Yeomans and Labour Standards Tribunal, (N.S.)* [1989] 1 S.C.R. 238.

history was really supporting, while my second example culminated in a "blended historical test" for jurisdiction that no academic historian would touch with a 10-foot pole. History itself, or at least the history that bears on these issues, is less the accumulation of simple brute facts than a string of stories that we keep retelling ourselves while adjusting the telling; the result is a compendium that can legitimately support a variety of different arguments.[15]

A third approach is the doctrinal or precedential mode—over time, the courts develop a language for explaining and applying particular elements of the constitution, and later decisions are filtered through the conceptual and historic framing of the earlier decisions. It is not that later courts cannot change direction if they really feel they have to—*stare decisis* was never this strong, especially on constitutional matters, and it is clearly less strong today—but they are very reluctant to do so, at least explicitly and directly.[16] In the study of constitutional law, it is sometimes difficult to make the leap from the bare words of the constitutional document to the details of modern judicial practice in applying those words; the explanation lies less in judicial wilfulness than in the layer-upon-layer accumulation of early explanations, each one shaping and constraining the next. Given that we don't think the Judicial Committee (our final court until 1949) was always as unanimous as its single-set-of-reasons decision presentation style seems to imply, some intriguing what-if historical scenarios can be generated; nonetheless, we are of course the product of a particular string of those scenarios (i.e., the ones that actually happened).

---

15 L.H. LaRue argues that what characterizes a great judge and a great decision is precisely the capacity to frame a decision within a compelling and purposeful historical narrative. See L.H. LaRue, *Constitutional Law as Fiction: Narrative in the Rhetoric of Authority* (University Park: Pennsylvania State University Press, 1995).

16 The splendid example from Canadian constitutional history is *Russell v. The Queen*, (1882) 7App Cas 829, a very curious decision of the Judicial Committee of the Privy Council that stands out from what we normally present as the evolution of the judicial interpretation of Canadian federalism; later courts employed a number of "their Lordships must have felt" conjectures to pave a logical road around it until it was effectively overturned in 1946.

This process is particularly attractive for concepts that are (to use Sunstein's lovely phrase)[17] "incompletely theorized"—which is to say, not subject to rigorous and objective definition. The history of the famous (or infamous) "peace, order, and good government" phrase from the beginning of section 91 of the Constitution Act, 1867 may be an example; it can only be understood today through its doctrinal history, and the literal words on the page no longer take us very far on this journey of meaning (even less so if you try to break them down into three distinct ideas linked by an "and"). Over time, as these readings of the text become embedded in the document as we understand it, this approach starts to look the same as the more historic approach, but it is logically different.

A fourth approach is pragmatism, or the prudential mode of interpretation—of several possible interpretations, pick the one that causes the fewest problems for government and society at that particular time, even if it is not on the face of it (on the other approaches) necessarily the strongest. This is sometimes also called "consequentialism," although that term is awkward because it sounds a bit like results-driven jurisprudence, which is not something judges feel comfortable with. In the 1980s, for example, the Supreme Court found that Manitoba had acted unconstitutionally when it turned itself into a unilingual province in 1899. Strictly speaking, this meant that every single statute that had been passed or amended since that date was invalid, with no legal force or effect; such a consequence was (to put it mildly) unpalatable. The Court therefore "discovered" a doctrine of constitutional necessity, which allowed them to say that those statutes would nonetheless remain enforceable for a limited period so long as Manitoba embarked immediately on the colossal project of translating every statute into French and then repassing (or, more correctly, passing the legislation in a valid form for the first time) both language versions through the legislature. As you will have gathered from my tone, you will look in vain for the phrase "constitutional necessity" in the text of the constitution, and in the earlier decisions of the Supreme Court or the Judicial Committee. Only on the basis of pragmatism can you

---

17 See Cass R. Sunstein, *One Case at a Time: Judicial Minimalism on the Supreme Court* (Boston: Harvard University Press, 2001).

defend this as a wise action by a responsible court, and not as an example of runaway judicial power. Sometimes, the Court simply must, in Weiler's lovely phrase, "make it up as they go along"—nevertheless, the legitimacy of the project is threatened if they do so too often.

A fifth approach is the structural mode—the judges work from the text of the document to derive the core ideas that are simply built into terms and phrases even though they are not spelled out in detail (not that it would be possible to draft a document that accomplished such a textual unfolding). This kind of interpretation is not based on historical documents or historical evolution but simply on the logical implications of a textual idea and the structural form it has been given. The paradigmatic example of this from Canadian constitutional history is the notion of federalism itself, which is notoriously difficult to define[18]—even more so for the judges of the Judicial Committee, who lived within a unitary state and had no experience whatsoever with the idea or its practice. We can read the early federalism decisions of the Committee as an exercise in gradually coming to grips with this idea, that is, in finding its logically built-in assumptions, and finding the central concepts (such as "balance") that do not appear in the document but must nonetheless steer its reasonable application to specific disputes over jurisdiction. "Balance" remains a central organizing concept in federalism jurisprudence to this day, which makes it tempting to see this in terms of either doctrine or history, but it can equally well function as an example of structure. An even more recent example is the invocation in the *Senate Reform Reference* to a basic "architecture" of federalism that means we cannot just read the text in a narrow technical way but have to relate it to the ideas and values behind it.[19]

And the sixth approach is the ethical mode—the judges must bring an ethical responsibility to the interpretation of a constitutional document,

---

18 Even more so today than it was in the nineteenth century, since the "American model" now shares the conceptual stage with the distinctly different "European model"—and this apart from the question of whether or not the European Union (which, at time of writing, may or may not even survive) does or does not oblige us to rethink our definitions to include it.

19 *Reference re Senate Reform* 2014 SCC 32.

and must not let the document itself steer them away from this priority. The standard example that tends to be used in this context is a judge in South Africa before the end of apartheid: given that we can all agree that apartheid is bad, and given that there was a plethora of statutes and governmental regulations and practices that promoted it, it seems obvious to us that such judges should have been bringing some higher standard or value to bear.[20] Graber raises the same question in a more geographically immediate context, suggesting that the accommodation of slavery within the US constitution presents directly the problem of "constitutional evil," as well as the difficulty of evolving a theory of the judicial role and constitutional interpretation process that would allow one to transcend such evil.[21] His basic point is that none of the standard theories of judicial interpretation allow us to say that Taney's *Dred Scott* decision[22] was "wrong" in the sense that the legal and logical train of thought in the majority reasons is impeachable; his conclusion is that the only way out of the box was the *deus ex machina* of a bloody civil war that, fortunately, was won by the "right" side.

The notion of an ethical standard that trumps mere text may seem attractive or even compelling in the extreme cases of apartheid or slavery, but it is much more problematic to apply as a standard technique of interpretation, even if it comes with the instructions "use only sparingly." We typically overcome the anti-democratic and counter-majoritarian overtones of a judicial power to overturn the actions of popular majorities by pointing to a constitutional document that was entrenched in a way that transcends temporary majorities—even those majorities that win several elections in a row. The text of such a constitutional document embodies some sort of entrenched multi-generational super-majority that can be counterposed to the immediate majority without discarding democratic values. However, if the judges are going to second-guess not only the

---

20 For an examination of these issues, see David Dyzenhaus, *Judging the Judges, Judging Ourselves: Truth, Reconciliation and the Apartheid Legal Order* (Oxford: Hart Publishing, 1998).

21 Mark A. Graber, *Dred Scott and the Problem of Constitutional Evil* (New York: Cambridge University Press, 2006); *Dred Scott v. Sandford*, 60 U.S. 393 (1857).

22 The USSC decision in 1857, which held that blacks could not become citizens of the United States, and that slavery could not be prohibited in the territories.

current majority and the government that speaks for it, but also the constitutional document that is the basis for that second-guessing in the first place, then this defence falls by the way.

The problem actually cuts deeper than this. Notice that the examples we tend to draw on (slavery in the United States before the Civil War, German judges when the Nazis were in power, South African judges under apartheid) are all safely in the past; we know with real confidence which side was clearly in the right, in a way that was much more problematic for people at the time. It is much harder to run the argument in the present tense, expecting judges to step in with solutions to ethically divisive issues before the consensus has formed that makes the answers clear. We tend to like the idea of judges acting decisively when the constitution was silent (or worse, when the constitution got it wrong) only when we basically agree with the choice the judges made; otherwise (as with *Dred Scott*) we use the story as a lesson against expecting too much from judges.

INTERPRETING THE BILLS OF RIGHTS

But we must take a further step back; before we try to decide what any specific section or phrase in the Charter should mean in practice, we have to ask what sort of a document a charter of rights or a bill of rights is in the first place, and what sort of consequences are supposed to follow from them. This is something that we have generally tended to take for granted—perhaps largely because of the example of our neighbour to the south, and the feeling that our Charter is in large part a consequence of gazing in the shop window and saying, "I want one of those"—but we shouldn't have, and our casualness may yet come back to haunt us.

Let me introduce this part of the discussion with a more everyday metaphor, which I will then cash in to make my point about Charter interpretation. Suppose that you, like many of us, discover one day that your favourite pair of pants is becoming a little tight around the waist, and you reluctantly contemplate the thought that perhaps you should lose some weight. But where will that thought take you?

For most of us, it will take us as far as simply saying, "I wish I could lose some weight." Maybe we even say it out loud, which we may regret if members of our family hear us. Maybe from time to time we say "no" to dessert (or, at least, to a second helping of dessert). Maybe, whenever anybody reminds us that we said we wanted to lose some weight, we agree that we said it, and we feel a bit embarrassed, and we try a little harder for a few days. But that is all that the "wish" format implies for us. There is nothing dishonest about our intentions, just something very human.

Now, suppose that the thought is dwelling on your mind a bit more, and come New Year's Day, you make this one of your New Year's resolutions; maybe you even write it down somewhere, and ask somebody in your family to remind you about it from time to time. This may take you a bit further down the track towards action, although we all know what happens to New Year's resolutions—performance may fall well short of potential. Still, there is nothing dishonest here, and nothing particularly surprising.

Perhaps you carry it a further step forward—you actually formulate a plan that has some realistic connection to this weight-loss thing, write it down, pin it to the fridge, and think about it so much that you actually do something about it. Sometimes. Maybe not often enough, but sometimes.

Or perhaps you make a sincere promise to someone you care about, with your hand on your heart or whatever: "I absolutely promise that come next Christmas, those pants will fit me again, and I will be able to bend over and tie up my shoes." Promise. Absolutely. This may or may not improve the chances that you will actually do something effective, and there is now massive embarrassment if you fail, but that is all.

Ratchet it up again: you sign up for a diet-and-exercise retreat during the summer—lots of carrots and lots of calisthenics, and not a chocolate bar in sight. You stick it out right through the whole two weeks or whatever, showing visible progress—at least for a while—and a much clearer demonstration of a powerful intention.

Or perhaps you sign a formal contract, a commitment that if you do not lose a stated number of pounds by a stated date, then there will be some sort of penalty—you will give up your summer vacation, or whatever—and your progress is formally tracked with weigh-ins at stated intervals in a neutral location. This certainly demonstrates that you are much more serious about your intentions, and maybe your performance comes closer to matching them; it is more likely that there will be identifiable negative consequences if you do not.

To create a fanciful top end, perhaps you could move to some imaginary country where they severely punish people who are overweight.

They put your routinely updated BMI number on your driver's license, along with your height and eye colour, and they imprison people for habitual or excessive pudginess—a sort of Singapore obsessed with calories rather than with clean streets.

My point is that the recognition of a weight problem, and even an intention of some kind to do something about it, is essentially ambiguous in its implications. There is a whole string of "somethings" of escalating degrees of severity that this might imply, and perhaps, at the moment my mind forms this thought, I am not even sure which one I mean. Certainly, anybody who overhears me enunciating my concern could easily misunderstand what I am sort of committing myself to, and how far along my notional continuum I really intend to go. The key word is "commitment" (not unattached to the notion of "consequences") and that is what my continuum tracks. The same observation applies to the concept of a bill of rights, which has at its core the thought that, in a society like ours, rights against government are a valuable thing; it is inherently ambiguous, however, as to exactly what course of action this justifies or demands.

First, a bill of rights might be a simple statement of principle and purpose, setting a standard against which a government asks us to measure it, although it may well be that the consequences are purely political, inviting the anger of an outraged public or the orchestrated indignation of an opportunistic opposition. The accounting will come, if at all, at the hands of the electorate in the next election; the courts need not be involved at all. This proposal might seem a little fanciful in the modern context—as Brian Mulroney famously said in a different context, "not worth the paper it is written on"—but it is not as far beyond the pale as you might think. Modern examples might include the fixed-election or balanced-budget legislation, which legislators have passed in various jurisdictions; there is never any real potential of judicial intervention (the legislation is typically drafted to preclude this) although the government invites embarrassment and confrontation when it reneges on the commitment.

Second, a bill of rights might be a simple guide to interpretation, that is, a set of instructions for judges on what they should have in mind as they deal with the meaning of statutes and regulations. People have rights, and all government legislation should be interpreted as intending to work around rather than over top of those rights unless the contrary intention is explicit and unambiguous. This really just extends the operation of the common law in English-based systems such as our own, since there have long been a set of presumptions built into the common law (no retroactivity, "beyond reasonable doubt" standards for criminal laws, ambiguities interpreted in favour of the taxpayer in tax provisions, etc.). These presumptions could be overcome by explicit statement, but will operate to the protection of rights absent such explicitness. As suggested in Chapter 1, this is transparently what the Diefenbaker Bill of Rights intended to do, and it says as much in section 2.[23] It follows, of course, that if the legislation is explicit, then the rights don't do you much good. By contemporary standards, this is pretty thin gruel, but that is precisely my point: those standards, the ideas of what a bill of rights actually accomplishes, are very much a moving target rather than any simple, timeless truth that is built into the concept of a bill of rights.

Broadening the notion a little, one might suggest what Tushnet calls "weak form" judicial review, by which he means a system of constitutional rights without judicial supremacy—which is to say, without automatically allowing the courts to have the final say in defining those rights and deciding their impact on legislation.[24] The point is that a judicial declaration of a violation, to which government will respond or not as it sees fit, is all there is; there is no judicial supremacy, just parliamentary supremacy that can absorb a judicial reprimand. Gardbaum explores the same idea under the rubric of a "commonwealth model" of constitutionalism, looking at constitutional rights in a way that does not simply mimic the way that this has played out in the United States.[25] Both are attracted by the Canadian Charter and its idea of a legislation override—section 33's

---

23 "Every law of Canada shall, unless it is expressly declared by an Act of the Parliament of Canada that it shall operate notwithstanding the *Canadian Bill of Rights*, be so construed and applied as not to abrogate, abridge or infringe or to authorize the abrogation, abridgment or infringement of any of the rights or freedoms herein recognized and declared...."

24 Mark Tushnet, *Weak Courts, Strong Rights: Judicial Review and Social Welfare Rights in Comparative Constitutional Law* (Princeton: Princeton University Press, 2009).

25 Stephen Gardbaum, *The New Commonwealth Model of Constitutionalism* (New York: Cambridge University Press, 2013).

notwithstanding clause—although most would agree that the shriveling of this legislative alternative has moved Canada very much towards the "strong form" of rights with judicial supremacy.[26]

Third, a bill of rights might be a flat catalogue of logically separate rights, each to be considered separately and confined by its own language. On this approach, there is no appropriate connect-the-dots interpolation—no "if it says 'a' and it says 'c' then it is reasonable to infer that 'b' is included"—and certainly no extrapolation based on an overarching and pervasive "spirit of the Charter" that somehow ties the whole thing together and therefore deserves judicial exploration in its own right. If I am reading some of the Supreme Court's recent decisions correctly, this is precisely the debate that the Court is beginning to have,[27] so I am not being fanciful in raising it.

Fourth, a charter could be a list of specific rights linked to an underlying central vision or purpose, not explicitly identified in the document but capable of being "teased out" in a rigorous and consistent fashion; this is a frozen rather than an evolving vision, complete in itself and not inviting any expansion or redaction. This is, you will recognize, American ("tea party" style) originalism; we are sometimes entitled to "read between the lines," but only in the same way that earlier generations would have read between the lines, and if you could somehow imagine talking to someone from one of those earlier generations about the matter, on this approach, the conversation would be mutually meaningful.

Fifth, a charter could be a list of specific rights linked to an evolving vision or purpose, developed through an ongoing conversation within the judiciary, and between the judiciary and the relevant public. Because this as an evolving rather than a static vision, it necessarily means that "what the Charter means" at one time is not necessarily, or not precisely, "what the Charter means" at another time. This is not because

---

26 Defenders of the courts would say "constitutional supremacy," but if the courts have the absolute ultimate say over what the constitution says, and how it applies to any dispute, this is a distinction without a difference.

27 I will explore this possibility in more detail in a later section.

the judges have changed their mind in any crass or "oops, sorry about that!" way, but because society itself has changed, and in the process it has changed how it thinks about itself—much of this thought being embodied in the Charter in the sense that judges work these new ideas into the way they interpret and apply the entrenched rights. Robertson suggests that this is the major dichotomy in the way that the judicial protection of rights works in the modern world—the distinction is between those courts and countries that work in terms of a static conception of protected rights, and those that work in terms of an evolving and developmental set of such conceptions. The United States is for him the prime example of the former, while the constitutional courts and councils of many European countries demonstrate the latter.[28] This implies a distinction between earlier decisions that the Court declares were "wrong the day they were decided," and those decisions that it treats more delicately as "no longer good law" (which implies that at one time they were, or at least could have been, "good" law).[29]

For all of these last three alternatives, we were probably thinking in terms of a charter that embodied a negative conception of rights—that is, a charter conceived so as to see government itself as the major threat to rights and liberties, such that the operative edge of the charter would be to prevent, or to annul retroactively, those actions of government that infringed on those rights. The purest expression of this is in the American Bill of Rights, with its "Congress shall make no law" format (its application subsequently extended, of course, to state legislatures as well), and the purest expression of a court using such a charter is one that finds a government action to be unconstitutional, and therefore null and

---

28 See David Robertson, *The Judge as Political Theorist: Contemporary Constitutional Review* (Princeton: Princeton University Press, 2010). Our own location within this dichotomy is ambiguous, and in any event the Canadian chapter is the weakest part of Robertson's otherwise intriguing book. See my review on the *Concurring Opinions* weblog at http://www.concurringopinions.com, entry for January 24, 2011.

29 I take the first phrase from Jack Balkin's article "'Wrong the Day It Was Decided': *Lochner* and Constitutional Historicism," *Boston University Law Review* 85 (2005): 677; a Canadian example would be McLachlin's extraordinary paragraph in *Health Service Workers*, discussed in a later chapter. "No longer good law" is a phrase with a solid pedigree within SCC decisions.

void and of no effect. There are a number of early Canadian Charter decisions that adopt precisely this point of view, treating it as axiomatic, that is, so obvious that it needs no real defence. Just as judicial review in a federal system traditionally involves dealing with the federal–provincial division of legislative authority in terms of keeping each government on its own side of the fence,[30] so this approach to the Charter suggests that it delineates a new, third zone with a double set of fences—one keeping the federal government, and the other keeping the provincial governments, off this new space.

Sixth, a charter could be understood to include positive obligations as well as negative constraints upon government. That is to say, it is not just a list of the things that governments cannot do (such that if they try to do them, they violate the charter), but also includes or implies a number of things that governments must do (such that if they fail to do them, that is also a violation of the charter, and they can be ordered to do it).[31] The Supreme Court of Canada started well back of this particular transition point, explicitly denying a number of times that the Charter gave it any such mandate; on a number of occasions in the last decade, however, it has put a toe over the line. In *Dunmore*,[32] for example, it premised a decision related to the freedom of association (in rather complicated circumstances—the decision actually found that it would be unconstitutional for the Ontario legislature to repeal a piece of legislation

---

30 There are of course problems with this geographic metaphor, which never worked particularly well and even less so in this era of activist government, but it is deeply engrained in our constitutional language—when courts find legislation constitutionally invalid on division-of-power grounds, the term they use is "ultra vires" meaning "outside the limits."

31 As something of a half-way station between the two: a court might not simply strike down a piece of government legislation as constitutionally invalid, but might also suggest how a similar purpose, or much of the same purpose, might be accomplished through legislation that would pass constitutional muster. There were a number of occasions, especially in the late 1990s, where the court was quite willing to provide this advice, which was sometimes taken by the government in question when it passed new legislation on the matter. A prime example is *R. v. O'Connor*, [1995] 4 S.C.R. 411.

32 *Dunmore v. Ontario (Attorney General)*, [2001] 3 S.C.R. 1016, 2001 SCC 94.

it had previously passed) on the special need of certain types of workers for legal protection for their organizing activities. In *Gosselin*,[33] it looked at the argument that "security of the person" included a right to an adequate level of social assistance, actively considering the possibility before deciding that a particular case was not the appropriate occasion for following through. Some of the more flamboyant critiques of the Supreme Court in the age of the Charter[34] imply that the Court has come well over this line on a permanent basis, although I prefer to see it as having flirted with this line and then retreated—I will illustrate my position in more detail in the following chapters. However, the point remains: it is possible to look at charter rights not as simply preventing governments from doing rights-violating things, but as actively requiring them to do rights-promoting things, such that inaction rather than action would be a charter violation.

I grant that it is too late in the day to take the first two options as serious suggestions on how to interpret the Charter; I include them for logical neatness, as well as to suggest a developmental sequence that is a bit less unfair to the Diefenbaker Bill of Rights. However, I think the last four are very much in play, such that the Supreme Court has, since 1982, moved gradually along the continuum and, to some extent, slowly back again, and that different judges on the Court have had, and continue to have, slightly different ideas of where they are right now with some suggestion of where they should be in the future.

CONCLUSION: INTERPRETING CONSTITUTIONS, INTERPRETING RIGHTS

In summary tabular form: what is a bill of rights all about?

I have tried to set these up as a conceptual progression—a kind of "charter intensity" metre—with each level taking us towards a more ambitious,

---

33 *Gosselin v. Quebec (Attorney General)*, [2002] 4 S.C.R. 429, 2002 SCC 84. Arbour, in dissent, concluded that there was such a right; McLachlin, for the majority, said in para. 82 that "One day s.7 of the Charter may be interpreted to include positive obligations" before going on to conclude that this was not the day.

34 See, for example, Philip Slayton, *Mighty Judgment: How the Supreme Court of Canada Runs Your Life* (Toronto: Penguin Group, 2011).

LEVEL	DESCRIPTION
Level One	Is the list of rights essentially a political commitment with political consequences, or *are they judicially enforceable* in any routine way?
Level Two	Are judges directing to interpret legislation in the manner most accommodating of the rights, or are they *explicitly directed to invalidate legislation* when it violates the rights?
Level Three	Are the rights a flat catalogue of separate free-standing rights, or *do they form a coherent package with an underlying principle or spirit* that can be drawn upon to "fill in the gaps" (interpolation) or to extend beyond the strict text (extrapolation)?
Level Four	Is the underlying principle or spirit of the Charter to be understood as a static vision grounded in a particular time and a particular set of actors, or is it *something that evolves and develops over time*, such that what the Charter means at one time may not be what it means at another? If so, what directs or constrains this evolution?
Level Five	When the legislation and the constitution are in conflict, are judges limited to findings of unconstitutionality, or *are judges to give discursive advice on how such measures might be made consistent with the constitution?* How general or specific should that advice be?
Level Six	The historic remedy for the unconstitutionality of legislation is the invalidation of the offending legislation in whole or in part. *Does the Charter require other remedies* in order to better realize the rights? If so, what might these remedies be, and what circumstances might direct or constrain their use?
Level Seven	Are Charter rights essentially or exclusively negative—protected FROM government action—or *are they in whole or in part positive rights*—protected BY government action? Does the Charter tell governments to "do no evil" or does it say "do good"?

more activist, and more socially intrusive conception of what it means to have a bill of rights. There was some real ambiguity about the intended and actual status of the 1960 Bill of Rights, which, barely clearing the first zone, may have been parked in the middle of the second; on the face of it, it is a set of instructions for judicial interpretation, not an invitation to findings of unconstitutional invalidity,[35] and the only clear and dramatic example of such a finding (the *Drybones* decision) simply emphasizes the fact that this was not a central meaning of the Bill. (For that matter, if racial characterization offends the Bill's right not to be discriminated

---

35 In the handful of cases where the Court or a minority wrestled with these ideas, the strongest wording they used was that the Bill rendered a statute "inoperative."

against, and if one section of the Indian Act offends this principle, then why not the whole statute?) The Charter of Rights clearly takes that next step, the needle clearly swinging at least into the third zone—but this just leaves the answers to my higher-level questions intensely controversial, and people who sincerely support the Charter might still be divided on the issue of how far down the continuum our Supreme Court should let the Charter take us. My thesis is that the Supreme Court has evolved through a number of different responses—a number of different locations on the table—but that it has now settled down at a point that is not as far along the continuum as some of its earlier suggestions. The following chapters will survey the trajectory of this evolution, describe its end point, and empirically support my end-of-revolution conclusions.

This helps to frame the challenge that was faced by the Supreme Court of Canada. It had gained a new set of responsibilities in the form of an entrenched Charter of Rights and Freedoms, vaulting it into the same politically charged role as that of the United States Supreme Court under the American Bill of Rights; however, where the American court had the advantage of two centuries of experience with judicial-political interaction (not all of it happy), the Canadian Court had nothing comparable. On the one hand, the American example gave Canadians a perhaps exaggerated feeling that this was well-explored territory; on the other hand, many Canadians were worried that too faithful a following of American ideas would subordinate Canadian law to American experiences.[36] Certainly, there were few distinctively Canadian practices that provided any guidance; as already discussed, the Supreme Court's experience with the quasi-constitutional 1960 Bill of Rights represented more dead end than springboard. Today, there are many courts in many countries that work with a variety of constitutional and quasi-constitutional rights documents, but in the 1980s, Canada was very much the second kid on the block (the Americans, of course, having been the first).

---

36 This latter fear was realistic but, in the event, greatly exaggerated; although there was an initial but not sustained surge of citations to American precedents in the early years of the Charter, very few of these actually involved adopting the American solution as opposed to surveying it, often as part of a broader sweep. See Peter McCormick, "American Citations and the McLachlin Court: An Empirical Study," *Osgoode Hall Law Journal* (2nd series) 47 (2009): 83.

That said, it is striking that there was so little delay out of the gate; the Charter came into effect in April 1982, and by 1984 the Supreme Court was handing down its first Charter decisions.[37] Considering that these cases had to work their way up through the trial courts and the provincial courts of appeal, and then be scheduled for oral argument with a reserved judgement following a year or so later, this is indeed quick turnaround. One might have thought that the Court would take its time working its way into the challenge of this new constitutional reality, dealing with easier issues before tackling the major ones, but this is not what happened—within a nine-month period between September 1984 and May 1985, they handed down five major decisions that set the stage for an ambitious application of the Charter.

More striking yet, this block of critically important "first look" Charter decisions were handed down by a Court that was still adjusting to a new Chief Justice; the death of Chief Justice Laskin on March 26, 1984, was followed by the appointment of Chief Justice Brian Dickson on April 18 of that same year. The general practice on the Supreme Court of Canada is for the new Chief Justice to be one of the most senior—almost invariably the single most senior—of the sitting associate justices. The appointment of Laskin himself in 1973 was one of only three counter-examples in the Court's history, but Dickson's appointment conformed to the more historic standard, and he became Chief Justice with eleven years of experience. This "promote the most senior" tactic has a double-stabilizing effect: firstly, the transition period of appointing an outsider as Chief Justice (the normal American practice) is completely avoided; secondly, if the new Chief Justice is a long-serving incumbent, there is less probability of a dramatic change of direction. Even so, however, it is extraordinary for the first year of a Chief Justiceship to have dealt so promptly and so confidently with so many aspects of this major new challenge.

---

37 In my opinion, *Skapinker* (*Law Society of Upper Canada v. Skapinker*, [1984] 1 S.C.R. 357) is the first case. Some would start the story with *Westendorp* (*Westendorp v. The Queen*, [1983] 1 S.C.R. 43) more than a year earlier, but although there was a Charter argument, Laskin's short decision for a unanimous Court does not even mention the Charter in passing, deciding the case on more traditional division of power grounds.

CHAPTER THREE

THE DICKSON COURT: THE CHARTER, FRAMED

THE DICKSON COURT AND THE CHARTER: THE "FIRST FIVE"

I will use the five major cases alluded to above (the "first five") to let the Dickson Court introduce us to the world of the Charter—the world that it was creating from the raw material that the politicians gave them in the constitutional amendments of 1982. I will do so not just by pointing out the outcomes of the cases (i.e., who won or lost, whether the rights claim was vindicated or contained, etc.) but by looking more closely at the reasons for judgement that the Court delivered. In the long run, it is the reasons that matter more than the outcome, because those reasons constitute the precedent that constrains subsequent courts and provides the concepts and the language within which the evolution of meaning will proceed. It is not that a future court cannot directly repudiate the argument and conclusions from an early decision; they can, although they generally try not to do so casually or too explicitly. Nor is it that a future court cannot significantly modify or qualify an earlier doctrine so as to steer it in a different direction; even so, the earlier decision still constrains the range of available choices. When I say the Charter revolution is over, you might think of the new Charter, metaphorically speaking, as a huge, surging river, where the reasons in every Charter decision build up the

49

dams and levees that progressively channel the flow of Charter ideas. It is not that there cannot be (to pursue the metaphor) a levee that is occasionally breached, or even, from time to time, a new dam that is put in place. Over time the scope for such change is steadily reduced, such that dramatic novelty becomes more difficult and incrementalism prevails.[1]

I will then add to this list a further five: two that were delivered six months later (*BC Motor Vehicle Reference* in December 1985 and *Oakes* in February 1986), another pair in 1989 (*Irwin Toy* and *Andrews*), and *Morgentaler* in January 1988, which was the blockbuster that made it absolutely clear that we were now in a different era—the dramatic flourish that solidly reinforced the developmental story I will be unfolding. This is a fast pace indeed, all the more so for a Court that some of us thought might be a little reluctant to accept the invitation to use the Charter to become a major political player. At the risk of some oversimplification, and therefore with a certain degree of trepidation, I will take these 10 cases as constituting the major part of the Dickson Court's contribution to Charter law. This is the Charter revolution in full swing. The story ends with the "odd one out" in the form of *Labour Reference* (actually three separate decisions, which were companion cases delivered on the same day on a single theme). These 11, I suggest, are the major part of the Dickson Court's Charter legacy.

HUNTER V. SOUTHAM

Hunter v. Southam[2] (reasons for judgement by Chief Justice Dickson) was the Court's first major Charter decision, with the oral argument heard on November 22, 1983, and the decision handed down on September 17, 1984. The case involved a search of the offices of Southam Inc. in Edmonton by the federal Combines Investigation Branch, operating under a warrant issued by the Director of Investigation and Research. The question at issue before the Supreme Court was whether the search

---

1 Pushing metaphors further than they should probably go: the Hoover Dam and the other dams that make up the broader system have become increasingly efficient at controlling the flow of the once-mighty and occasionally destructive Colorado River, to such an extent that the Colorado River no longer reaches the ocean.

2 *Hunter et al. v. Southam Inc.*, [1984] 2 S.C.R. 145.

violated section 8 of the Charter, which provided that "Everyone has the right to be secure against unreasonable search and seizure." The outcome was the finding that the challenged warrant process violated the Charter, and the Court mandated a stricter set of procedural requirements. What is important for my purposes, however, is the careful and extended discussion of the frame within which the Court understood its new responsibilities.

The decision began by acknowledging that the wording of the Charter, in this as in other sections, was "vague and open" (154), and went on to acknowledge that the task of interpreting a constitution is crucially different from that of construing a statute because of the greater difficulties of amending the constitution (155); in other words, even when the wording of the Charter simply repeats phrases that used to be in statutes like the Criminal Code (which is true of many of the elements in the Part headed "Legal Rights," which contains sections 7–14), it does not follow that the interpretation of the constitutional words will be the same as, or constrained by, the earlier interpretations of the earlier statutory words. With respect to the immediate section, the Court acknowledged a history of the concept of reasonable search and seizure that grows out of a common law concern for property rights, but insisted that this fact did not settle the immediate question.[3] Instead, they said the right tactic was to "interpret specific provisions ... in the light of (the Charter's) larger objects" (117).

The key word in that paragraph is "purpose," and "purposivism" is the central motif of the Dickson Court's subsequent Charter jurisprudence. The most important pair of sentences in the decision describes as "obvious" the fact that "The *Canadian Charter of Rights and Freedoms* is a purposive document" (156); "purposivism," however, necessarily denies "textualism." The supporting argument, drawing on quotations that condemn "the austerity of tabulated legalism," picked up the "living tree" phrase from a Judicial Committee decision of the 1930s and endorsed a "large and liberal interpretation" rather than a constrained one.

---

3 This seems to be a recurrent feature of Dickson's style—a careful and solemn exposition of some element of law (in this case, the Criminal Code jurisprudence; in other places, the American jurisprudence) that is abruptly set aside in a single sentence as not being relevant to the Court's immediate challenge as the argument heads off in quite a different direction.

This is a very bold statement of an ambitious program. It is clear that Charter provisions are vague and open, and they have to be interpreted liberally as part of a purposive document in a way that is not unduly deferential to, or constrained by, the common law past. Nevertheless, (as often happens when courts are making such strong claims) it is promptly fenced in from another direction. What follows is the key comment, which I quote at some length because it is important:

> It is the legislature's responsibility to enact legislation that embodies appropriate safeguards to comply with the Constitution's requirements. It should not fall to the courts to fill in the details that will render legislative lacunae constitutional. (169)

To paraphrase: it is not the referee's job to help you score a goal, but only to blow the whistle if you have tripped somebody on your way to the net (or vice versa). The vision is ambitious in one direction—the purposive interpretation of vague provisions—but constrained in another—the only available remedy is to strike down offending laws. This should not be taken completely literally; unlike referees who simply blow the whistles and get on with business, the Court explains itself at length, and in explaining how you got it wrong this time they are necessarily and unavoidably giving strong hints as to how to get it right next time. If they weren't giving these strong hints—if they only gave "constitutional/unconstitutional" declarations, without any explanation whatever—ours would be quite a different system. Still, compared with the rights-enforcement stance repertoire subsequently developed by the Court, this element of self-restraint is well worth noting.

SINGH

I have already discussed something of the content of *Singh*[4] in terms of "the Bill of Rights we could have had, with a different Supreme Court," the point being that Beetz and his two colleagues simply ignored the "new" Charter to find that the government's actions policy was invalidated by

---

4 *Singh v. Minister of Employment and Immigration*, [1985] 1 S.C.R. 177.

the "old" Bill of Rights. In practice, however, *Singh*'s lasting influence on law and precedent was through the reasons of the other trio of judges (Wilson writing, Dickson and Lamer signing), whose analysis centres itself on the Charter from start to finish.[5]

The case involved refugee claimants who were already within Canada but were facing removal from the country, and their argument was that the proceedings of the Immigration Department for dealing with appeals from this initial decision violated Charter rights. Essentially, that right to appeal involved only the opportunity to submit written arguments against the minister's determination that they were not Convention refugees, without any appearance in person before the appellate decision maker and without having been given any information about the reasons for the minister's determination such that they might make a focused response.

At first, it might seem as if there were a preliminary question that finessed the Charter altogether—that is, the question of whether people who were physically in the country without having been officially and legally admitted were among the rights-enjoying people in the first place. On the American understanding of the power of the national government to "expel or exclude aliens," an argument along these lines would generally be successful, and Wilson alludes to this possibility in paragraphs 52–56 of her decision. Although the most obvious way to get to a Charter issue is through your claim that your own rights have been violated (as contemplated by section 24 of the Charter, which begins, "anyone whose rights have been violated ...") there is yet another access point. That is section 52 of the Constitution Act, 1982, which declares that the constitution (including the Charter) is the "supreme law of Canada," such that any law that is "inconsistent" with the constitution is null and void, and that, from this angle, it does not matter whose rights have been infringed upon. In any event, Wilson simply conflated these two elements in a way that more recent decisions probably would not—if there is a rights violation, then

---

5 It is mildly interesting that on the face of it, Wilson was originally writing a majority judgement for the Court, but suffered defections that turned this into a 3–3 split. This is the clear implication of Beetz's comment of "having read the reasons" of Justice Wilson clearly acknowledge that Wilson was writing first, which is to say writing a judgement.

section 52 renders the legislation or regulation null and void, and section 24(2) directs the Court to find an appropriate remedy.

There were three significant aspects of the case that Wilson had to work through. The first involved the meaning of the "principles of fundamental justice" in section 7; Wilson limited herself to finding that, like the same phrase in the Bill of Rights, it included (without being limited to) the idea of natural justice, which in turn included the idea of "procedural fairness." Although Wilson accepted the idea that such fairness might not always require an in-person hearing, it certainly did so when personal credibility was an important aspect; furthermore, it was problematic that the person had no right to know the argument against them.

The second was the broader question of how to unravel the meaning of section 7, which is by no means obvious—indeed, it provides a splendid example of the problems of documentary interpretation. Section 7 proclaims the right to "life, liberty and the security of the person"—but is this one right, or three? (Given that the section ends with "and the right not to be deprived thereof except in accordance with the principles of fundamental justice," we are really asking if this section involves one single right with some sort of built-in limitation, or two separate rights, or a list of four rights, making its decipherment even more challenging.) If it were only one right, a right to life/liberty/security, then the three elements would limit each other—a threat to liberty alone would presumably matter less if it didn't somehow engage the others. On the other hand, if it were three different rights, then each one would seem to be claiming a very expansive and free-standing interpretation, and finding a "right to life" in the Charter (given the abortion debate) would create its own problems. Wilson essentially tried to find a middle ground—not a single right, not three separate rights, but a right with three separate "elements"—and this is pretty much where the Court has stayed on this important issue, although in its current language it tends to refer to a life "interest," a liberty "interest," and a security "interest" within the single right. This is neither as limiting as the single-right package, nor as wide-open as the three free-standing rights. Those with a bent for theological history might find themselves thinking of the Christian doctrine of the Trinity.

The most striking aspect of the *Singh* decision, however, involved its approach to a remedy, and its treatment of the suggestion of a "reasonable limit" argument that might save the legislation in spite of the violation. The remedy, which seems innocuous, was for the immediate claim to be remanded to a full hearing on the merits in front of the Immigration Appeal Board, and Wilson had already suggested that this had to involve some information as to the basis for the government's argument in rejecting the application. In fact, it is not innocuous at all, because ours is, sadly, the age of the refugee, with unprecedented numbers of people trying to escape from dangerous or intolerable situations (and some comparable number trying to join in for more prosaic considerations). Suddenly substituting the new Wilson requirements for the prior, more bureaucratic and clearly slanted, procedures was nothing short of devastating, and it is probably not an exaggeration to say that Canada's refugee determination system has never fully recovered. Although Wilson stopped short of setting the test for section 1's reasonable limits (this would await a later decision), she was adamant that "a balance of administrative convenience does not override the need to adhere to these principles" (para. 70). No matter that Canada's existing procedures were comparable to those of other Western and Commonwealth countries, and no matter that the UN Commissioner on Refugees had spoken positively of them; the new standard was the Charter, a uniquely Canadian document with its own terms and standards.

If *Hunter* established that the Court was going to treat the Charter as accomplishing a major transformation of Canadian law, then *Singh* established that reasonable limits are not going to be used as a magic wand for governmental convenience. There is going to be considerably more at stake in section 1 than merely "technical violation, but looks reasonable to me"—not blinking at the total disruption of the Canadian refugee system clearly shows that the Court is not going to be easily satisfied.

BIG M

What was at issue in the *Big M* case[6] was the Lord's Day Act, a piece of federal legislation, first passed in 1906, that strictly limited what could be done on Sunday; with a handful of exceptions, stores could not do

---

6 *R. v. Big M Drug Mart Ltd.*, [1985] 1 S.C.R. 295.

business, and although sports games could be held, they could not charge admission. A drug store in Calgary challenged the law on the basis that it violated the freedom of religion. To be sure, this is curious on the face of it, but note once again the comments above about two different routes to the finding of a Charter violation and a remedy: under section 52, anyone can challenge a law as violating Charter rights, and it does not strictly matter whose rights are being violated; under section 24, anyone can challenge a law and seek a variety of remedies if their rights have been violated. Therefore, even though religion is not something that corporate entities can have or seek,[7] Big M Drug Mart can still ask the court to decide if the Lord's Day Act violates (somebody's) freedom of religion.

At first glance, this looks easy: What could be clearer than a case involving a law that is based upon the sacred day of a particular religion and requires everyone (whether or not they adhere to that religion) to observe it in certain ways (with the purpose being made all the more unambiguous by the very name of the legislation: The "Lord's Day" Act)? Subtle, it isn't. But Charter cases are seldom really that easy, and in its typical early-days-of-the-Charter style, the Dickson Court used this case not only to answer the immediate case but to set the direction and the tone for future cases.

The first problem in the way of a straightforward answer was a precedent from a case involving the Bill of Rights—*Robertson and Rosetanni*[8]—in which the Supreme Court had held that compelling Sunday observance did not violate freedom of religion because adherents of other religions were still free to observe their own holy day (say, Saturday) by closing for that day as well; nothing in the instruction to "close on Sunday" prevented you from worshipping on your own day, nor did it compel you to use Sunday to worship in a Christian manner. As Ritchie had put it for the majority in *Robertson and Rosetanni*, "I can see nothing in that statute which in any way affects the liberty of religious thought and practice of any citizen of this country" (657–58). Therefore, no violation. It might be a little unfortunate if your beliefs require you to lose business by closing on an additional day of a statute-shortened week, but that is your own decision and

---

7 This is not completely true, because sometimes, especially for smaller stores or companies, the courts will treat the store as having the same religion as its owners.

8 *Robertson and Rosetanni v. The Queen*, [1963] S.C.R. 651.

your own choice. Indeed, that is what "freedom of religion" looks like, in that you are free to make the choice.

The second problem was the temptation of the very extensive juris-prudence in the United States involving the freedom of religion, and Dickson did indeed review some of this case law. However, he did so only in order to set it aside as irrelevant. There are three different aspects to the American treatment of freedom of religion. One stems from the anti-establishment rule—no law "establishing" a religion—with an extensive doctrine on what constitutes "establishment" and what sorts of government actions would accomplish it. A second involves "freedom of religious speech," and this can be treated simply as a subset of the right to freedom of speech, which Americans have long treated as pre-emotively important. The third, always the weakest of the three in jurisprudential terms and even more so since *Smith*,[9] has been the "free exercise" clause.[10] The major elements of American case law, then, are not directly useful, and the element that might have been the most useful is the most under-developed. This example makes a very important point: our Supreme Court's treatment of Charter law has in many important respects been distinctly and consciously separate from the American experience with the Bill of Rights, largely refuting the profound concerns that our act of entrenchment would have served as a major open pipeline to American doctrines and ideas, so as to make the USSC a partner (and maybe a senior partner) in the development of Canadian constitutional law. By and large, this simply has not happened.

The acknowledged historic purpose of the legislation was "the com-pulsion of sabbatical observance" (para. 87); contrary to any suggestion that this original purpose might have vanished behind something more secular (such as a common day of rest),[11] Dickson rejected the notion

---

9 *Employment Division, Department of Human Resources of Oregon v. Smith*, 494 U.S. 872 (1990), which held that otherwise valid laws of general applicability are not invalidated by incidental conflict with the requirements of religious belief.

10 As Dickson points out in paras. 73–77, the USSC actually consistently upheld Sunday observance laws against First Amendment claims on the grounds that they had over time lost their religious overtones and become purely secular labour legislation.

11 As noted in footnote 98, this is exactly what the United States Supreme Court was completely comfortable with accepting.

that "the purpose of legislation may shift, or be transformed over time by changing social circumstances" (para. 89), both because "[n]o legislation would be safe from a revised judicial assessment of purpose" (para. 90) and because it would completely undermine our fundamental legal notions about the nature of Parliamentary intention (para. 91). Although this could well have been enough to settle the matter, Dickson went on to sketch the basic framework of freedom of religion; this involved reframing "freedom of religion" in terms of equality in the enjoyment of fundamental freedoms (para. 94)—which of course is violated if some people do, and others do not, have their special practices or their special days of worship formally supported by the coercive power of the state.[12] Without the words "no shifting purpose" and "equality of religion" (neither of which appears in the Charter), the Charter jurisprudence on freedom of religion would have started in a rather different direction.

Dickson strikingly identified four basic elements to the freedom of religion (para. 94):

- the right to entertain such religious beliefs as a person chooses
- the right to declare religious beliefs openly and without fear of hindrance or reprisal
- the right to manifest religious belief by worship and practice
- the right to manifest religious belief by teaching and dissemination

This is a very nice, neat package (although my own preference would be to reverse the last two to create a steadily escalating ladder of potential practical difficulties). In terms of the immediate case, which was arguably already resolved by inserting an equality concept within the freedom of religion, this expansion does not seem strictly necessary, but the Dickson Court's style was to sketch broad principles in general terms and

---

12 He also defines freedom directly as "the absence of coercion or restraint" (para. 95). As I will describe later in this chapter, the Supreme Court has, at least briefly, contemplated stepping beyond this simple statement to a more intrusive concept of freedom.

then to leave it to later courts to expand upon or refine that framework. Ultimately, it took surprisingly long for the second shoe to drop; it was two decades before the Court returned in a focused way to the scope and meaning of freedom of religion under the Charter, as I will discuss in a later chapter.

One further point of note: Trudeau defended the Charter as part of "the people's package," which was a rhetorical counterpoise to the "premiers' package" of more powers for provinces; *Big M*, however, was not "people," but rather a major business corporation. (For that matter, so was *Southam*, and so was *Irwin Toy*, discussed below.) *Big M* was about "freedom of religion," but it was also about the right of a business to stay open and to make money right through the week; the flip side of this was the fact that it might induce (even compel, through the terms of employment) employees to work on Sunday, even if they would rather not do so for religious or other reasons. This was the aspect of the case that surfaced in the follow-up to *Big M*, namely, *Edward's Books*.[13] This time, it was not a federal "Lord's Day" Act within the federal criminal power that was involved, but rather a provincial statute within the provincial jurisdiction over property and civil rights that was part of the regulation of business hours. Nonetheless, it was still legislation that sought to make the same day of the week a "general day of rest" for personal and family purposes. This time the Supreme Court found it valid, as promoting a "common day of rest" for families, although, ultimately, this was simply a rearguard action; all readers will know (will take it for granted) that Sunday is, for commercial and business purposes, very much like every other day of the week. This follow-up episode reminds us that rights are a two-edged sword, and that, sometimes, all that is at issue is who gets cut.

OPERATION DISMANTLE

Strictly speaking, this case[14] has not cast the same shadow as some of the others—for example, it has not been cited particularly often—but in an important way, the Court used this case to put the Charter marker higher

---

13 *R. v. Edwards Books and Art Ltd.* [1986] 2 S.C.R. 713.

14 *Operation Dismantle v. The Queen*, [1985] 1 S.C.R. 441.

on the wall than many expected, and so it deserves to be included in the dramatic opening flurry of Charter cases.

Operation Dismantle was a protest organization that was concerned, among other things, with the American testing of cruise missiles in northern Alberta in the early 1980s. Then, as today, a major outlet for such sentiments was public demonstrations and protests, but Operation Dismantle chose a different tactic that had only recently become available: a Charter challenge. The organization made an application to the federal court to set aside the Canadian government's decision to cooperate with these tests on the grounds that their section 7 rights to life, liberty, and security of the person were violated—these were said to be put at risk in one sense if the perfection of yet another weapon system made major nuclear war more likely, and in a second sense if one thinks of Canadian cooperation in this testing as making Canada a more tempting target in the case a nuclear war did break out.

This is a pretty ambitious challenge. For one thing, it does not involve a statute or a government regulation that is being enforced (or even potentially might be enforced) against specific individuals who would be particularly, and allegedly unjustifiably, disadvantaged; rather, it involves a cabinet decision reached on the basis of confidential internal debates. For another, it involved foreign relations, a policy area inside which the courts of Western countries (including Canada) have tended to be rather more deferential; in Commonwealth countries, the notion frequently invoked is that foreign relations is an exercise of the royal prerogative. Especially in the early days of the new Charter era, either or both of these might have given the courts some reason to hesitate (and this was as true of the lower courts as of the Supreme Court) but in fact it did not. The courts accepted in principle the argument that they should be willing to call the government to account for what went on within the cabinet room—even to call for evidence as to what had happened; they did not accept the notion of an unreviewable or less reviewable royal prerogative, and they did not think that the case was somehow off limits because it involved foreign rather than domestic policy.

That said, it is mildly disappointing to find that their decision was to grant the government's motion to have the application summarily dismissed before even calling for any evidence. (The trial court had turned down this motion, but the federal Court of Appeal reversed this decision, and it was this appeal that was before the Supreme Court.) The reason was that the factual claims in the case were not capable of juridical proof. How would one prove in a court of law whether better weapons made war more likely because they were easier and more dependable to use, or less likely because of the enhanced certainty of mutual destruction after a nuclear exchange? Rhetorical flourishes aside, how could we know? It is also worth noting that Wilson's more vigorous reasons, originally written as the majority judgement, became a solo concurrence when Dickson persuaded the other members of the panel to join his own moderately worded reasons.[15] Finally, as Mandel points out,[16] there is a message in the fact that Operation Dismantle poured all of its financial resources and all of its energy into a judicial strategy that failed, after which the organization folded.

All this conceded, it is more than a little astonishing that the courts would, a few short years after the entrenchment of a new Charter of rights, be asserting their right to call cabinet to make an accounting for a decision, shrugging off royal prerogative arguments and expressing indifference to the fact that all this was related to a case involving foreign rather than domestic policy. It exemplifies what I have always thought of as the *Marbury* gambit,[17] whereby a Court makes an audaciously bold claim about its own power but "sugarcoats" it by either not using it in the immediate case or using it in a way that actually satisfies rather than annoys its opponents: "We could demand the cabinet give an accounting for a foreign policy decision—but we won't do so this time." A third of

---

15 We know this because strict Court protocol is that the draft reasons for the majority are written first and minority reasons are only written and circulated afterward—and Dickson's judgement specifically acknowledges having read Wilson's reasons and adopting her statement of the background facts.

16 See Michael Mandel, *The Charter of Rights and the Legalization of Politics in Canada*, rev. ed. (Toronto: Thomson Educational Publishing, 1994).

17 My reference is to the decision of USSC Chief Justice John Marshall in *Marbury v. Madison*, 5 U.S. 137 (1803), which asserted the power of the Supreme Court to annul legislation by finding it unconstitutional, only to use the power to declare unconstitutional a statute that would have required the Supreme Court directly to defy newly elected President Jefferson in a way that was sure to provoke a vigorous response. But when the USSC next used this power decades later, it had not only a prior case to cite as precedent but also one that had gone largely unremarked at the time.

a century later, the Court still has not actually followed through on this (as demonstrated recently by their reticence in *Khadr*,[18] where they found that the government had violated *Khadr*'s rights but left it to the government itself to decide what to do about it). The marker is still out, but this case is still part of the relentless drumbeat of the early days of the Charter revolution.

THERENS

Therens[19] raised the question of the constitutionality of Breathalyzer tests: given that there is a Charter right to "retain and instruct counsel" upon "arrest or detention," does it constitute detention for a police officer to stop a driver and request a breath sample? In practical terms, does one have the right to say, "Not until I speak to a lawyer"? If you say, "I am not doing so until I talk to my lawyer," have you committed the Criminal Code offence of refusing to blow?

At first glance, the Supreme Court had already dealt with this issue only five years earlier—in *Chromiak*,[20] the Supreme Court had unanimously decided that such a police request did not constitute detention, that it did not trigger the right to counsel, and that a refusal on those grounds did not escape the charge of refusing to blow. Somewhat surprisingly, every judge on the *Therens* panel agreed that a police stop resulting in a Breathalyzer request was, no question about it, a detention within the fair meaning of that term and triggered the right to counsel. For those of us accustomed to the later style of Charter decisions, the *Therens* panel seemed surprisingly anxious to make the point that it was only targeting discretionary police actions, and not in any way challenging the validity of the statute or the wishes and intentions of Parliament.

Notice the tightrope that the Supreme Court was walking in this decision. On the one hand, all legal documents, including the Charter, include English words that have a meaning that has been established

---

18 *Canada (Prime Minister) v. Khadr*, [2010] 1 S.C.R. 44, 2010 SCC 3.

19 *R. v. Therens*, [1985] 1 S.C.R. 613.

20 *Chromiak v. The Queen*, [1980] 1 S.C.R. 471. This was a Bill of Rights decision, so the relationship between *Chromiak* and *Therens* is much the same as the relationship between *Rosetanni* and *Big M Drug Mart* discussed above.

through decades or centuries of usage—both a general public meaning that you would use in conversation, and a possibly a more technical or focused meaning when they are used in statutes or by judges. A word that is put in a legal document carries that meaning with it; this is how people are able to understand the law such that they can know if they are choosing not to obey it. This is particularly true of not-at-all-new frequently used terms like "detention." On the other hand, the Charter is a deliberate innovation and a break from the past in many ways, and this is largely defeated if past practices and past meanings are imported too routinely and casually. Nobody is surprised by the suggestion that reusing old words and concepts within a formally entrenched document like the Charter would give them greater weight and more teeth, but it is a little more surprising that those old words and terms would, through that process, gain a somewhat different meaning. This is what happened here, however, with the Court being unanimous both in 1980, when the word meant one thing, and again in 1985, when the word meant something that is directly opposite.[21]

Reading the *Therens* decision is a bit confusing, because all the analysis and discussion of the meaning of Charter sections are found in the reasons of Le Dain, although, ultimately, his are dissenting reasons on a panel whose final decision went the other way. On a closer reading, it is clear that it was Le Dain who was assigned the writing of the judgement of the Court at conference,[22] which means that most or all of the other sets of reasons (none of which are labelled "the judgement of the Court") were written by judges who initially agreed with Le Dain. This is one of those unusual cases where a division as to outcome is not at all a division as to the important part of the reasons; although Le Dain agrees with everyone else that a Breathalyzer request is a detention triggering the

---

21 Of course, the 1985 Court could have said that the 1980 Court was wrong— which would have been a bit unusual because most of the 1985 judges had also served on the 1980 panel—but what they said was that it was the entrenchment of the Charter that explained the difference.

22 Clear, that is, because every one of the other sets of reasons starts with "I have read the reasons of Le Dain" but Le Dain makes no reference to reading any other reasons—the first set of reasons circulation within the Supreme Court is always the set of reasons written by the justice who has been assigned the judgement.

right to counsel, he is (and his colleagues are not), in the immediate case, willing to give the police constable a "good faith" defence because of the signal the Court had sent in *Chromiak*. The reasons given in dissents do not often constitute binding precedents, but this is one of those rare occasions when they do. Of course, the critical message in *Therens*—that which makes it part of my initial "big five"—is that Criminal Code and Bill of Rights precedents from pre-Charter cases will not bind and will not necessarily even guide decisions on similar issues under the Charter. The fact that many readers find themselves saying "Well, of course" is itself confirmation of the importance of establishing this fact very early in the Charter jurisprudence.

FOLLOWING UP

"Fast out of the gate" is one thing, and a very important one; "no subsequent sign of slowing down" is, however, equally important, and I will continue my walk through the cases by substantiating this description of the continuing evolution of the Dickson Court's Charter jurisprudence.

BC MOTOR VEHICLE

In *BC Motor Vehicle Reference*, the Supreme Court was asked by the BC government to consider the constitutionality of legislation that made it an offence to drive a motor vehicle without a valid license, the problem being that this was an absolute liability offence—it didn't matter if you were unaware that your license had become invalid, or even blamelessly unaware (e.g., if the letter telling you your license was suspended had gone astray).[23] This brought section 7 of the Charter into play, and since it is straightforward to find that the "liberty interest" is engaged (i.e., if you are found guilty, you can go to jail), this carries our attention to the

---

23 What is involved here is not the infamous "ignorance of the law is no excuse" but rather the better pedigreed notion of *mens rea*: in order to have committed a crime, you must not simply have done something that is wrong (the *actus reus*) but you must have done it with the intention and the knowledge that you are doing something wrong (the *mens rea*). Absolute liability offends the expectation of some blameworthy intention.

second half of the section: Given that the statute violates your right to life, liberty, and the security of the person, does it do so in a manner and for a purpose that accord with the principles of fundamental justice? This in turn requires an answer to another question: What on earth are the principles of fundamental justice?

This is a slightly complicated question. Historically, in the English-speaking world, the phrase we would have expected in this part of the Charter is "without due process of law," and this is indeed what we find in the US Bill of Rights (in the Fifth and Fourteenth Amendments) and in Diefenbaker's 1960 Canadian Bill of Rights.[24] This was generally understood as relating to aspects of legal proceedings through which individuals can seek to have their rights recognized and respected. In American jurisprudence, however, there has come to be a notion of "substantive due process"—this means, crudely, that there are some rights so important that one cannot be deprived of them by government through any process whatever. This has been connected to such famous (and infamous) cases as *Dred Scott*[25] (which held that slavery could not be prohibited in the territories), *Lochner*[26] (which, in the name of freedom of contract, invalidated certain regulations on business), and *Griswold*[27] (which found that a law against using contraceptives violated a right to privacy). Anxious to avoid this development, and worrying that an entrenched Charter that simply echoed American terminology would open the floodgates to American influence, the drafters of the Charter opted instead for the alternative wording from another part of the 1960 Bill—the "principles of fundamental justice." However—as those drafters testified before the courts in this case—what they really had in mind was what "due process of law" historically meant before it (sometimes) acquired these substantive overtones.

Lamer, for the Supreme Court, was unconvinced—and I have to admit that I don't blame him, because "principles of fundamental justice"

---

24 The Canadian Bill of Rights does use the phrase "principles of fundamental justice" but in a different part of the document with a much narrower application, applying only to the right to a fair hearing.

25 *Dred Scott v. Sandford*, 60 U.S. 393 (1857).

26 *Lochner v. New York*, 198 U.S. 45 (1905).

27 *Griswold v. Connecticut*, 381 U.S. 479 (1965).

certainly seems, on the face of it, to be carrying some substantive weight—much more so than the apparently transparent proceduralism of "due process of law." He was making a broader and much more important point, which was that even the speeches and declarations of prominent figures involved in the Charter process were "inherently unreliable" as a source of meaning (50), the more so because the Charter was the product of a "multiplicity of individuals" such that no one small set of them (even the federal civil servants who did the initial drafting) could speak for them all (51). Even if some initial intention could be determined, using this as the basis of determination risked allowing rights to become "frozen in time" with little or no possibility of growth or development. Similarly, the principles of fundamental justice "cannot be given any exhaustive content or simple enumerative definition" (67) in the immediate case; their meaning would have to unfold as the courts dealt with other alleged violations. Although it was an absolute liability offence that gave rise to the immediate case, Lamer was not willing to say that all absolute liability offences necessarily violated the constitution (just that this one did), the constitution being something that would unfold over time as well (75–76).

This seems to leave the Supreme Court in a slightly curious corner: as Petter points out, the Supreme Court had embraced purposivism as the major element of its interpretive strategy, but had simultaneously rejected the originalist overtones of attaching particular, let alone pre-emptive, importance to the stated intentions of the original drafters and architects of the Charter.[28] Whose purposes are we talking about? And how are they to be discovered? How can you have purposes that are not connected to a specific and identifiable purpose-willing mind or entity? You can say that the actual words prevail over the stated intentions, or vice versa, and either would be intelligible, but how can you say both that the actual purposes don't matter even when they can be ascertained, and also that interpretation must avoid the word-locked "austerity of tabulated legalism" (as Dickson described it in *Hunter v. Southam*) by being informed by a purposive analysis?

---

28 Andrew Petter, "Charter Legitimacy on Trial: The Resistible Rise of Substantive Due Process," in *The Politics of the Charter: The Illusive Promise of Constitutional Rights* (Toronto: University of Toronto Press, 2010), 61; originally published in *Supreme Court Law Review* 9 (1987).

This is reminiscent of an old academic joke: Were William Shakespeare magically transported through time to take a contemporary university course in Shakespeare's plays, would he be able to pass the course? Of course he would know a great deal about the plays on the basis of having written them, but he would be without the benefit of the centuries of interpretation and analysis those plays have undergone, and the understanding of the ways in which they have been absorbed into popular culture. If it were the Supreme Court doing the grading, the answer would clearly be "no," with Lamer dismissing as irrelevant the fact that he was the one who put the words on the page in the first place. My jibe is not entirely fair, because as Barak has demonstrated at considerable length,[29] there is a lot more to the judicial concept of purposiveness than originalist conjectures about legislators' states of mind; nonetheless, the appeal of pursuing purposive interpretation had seemed to be its promise of some middle ground between sterile legalism and pure judicial discretion rather than the subtle philosophical interplay between "subjective"[30] and "objective"[31] purpose (not to mention the further idea of "ultimate"[32] purpose). In the event, the approach seemed to deny transparency in favour of an oracular court with privileged knowledge that is available to the judges but not to others—very much a "just trust us" approach, like the automobile ads on TV that tell you "Don't try this at home, we are professionals." With respect to an entrenched Charter, many of us would like to be able to do at least some of it at home.

OAKES

Mr. Oakes was charged with possession of heroin, and with possession for the purpose of trafficking (which was by far the more serious charge), and the way that the law was drafted meant that, once possession of a prohibited drug beyond a rather modest amount was proven, it was the responsibility of the accused to prove that it was not for the purposes of

---

29 Aharon Barak, *Purposive Interpretation in Law* (Princeton: Princeton University Press, 2005).

30 *Ibid.*, chap. 6.

31 *Ibid.*, chap. 7.

32 *Ibid.*, chap. 8.

trafficking.[33] This is a "reverse onus" clause—that is to say, instead of the normal situation in which the burden is on the Crown to prove that a person is guilty of a crime, the burden has been reversed and it is now the person who must prove they are not guilty. This is a transparent violation of the presumption of innocence in section 11 of the Charter, as was not even disputed by the Crown, so the critical question was whether it constituted a "reasonable limit" under section 1 of the Charter, such that it could remain a valid law despite the violation of section 11.

Up until this point, the Court had dealt with the section 1 issue somewhat opaquely—that is to say, it would hear the argument on the specific case, and then say whether the limit on the right was or was not reasonable under the immediate circumstances. Over time, this gave some sense of where the boundary line was located, but in a general rather than a specific way. In *Oakes*, Dickson grasped the nettle to lay down a test for the application of section 1, one which would make clear the logical steps that the Court would follow in deciding whether or not section 1 saved a rights violation, and would therefore make it clear both to challengers of statutes and to governments defending those statutes what standards had to be met and in what terms.

The judicial creation of tests of this sort is part of an interesting dialectic; they represent the Court restricting its own freedom of action in the future. Before *Oakes*, the Court was in a position (to be crude) to "make it up as it went along" and operate in terms of a "reasonableness" defined as whatever looked reasonable to that particular panel on that particular day under those particular circumstances. As a justice of the USSC once said in a somewhat different context, "I may not be able to define it, but I know it when I see it."[34] Because judges are not as fickle as that sentence makes them sound, this would, over time, add up to some degree of predictability, while allowing for the capacity to "drift" over time with changing judges and changing circumstances. A test, however, promises that the Court will follow a set logical process that it has declared in advance, and it will explain the way it answers this particular question with specific and careful reference to the test. Furthermore,

---

33 *R. v. Oakes*, [1986] 1 S.C.R. 103.

34 The Justice was Potter Stewart, and the case was *Jacobellis v. Ohio*, 370 U.S. 184 (1964).

since the litigants know the test, they can target their evidence and their arguments on it. The pre-commitment of this self-constraint makes the Court more predictable (although, since it is self-imposed, it can also be self-modified).

The "*Oakes* test" lays out the following procedure:

> First, the party challenging the statute must establish a prima facie case that the statute violates a Charter right: first, we define the right; second, we consider how the statute relates to the right; and then, only if there is a good "first look" argument that the right is violated, we proceed to the second step.
> Second, the government defending the statute must establish:
>> that the statute serves a purpose sufficiently important to justify the violation of a right, relating to concerns that are pressing and substantial
>> that the rights violation passes a proportionality test, or demonstration
>> that the rights violation has a rational connection to this purpose, and is not arbitrary or unfair
>> that the measures infringe the rights as little as possible[35] to achieve the purpose
>> that the benefit from the violation of the right is proportionate to the deleterious effects of the violation on any groups or individuals

At first glance, this seems to turn the Charter into something of a cruel game, like the adult that holds something out to a baby and then snatches it away just as the baby reaches for it (although the comparison is not perfect because the babies seem to enjoy it while rights claimants certainly do not). The more generously we define and describe the guaranteed rights (and this was an early tendency in the Court), the more

---

35 Taken literally, this is of course impossible—one could always come up with some alternative mechanism or process, albeit possibly an extremely difficult or expensive one, that would be just a tiny bit less rights-intrusive than the present one while accomplishing the same objective—and the Court subsequently relaxed this to require that the infringement be as little as *reasonably* possible.

work has to be done by the reasonable limits test; thus we play the game more often, and the broad expansive rights seem to mean a lot less in actual practice.

I don't think this is quite right; I think what is happening is a little more subtle than a simple game of offer and snatch. To change metaphors, I think of this as something of a "Charter three-step"; meeting the prima facie case for a Charter violation is two steps forward, and the successful section 1 claim is a single step back. We did not go all the way to a statute-striking finding of a Charter violation, but we did establish a broad statement of a right, we did oblige the government to go through the demanding process of proving the reasonableness of the limits.[36] Furthermore, we have effectively put the government on notice that any other statutes that similarly enter this notional zone will certainly be challenged and may or may not clear the same test—that is to say, we have imposed a cost that will make governments at least a little more hesitant to pass legislation that tests the limits of the reasonable-limits finding. (If relevant circumstances change, the same statute may not survive a later test, as Quebec discovered with respect to its language legislation when the Court found that, because the French language was now less threatened, the acceptable scope of rights-limiting legislation to promote that less-threatened language was reduced as well.) This is not the whole game, to be sure, but it is considerably more than nothing; it can thus be described as a three-step rather than a two-step (forward and back).

My point is not that the test as laid down is much more than a reasonably logical way of dealing with the reasonable limits question; to be blunt, it is not rocket science. In fact, as Huscroft[37] and Hogg[38] point out, it is not even original to Dickson, as it appears in a United States

---

36 It would be defeated, of course, if the Court is too perfunctory in accepting the government's claims in this regard, which it sometimes can be.

37 Grant Huscroft, "Rationalizing Judicial Power: The Mischief of Dialogue Theory," in James B. Kelly and Christopher Manfredi, eds., *Contested Constitutionalism: Reflections on the Canadian Charter of Rights and Freedoms* (Vancouver: UBC Press, 2009), 58.

38 Peter Hogg, *Constitutional Law of Canada, 2012 Student Edition* (Toronto: Carswell, 2012), 38.

Supreme Court decision[39] that is not even cited by Dickson.[40] What matters is not whether it is original or brilliant, but whether it is proclaimed and (reasonably closely) followed by the Court in a way that makes the application of the "reasonable limits" test considerably more predictable for litigants and governments, and removes the Court from any appearance of I-know-it-when-I-see-it jurisprudence. This is what makes *Oakes* one of the most important cases (and easily the most frequently cited case) in the body of Charter case-law; the question of how much more predictable it has made the Court, or whether it has surreptitiously been "moving the goal posts" over the years, is harder to answer.

IRWIN TOY

The Province of Quebec passed legislation limiting the kind and the amount of television advertising that could be directed at children, and the Irwin Toy company challenged the legislation as a violation of the freedom of expression.[41] (They also argued that the province did not have the authority to regulate television advertising directed at children because broadcasting is federal jurisdiction, but this was a long shot because the Supreme Court had ruled in 1978 that such regulation was valid.[42]) In a highly unusual triple-authored set of reasons[43]—Dickson combining with Wilson and Lamer—the Court chose to use this case as an opportunity to

---

39 *Central Hudson Gas and Electric Corp. v. Public Service Commission*, 447 U.S. 557 (1980).

40 For that matter, Cohen-Eliya and Porat argue that a well-developed version of this proportionality test can be found in nineteenth-century Prussian administrative law, from which beginnings it has become a major global element of constitutional law. See Moshe Cohen-Eliya and Iddo Porat, *Proportionality and Constitutional Culture* (Cambridge: Cambridge University Press, 2013).

41 *Irwin Toy Ltd. v. Quebec (Attorney General)*, [1989] 1 S.C.R. 927.

42 *Attorney General (Que.) v. Kellogg's Co. of Canada et al.*, [1978] 2 S.C.R. 211. Triple-authored judgements are considerably rarer than double-authored ones; I have only been able to find a single example other than *Irwin Toy*.

43 Co-authored reasons have become more common in recent years, now accounting for about one set of reasons in 10, but before 1995 they were highly unusual; *Irwin Toy* is one of only two co-authored judgements (*Sparrow* is the other) handed down by the Dickson Court. See Peter McCormick, "Sharing the Spotlight: Co-Authored Reasons on the Modern Supreme Court of Canada," *Dalhousie Law Journal* 34 (2011): 165.

deal with the much broader issue of the definition of "expression" for the purposes of the Charter.[44]

To begin with the obvious, it should be noted that the Canadian protection is not for "freedom of speech" but for the deliberately and explicitly broader notion of "freedom of expression," and this, the majority says, is a protection which covers both a content and a form. With truly splendid brevity, they say, "Activity is expressive if it attempts to convey meaning," and, "That meaning is its content." At the prima facie level, which is sufficient to trigger a full section 1 analysis, this means that any activity that has as its purpose the conveying of a meaning is protected activity, and so there is literally no activity, at least theoretically, that could not be considered protected on this interpretation. Their striking example is parking a car: "For example, an unmarried person might, as part of a public protest, park in a zone reserved for spouses of government employees in order to express dissatisfaction or outrage at the chosen method of allocating a limited resource." It is probably not a good idea to take this invitation too literally the next time you are frustrated with looking for a parking space.

Although content can be conveyed in "an infinite variety of forms of expression" the Court sets one firm line:[45] "violence as a form of expression receives no such protection." It certainly conveys meaning when somebody punches you in the nose or throws a rock through your window, but they cannot invoke the Charter to shield that action from an official state response.

There is one more aspect of the case that needs to be considered, and that is the fact that we are not dealing with a person expressing unpopular ideas, or even with someone parking in a prohibited zone in order to

---

44 Actually, the Court had started with a seven-judge panel for the oral argument, but Estey and Le Dain had both left the Court by the time a decision was handed down; and since Beetz and McIntyre wrote a dissent, these three co-authoring judges constituted the entirety of the decision-delivering majority of the panel. It is a bit unusual to have had such a major decision handed down so confidently by what had been reduced through attrition to such a minimum panel.

45 Although, typically for the Dickson Court in its "first wave" of Charter decisions, it does not actually draw a line, saying instead that there is no need to draw the line at this time beyond making it clear that violence is always and necessarily on the wrong side.

protest a rule; we are dealing with TV advertising for the purpose of sell-ing products for profit—what the literature calls "commercial speech." In the United States, for example, although "freedom of speech" (expanded by judicial interpretation so that it might as well say freedom of expres-sion) is the core of the First Amendment that has become so iconically important, it was long accepted that differences in content would consign various examples or means of communication to different "levels of scru-tiny" for constitutional purposes. Only in 1976 was it clearly accepted that "commercial speech" was deserving of a rigorous level (albeit not yet the highest level) of protection against government regulation.[46] It is therefore striking that in this, the very first major decision on the freedom of expression,[47] the Supreme Court of Canada was already treating com-mercial expression as part of the broader category of protected expression for constitutional purposes: "Surely it aims to convey a meaning, and can-not be excluded as having no expressive content. Nor is there any basis for excluding the form of expression chosen from the sphere of protected activity." When the Charter constrains government activity, it does not do so only to protect individuals, but also to protect corporate activities that can wear the same identifying cloak.

This is just the first step, however, of the recently established *Oakes* test: the claimant has made a prima facie case that the legislation vio-lates a Charter right.[48] In this case, although I will not follow the logic in detail, the Quebec government was able to make a convincing argument that the legislation in question was a reasonable limit directed towards a significant purpose that was tailored to accomplish its ends with minimal interference with the right. Nonetheless, this case already hints at a real

---

46 The case was *Virginia State Board of Pharmacy v. Virginia Citizens Consumer Council*, 425 U.S. 748 (1976). This case is *not* cited in *Irwin Toy*.

47 I should note that they had also made the point four months earlier in *Ford v. Quebec (A.-G.)*, [1988] 2 S.C.R. 712.

48 There is a terminological question here: if we ultimately find that a limit was indeed justified under s.1, can we really use the word "violation" to describe the find-ing that led to the s.1 enquiry in the first place? The answer clearly is, yes; in *Oakes*, paragraph 68, where Dickson describes section 1 as being invoked "for the purpose of justifying a *violation* of the constitutional rights and freedoms the Charter was designed to protect" (emphasis added).

problem with the perfectly plausible procedure of adopting a very generous and expansive notion of a protected right—it really leaves section 1
to do all the work. Pretty well anything that conveys any meaning at all
(and is not violent) is protected prima facie, but there are lots of things
that convey objectionable meaning or that do so in objectionable ways;
the standard example from the US is a person who (falsely) shouts "Fire!"
in a crowded theatre. When section 1 does the work and everything is
protected expression, but lots of regulations are nonetheless reasonable,
it really does support the impression of a section 1 game of "offer and
snatch" with respect to rights—rights that are protected in general but
often, even usually, not in the specific.

ANDREWS

Andrews[49] seems a little late to qualify for my "first early take on the
Charter" rubric, but this appearance is misleading; unlike the rest of the
Charter, which came into effect on April 17, 1982, the "equality rights"
section of the Charter came into effect three years later. The delay was
to allow Parliament and legislators some time to do a review of their
legislation—much of it drafted in a different time and guided by a different set of expectations on such matters—and then to make the appropriate
changes to bring it into line with these new constitutional requirements.
For a non-trivial number of statutes, such retrofitting was simply not feasible, and the appropriate adjustment was simply to repeal the legislation.
This was generally done through a series of massive omnibus bills making
minor amendments to long strings of statutes. This meant that, although
the first set of Charter cases worked their way up the judicial pyramid
and began arriving before the Supreme Court in 1984, the first equality
rights cases took several years, and *Andrews* was the Court's first major
take on section 15. The date notwithstanding, it clearly belongs in this
early impact set.

The case was brought by a British subject who was not admitted by
the BC bar to the practice of law because he was not (as their rules then
required) a Canadian citizen, although he met every other requirement

---

49 *Andrews v. Law Society of British Columbia*, [1989] 1 S.C.R. 143.

for admission.[50] The giving of reasons for this decision is slightly unusual (and very much like *Therens*, discussed above) in that the section 15 analysis is provided by Justice McIntyre, even though he ultimately wound up writing a dissent because the majority of the panel disagreed with him as to whether the section 1 "reasonable limits" clause could save the legislation in question. McIntyre thought it could, while the majority of the panel thought it could not, with Wilson delivering the reasons that took the majority in this other direction. This renders the case another demonstration of the fact that interesting things can happen between the conference that follows oral argument and the actual handing down of the Court's decision.[51] Given the section 1 process, though, of first having to find that there is a prima facie case for a violation, the critical part of *Andrews* is found in the reasons by McIntyre, their status as a dissent notwithstanding.

McIntyre began by disagreeing with the reasons of the British Columbia Court of Appeal,[52] which had suggested that the discrimination that was inconsistent with the Charter was discrimination that was "'invidious or pejorative' in nature, in that it must result from an unreasonable classification or unjustifiable differentiation" on the grounds that it would "trivialize" the Charter for any and every distinction to trigger section 1 scrutiny. McIntyre rejected this line of argument, which would have imported ideas of reasonableness and fairness into section 15 itself instead of (or even in addition to) considering such aspects of the case within the section 1 analysis. He did not adopt the option that the British Columbia Court of Appeal had rejected (but that constitutional expert Peter Hogg had explicitly recommended) of treating every legislative

---

50 The fact situation therefore was very similar to that in *Skapinker v. Law Society of Upper Canada*, [1984] 1 S.C.R. 357, arguably the Court's first Charter case; but because of the three year delay for the coming into force of the s.15 equality rights, that case was argued—unsuccessfully—in terms of a violation of s.6 mobility rights.

51 For a more thorough treatment of these "swing" judgements, see Peter McCormick, ""Was it Something I Said?" Losing the Majority on the Modern Supreme Court of Canada, 1984–2011," *Osgoode Hall Law Journal* (2012).

52 Ironically, those reasons for a unanimous panel of the B.C.C.A. were written by Justice Beverley McLachlin, who was elevated to the Supreme Court less than two months after this decision was handed down, and became Chief Justice a dozen years later.

distinction as a prima facie violation; this would have replicated the experience of "freedom of expression" described above, where all speech is free but many limits are ultimately justified. Instead, he found a third option, which was to focus on the "grounds" rather than simply "the discrimination." Section 15 has a somewhat confusing structure; it is labelled "equality rights," but it unfolds this as equality before and under the law and a right to equal protection and benefit of the law "without discrimination" and in particular, without discrimination on a listed set of criteria such as race, religion, sex, or age.[53]

We can therefore narrow the scope of the discrimination that is a prima facie violation, not by the "reasonableness" test of the BC Court of Appeal, but by identifying what the listed criteria have in common and then extending the protection to unlisted criteria only if they share these essential features. Starting with *Andrews*, these criteria have been thought to be personal characteristics that are either immutable or changeable only with exceptional difficulty. Lack of citizenship, although it is not one of the enumerated categories, is a "good example" of what the Charter language contemplates. (La Forest's separate reasons ratchet up the rhetoric by describing them as "an example without parallel of a group of persons who are relatively powerless politically, and whose interests are likely to be compromised by legislative decisions.")[54]

What strikes me as unusual about this case is that, although these are the Court's first major statements about equality rights, the occasion that was seized by the Court did not hinge on one of the enumerated categories, but rather explicitly expanded that set in a non-trivial way by defining and then using the notion of analogous categories; I would have thought that it would take the Court two or three major cases to work up to this potentially ambitious expansion. This case remains important today; at

---

53 The standard label in the case law and the literature for this list is the "enumerated categories" (even though they are not in fact numbered) and the broader set of conceptually similar grounds as "analogous categories."

54 McIntyre mentions in passing the phrase "discrete and insular majorities" (from the famous "footnote 4" in *United States v. Carolene Products Co.*, 304 U.S. 144 [1938]) which have played an important part in American constitutional law. Wilson's short majority reasons pick up on this in a more focused way, making this a rare example of American ideas and terminology being imported into Charter law.

one point, we might have thought that the *Law v. Canada* case (discussed in the next chapter) had redefined the Court's equality rights doctrine in a major way that relegated *Andrews* to the history books, but a more recent decision by the McLachlin Court (also discussed in the following chapter) has restored *Andrews* to something close to its earlier prominence.

THE BLOCKBUSTER: *MORGENTALER*

Morgentaler[55] was without a doubt the clearest signal that the Charter's reception by the Supreme Court had indeed taken us into a new era of Canadian politics with a new balance between elected governments and an appointed Supreme Court. It dealt with abortion, arguably the most divisive and potentially explosive social issue in Western societies in the last third of the twentieth century[56]—something that the Court could have been excused for sidestepping. If one looks closely, the decision was not only divided (seven judges writing four sets of reasons) but also delicately nuanced—nowhere close to the definitive settling of the issue that it is now widely accepted as having been. This nuance is a nice display of the Dickson Court's careful balancing act: firm statements of Charter meaning, open for future development, made in such a way as to avoid an unnecessarily direct confrontational showdown with the government.

The case involved three doctors who were accused of performing abortions in a Toronto clinic in a manner that contravened the abortion sections in the Criminal Code, which essentially criminalized abortions unless they were handled by an appropriate committee through an appropriate procedure. Morgentaler had for years been a crusader in favour of a woman's right to abortion, and he and his colleagues had been before the courts previously—generally doing better with juries than with judges—but this was the case which made it to the Supreme Court as a Charter case. At first glance, it might seem a little curious that a core women's rights issue surfaced in the context of a criminal case with three male defendants, but,

---

55 *R. v. Morgentaler*, [1988] 1 S.C.R. 301; I specify 1988 because Dr. Morgentaler was also before the Supreme Court both earlier (in 1976) and later (in 1993).

56 Gay rights is arguably on the same short list and would be dealt with by the Lamer Court during the 1990s, as discussed below.

again, this is entirely consistent with section 52 of the Constitution Act, 1982 (a statute is invalid if it conflicts with the constitution by violating anybody's rights, not just the defendant's). It is more problematic, however, for section 24(2) of the Charter, which suggests that you can explore a broader set of remedies if it is your own rights that have been violated.

The very divided decision (four sets of reasons on a seven-judge panel, none signed by more than a pair of judges) centred on section 7 of the Charter—the right to life, liberty, and security of the person—and the core issue was whether the Criminal Code provisions violated women's right to security of the person. Essentially, the Criminal Code said that abortion was a crime, but not if it was approved by a hospital-specific Therapeutic Abortion Committee with several medically qualified members and performed under their aegis. For two members of the panel (McIntyre and La Forest), this logical structure and process completely satisfied Charter requirements such that they would have upheld the Criminal Code sections, but their five colleagues, in three different sets of reasons, held otherwise. The problem was that not all hospitals had established Therapeutic Abortion Committees (indeed, there were entire provinces where none existed), nor did they all deal with the applications made to them in an equally timely fashion. A further problem was that the notion of "health" (from the text of the Code) was not defined clearly or applied identically by different committees. Women in different parts of the country did not enjoy equal access to abortion through the established channels, and this violated the security rights of women in the less-accessible or not-at-all-accessible parts of the country.

For two pairs of judges (Dickson with Lamer, and Beetz with Estey), this was sufficient to find that the relevant sections of the Criminal Code violated section 7 of the constitution, although their reasons suggested slightly different sets of adjustments that would suffice to bring the law into conformity with the Charter; the statute was procedurally flawed, but not substantively inappropriate. As Dickson wrote, "Simply put, assuming Parliament can act, it must do so properly" (73). The point I am making is that Parliament could indeed act.[57] Only a single judge on

---

[57] The wording is mildly provocative, but there was no indication that anything in particular should be read into the "assuming" qualifier at the start of the sentence.

the Court, Justice Wilson, wrote her own separately concurring reasons (i.e., agreeing with the outcome but not with the analysis that led up to it), eloquently defending a woman's right to abortion. Despite the solitary nature of her position on the panel—no other justice signed on to her reasons—hers is probably the meaning that most people take from the decision. The Mulroney government spent several years attempting to amend the Code so as to address the procedural flaws, but failed to get the amendments through Parliament, admitting defeat after the bill famously went down to a tied vote in the Senate.

There is something that is (on the one hand) curious but (on the other) very informative about the outcome. The Supreme Court's 1988 decision effectively settled the abortion issue in Canada, leading to virtually unfettered access to abortion on demand, unrestrained by any Criminal Code provisions. There are still some organizations passionately opposed to this outcome, and laws limiting protests outside abortion clinics are on the books and occasionally in the news. Backbench MPs briefly raise the issue in Parliament, but, effectively, abortion has disappeared as a significant political issue. Most people would explain this in terms of the Supreme Court decision—probably in terms of a woman's "right to abortion"—but there is no such declaration in the Supreme Court decision, except from a solitary outlier. In one sense, this shows the power of the Court in striking down the statute (at least until it could be appropriately revised, which turned out to be never); in another sense, this shows the real limitation of the Court, in that it cannot control the broader meaning and impact of its decisions, which can wind up being rather different from anything the Court said or (on the face of it) intended.

It is worth noting that even in this early case, section 7 was already starting to "float away" from the other rights in sections 7–14, a block that is identified in the Charter as "legal rights." At first reading, it looks like this is a set of rights that relate to what happens when you are directly involved with judicial—even more narrowly, criminal—proceedings, with section 7 as a general introduction to the more focused rights of sections 8–14. Already in 1988, section 7 was being read as something of a free-standing section, linked to, but by no means limited by, the more specifically judicial/criminal rights that followed it. The rise of the importance of section 7 is one of the less anticipated and more significant developments of Charter interpretation.

THE ODD ONE OUT: *THE LABOUR TRILOGY*

If *Irwin Toy* was the opening act for the major issue of freedom of expression under the Charter, and *Big M* played the same role for freedom of religion, and *Andrews* raised the curtains on equality rights, then the *Labour Trilogy* seemed well positioned to do the same thing for the freedom of association. As I will explain, this did not unfold in anything like the same way, and it stands out as a curious anomaly in what was otherwise a dramatic and confident exposition of the Charter that the Court was taking very seriously indeed.

As the label implies, the *Labour Trilogy* was not one case but three: a reference case on a piece of Alberta legislation that would have denied certain sets of provincial employees the right to strike;[58] another case involving collective bargaining and the federal government's wage and price controls;[59] and a third case involving "back to work" legislation as the Saskatchewan government intervened in a labour dispute involving dairy workers.[60] These were "companion cases" in that they raised related issues and were assigned to exactly the same panel of Supreme Court judges; furthermore, two of them (PSAC and RWDSU) were argued on sequential days, and all three decisions were handed down on the same day. More to the point, the divisions in the panel were exactly the same for all three cases; the *Alberta Labour Reference* was the first of the three (i.e., it goes first in the *Supreme Court Reports*), and the other two can be taken as variations on this basic theme, although the triplication of the results make the message unusually emphatic.

Dickson assigned himself the initial drafting of the majority reasons, and he sketched a very broad conception of the freedom of association as "the freedom to combine together for the pursuit of common purposes or the advancement of common causes" (para. 23) which had been an important part of human endeavours "throughout history" (para. 23). The freedom of association, said Dickson, was "the cornerstone of modern labour relations" (para. 24) and a response to "the inherent inequalities

---

58 *Reference re Public Service Employee Relations Act (Alta.)*, [1987] 1 S.C.R. 313.
59 *PSAC v. Canada*, [1987] 1 S.C.R. 424.
60 *RWDSU v. Saskatchewan*, [1987] 1 S.C.R. 460.

of bargaining power in the employment relationship" (para. 24). He set himself three questions—Are trade unions accorded any constitutional protection? What approach is taken to the nature of freedom of association? What is the nature of activity that is protected?—and surveyed English, Canadian, American, and international law and jurisprudence to find an expansive answer. He denied (para. 73) that the Charter protected only those rights that clearly existed before entrenchment, and he denied as well (para. 85) that the freedom of association focused on political issues rather than economic activities. He concluded that what was protected is not only association for other Charter-protected activities, but action that follows from the common interests of legitimate association; otherwise, adding a "freedom of association" would be "mere surplusage." Indeed, his ultimate conclusion was that the Charter also provided "protection of their freedom to withdraw collectively their services" (para. 96)—that is to say, the right to strike—which was a daring high point the Court has never since reached. All this, of course, was within the frame of section 1 and its reasonable limits, but in the immediate circumstances of the Alberta legislation (and the legislation in the companion cases) he did not find that there was such a reasonable limit.

The tone and the analysis is clearly consistent with Dickson's style of decision-making in the major Charter decisions he had delivered during his Chief Justiceship, but although his reasons were drafted as the majority judgement, a swing of support left him (and his lone ultimate supporter, Justice Wilson) writing a dissent. McIntyre instead wrote reasons adopting precisely the idea that Dickson had rejected: the freedom of association merely allows people to do in the company of others what they are already free to do as individuals under other provisions of the Charter (para. 155). That is to say, it is, in the end, mere surplusage. McIntyre included what strikes me as a rather sharp rebuke to Dickson, warning that "the *Charter* should not be regarded as an empty vessel to be filled with whatever meaning we might wish from time to time" (para. 151). Curiously, though, even McIntyre could not hold the majority, and the very short reasons that ultimately constituted the judgement of the Court (so-labelled in the *Supreme Court Reports*) were written by Le Dain, who flatly declared that collective bargaining rights "are not fundamental rights or freedoms" but rather "the creation of legislation" (para. 144). He concluded by finding it "surprising" that the Court would consider "substituting its judgement" on this matter for that of the legislature, which involved a review of legislative policy for which the Court really was "not fitted."

It is intriguing that although Dickson clearly led his Court as few other Chief Justices have done and personally delivered many of the major decisions (especially the Charter decisions) for which his Court is remembered, he could not do so in this one significant instance. Furthermore, the case is all the more important for the fact that it so clearly raised class issues and practical divisions within society in a way that many other Charter cases did not. It cannot be denied that corporations did rather well in the early Charter cases, using freedom of expression and freedom of religion in ways which enhanced their capacity to make profits, while the unions struck out even on the section they thought spoke directly to them. The issue of what the Charter means for organized labour and collective bargaining will re-emerge in a later chapter.

CONCLUSION

At the end of Dickson's Chief Justiceship in 1990, the Supreme Court's Charter jurisprudence had clearly established a number of guiding principles and characteristics:

1. A purposive approach, accommodated by a "broad and liberal" reading of the text.
2. A flexible, open, and evolving approach to rights and the Charter, explicitly avowing a document whose meaning will change over time and avoiding a chiseled-in-stone tone for its findings.
3. A lack of constraint by legislative history or pre-Charter jurisprudence (purposivism without originalism).
4. A lack of restraint by older presumptions about the special status of cabinet deliberations or foreign policy.
5. No excessive deference to or acceptance of the ideas and doctrines that the USSC had developed for its much longer-standing entrenched Bill of Rights.
6. More generous standing rules to permit the entry of a wider range of litigants.

7. A lack of sympathy to governmental convenience or cost in terms of reasonableness of limitations.

8. A willingness to tackle the most politically controversial issues.

9. A setting down of (very) broadly defined approaches to fundamental freedoms (especially speech), and also to equality (i.e., moving beyond the "enumerated" categories).

10. An attachment of vigorous meaning to some of the more opaque and potentially government-friendly phrases in the Charter (e.g., "reasonable limits" and "fundamental justice").

This is certainly value-for-money for the new Charter and the newly reorganized Court that was putting flesh on the textual bones. The emerging doctrine centred on a single concept (which is a bit reductionist but still worth doing): "purposivism" is the key idea. However, as it was developed by the Dickson Court, this had no overtones of originalism in any of its variants, but rather organized itself around some question like, "What kind of a Canada does the Charter want us to have?"

CHAPTER FOUR

THE LAMER COURT: THE CHARTER EXPANDED

The Lamer Court is the second of the three to have dealt with the Charter. Lamer became Chief Justice on July 1, 1990, when Dickson stepped down, almost a full year before he reached retirement age. Lamer's appointment was not a surprise, given the practice for a senior serving member of the Court to become Chief Justice when a vacancy occurs. (On some accounts, there is an emerging convention for a French/English alternation for Chief Justices, which this appointment also satisfied, although I am not fully persuaded that there is any such convention.) Unlike the American practice of bringing a new Chief Justice from outside the Court, the Canadian practice of promoting seniority from within implies a considerable degree of continuity within the Court from one Chief Justiceship to the next, an expectation reinforced by the fact that Dickson and Lamer tended to vote together on divided panels.[1]

I have described the major elements of the Charter revolution as having been accomplished by the robust jurisprudence of the Dickson Court in the Charter's first half-dozen years of court cases. The Lamer Court's contribution to the continuing development of the Charter came

---

1 See Peter McCormick, *Supreme at Last: The Evolution of the Supreme Court of Canada* (Toronto: Lorimer Press, 2000), chap. 7.

in two forms. The first was the not-unexpected expansion of doctrine, continuing to press forward with unsettled or incompletely resolved issues (such as gay rights) and to flesh out Charter jurisprudence both with more specific details and with conceptual frameworks to consolidate differences within the Court (such as equality rights more generally). If there was an underlying theme to this, it was perhaps the reshaping of Charter doctrine to give greater emphasis and a stronger role to the notion of human dignity, a recurrent tendency of Lamer Court decisions that arguably peaked just before the end of the decade; the *Law* case, which I discuss below, is perhaps the high-water mark in this respect. The second was a willingness to explore a considerably wider repertoire of remedies for Charter breaches; where the Dickson Court had generally declared offending legislation void in whole or in part, the Lamer Court was more prepared to advise as to the appropriate legislative reworking of offending legislation, or to use the remarkably open invitation of section 24 to fashion its own solutions, or both. This was accompanied by a more flamboyant enthusiasm for the Court's new and powerful role—all too delightfully epitomized by the famous interview in which Lamer said of his own Court, and its vigorous invocation of the Charter, "Thank God we're here."[2]

THE LAMER COURT AND GAY RIGHTS

In terms of equality rights, one of the Lamer Court's significant moves was to extend the analogous grounds of section 15 to include sexual orientation. This happened in a slightly curious two-step process. The first critical case in this respect was *Egan v. Canada*,[3] in which a person in a gay relationship asked the court to uphold his right to a dependent's allowance derived from his partner's old-age pension. (Since the person in question was actually entitled to his own pension instead, this would

---

2 The quotation appears in Janice Tibbetts, "Politicians Duck Divisive Issues, Chief Justice Says," *National Post*, July 12, 1999, A4, cited in Grant Huscroft, "'Thank God We're Here': Judicial Exclusivity in Charter Interpretation and Its Consequences," *Supreme Court Law Review* 25 (2nd series) (2004): 243.

3 *Egan v. Canada*, [1995] 2 S.C.R. 513.

have the effect of reducing the payment to which he was entitled, but this is irrelevant to the legal issues involved.) In a fragmented judgement, the Court agreed that sexual orientation was included in section 15 as an "analogous ground" (not one of the listed prohibited grounds for discrimination, but like the items on that list in being a personal characteristic that is immutable or that cannot be changed without real difficulty). However, a plurality of the Court found that the government's policy was ultimately not a violation of that right because that policy was grounded in the "functional realities" of the family interests that were embedded in the legislation. Although Sopinka and his "swing vote" broke the tie between the two major groupings into which the panel divided, he did so by being the only member of the panel to find a Charter violation that could still be saved by section 1's "reasonable limits" so as to allow the legislation to stand. In broader terms, this was seen by many critics as part of an alarming trend that threatened to contain section 15's implications unacceptably; they spoke of an "Equality Rights Trilogy"[4] in ways that evoked comparison with the 1987 "Labour Trilogy"—that is to say, a set of judicial decisions that effectively strangled the broader hopes of an initially promising constitutional provision. The Court responded to these concerns in the *Law* case, which I will discuss below.

If you have to lose a court case, this is definitely the way to do it. The Court had definitively and unambiguously found that sexual orientation was protected by section 15, not because it was listed specifically, but because it satisfied the conditions the Court had developed for invoking analogous grounds (i.e., "immutable personal characteristics"). So long as the "functional realities" internal test for these analogous grounds did not turn out to have a long shelf life—and as far as I can work out, this was Gonthier's idea that disappeared fairly promptly from the Charter jurisprudence—this surface defeat was really a deeper victory, to be cashed in later. The cashing in was clearly accomplished in *Vriend v. Alberta*,[5] which I will discuss below in terms of its contribution to the

---

4 The other cases in the trilogy were *Miron v. Trudel*, [1995] 2 S.C.R. 418 and *Thibaudeau v. Canada*, [1995] 2 S.C.R. 627, the first dealing with the exclusion of common-law spouses from routine automobile insurance coverage, and the second dealing with the taxation of support payments following the breakup of a marriage.

5 *Vriend v. Alberta*, [1998] 1 S.C.R. 493.

Lamer Court's exploration of Charter remedies.[6] However, given that gay rights has been one of the more divisive issues in Canadian society over the preceding decades, the Court's willingness to settle the issue for legal and constitutional purposes is striking, the more so because it had already dealt equally vigorously with the even more divisive issue of abortion rights.[7]

The divided decision in *Egan* mentioned above was actually symptomatic of a deeper problem—although the Dickson Court decision in *Andrews* was accepted as the bedrock starting point for the Court's section 15 jurisprudence, there were diverging ideas within the Court as to where the logic should take them. This sometimes resulted in a multiplicity of judgements and plurality decisions (that is, cases in which there was no single outcome-plus-reasons that drew the signatures of a majority of the members of the panel); other times, it resulted in narrow majority outcomes as one group or another prevailed because of the details of the immediate case or because of the composition of less-than-full panels. The Court finally grasped this nettle in *Law*.

THE LAMER COURT AND EQUALITY RIGHTS

Law v. Canada[8] was arguably the Lamer Court's most ambitious undertaking. It was an attempt, authored by Iacobucci, to fundamentally reshape the judicial framework for dealing with equality cases, responding to the

---

6 I will not discuss the reasons for that decision in any detail—once it is established that sexual orientation satisfies section 15's analogous grounds, and once there is no "functional realities" speed bump put in the way, then a prima facie case for a Charter violation is easily established, and we are into section 1's "reasonable limits" and remedy issues. This, rather than the substantive issue, is the major interest in *Vriend*—it is the prime example of one of the Lamer Court's additions to the repertoire of Charter remedies, as will be discussed later.

7 Strictly speaking, there is still no "right to abortion" that has ever been recognized by the Supreme Court in Canadian constitutional law, but working the issue into a broad reading of the section 7 right to "life, liberty and security of the person" has made it so difficult for the government to legislate, not least by priming public opinion on the issue, that it might as well be.

8 *Law v. Canada*, [1999] 1 S.C.R. 497.

differences and divisions that had emerged in a decade of equality case decisions. Some judges (such as La Forest and Gonthier) continued to look for an internal limiting principle within equality rights to deflect rights claims short of the section 1 reasonable limits process, while some (most notably L'Heureux-Dubé, who makes this argument again in her short, separate reasons in *Law*) wanted to expand the scope of section 15's anti-discrimination bite well beyond enumerated and analogous grounds; still others wanted to stay with the simpler framework of *Andrews*. In *Law*, Iacobucci sought to consolidate these trends, and to establish a central logic around which the challenges to legislation and policy on equality grounds could be organized, expanding upon the bare-bones procedural framework that could be found in *Andrews*. Put differently, the target was a decision that would do for equality rights what *Irwin Toy* had done for freedom of expression: set a solid and comprehensive basic frame that could be explored for its details (such as the interaction with section 1) but would not need to be revisited or modified in its basic contours. Although initial trends were promising, *Law* ultimately failed, and in a later section, I will be discussing the case where the Court itself (sort of) said so.

The *Law* case involved the legislative and regulation framework for old-age pensions—specifically, the provision that a person below a certain age could not gain survivor's benefits for a deceased spouse in the absence of a demonstrated handicap or disability. The case is interesting as well for demonstrating the increasing tendency of equality rights cases not to focus on the "big," broad sweep issues (men versus women, young versus old, etc.) but rather to involve multiple cross-cutting distinctions that tend to create very small claimant categories—in this case, young, non-handicapped widows of deceased old-age pension recipients, a group small enough that it almost looks like caricature simply to describe it.

I will not attempt to summarize the complexity of Iacobucci's analysis, because it is very extended and rather complicated. Instead of the relative simplicity of the three stages of *Andrews*, we now have 10 stages, four of which included several identified substages. There is also the new critical factor of "comparator groups" which must be correctly chosen and described in order for the case to succeed—one is not discriminated against *tout court*, but rather discriminated against because one is a member of an identifiable group that is treated by government in a way that is disadvantageous in comparison with the way that another group, the "comparator group," is treated. It follows on the earlier shift in equality rights jurisprudence, from "equality" in a strictly formal sense to "freedom from discrimination," and it continues to ground the prohibited grounds of discrimination in immutable personal characteristics, but now firmly anchors the analysis to the proposition that what is prohibited is discrimination (that is to say, differentiated treatment) that involves denigration or a denial of human dignity. It is also worth noting that this case represents arguably the high-water mark for the Lamer Court's exploration of "human dignity" as a central organizing concept for the interpretation of the Charter, in the same sense that "purposiveness" was the comparable central organizing concept for the Dickson Court.

The case is important for its ambition: while insisting that it was not a formal or final test, it would have permanently set the framework for the resolution of future equality cases. For a number of years it was by far the most frequently cited case in the Supreme Court's Charter equality cases, clearly eclipsing its predecessor *Andrews*; to argue equality, you simply had to locate your case by reference to *Law*. More recently, however, it has been set aside; in an unusually candid way, the McLachlin Court acknowledged the difficulties with *Law*, denied it the pre-eminence it briefly seemed to have gained, and effectively resurrected *Andrews* as the leading precedent case. The case in which they did so was *Kapp*, described in the next chapter. Readers will note how well this recent tone of moderation, containment, and partial retreat fits with my overall theme.

THE LAMER COURT AND FREE SPEECH OR OBSCENITY

The problem with the right to freedom of expression is that it simply cannot mean that all expression is absolutely free of legal constraint or consequence; the simple slogan is completely misleading. There are still problems with slander and libel, false advertising, selling secrets to the enemy, and openly publishing information about how to make bombs or manufacture deadly toxins, not to mention all the obvious problems about privacy rights. More immediately and even more obviously, there is a problem with pornography, that is, with the kind of pictures and movies that some people like to look at but which other people find deeply offensive.

The Lamer Court's definitive answer to this was *Butler*,[9] which is still the leading case on the issue. Butler was the owner of a video boutique selling adult materials in Winnipeg, and was charged with a string of violations of the laws regarding the distribution of obscene material. His perfectly obvious and predictable defence was the Charter right to freedom of expression. Given the sweeping general doctrine in *Irwin Toy*, there was unquestionably a prima facie violation, and therefore the weight fell on "reasonable limits" in section 1 of the Charter. The trial judge found that most of the charges were brought under sections of the Criminal Code that were such a reasonable limit, and so Butler was convicted on 16 counts. A divided Manitoba Court of Appeal decided that the films in question depicted "mere physical activity" that conveyed no meaning and therefore did not raise "freedom of expression" issues in the first place, which led to the same end point of upholding the convictions.

The Supreme Court of Canada, however, agreed instead with the trial judge, finding a Charter violation, and much of the explanatory efforts were devoted to a "reasonable limits" analysis. They identified the objective of that part of the Criminal Code as "the prevention of harm" to society, and this being a valid objective, and the criminal sanction being reasonably connected to the objective, the law was a reasonable limit.[10] Characterizing the Criminal Code in this way is actually a little tricky; the section in question had been passed in 1959, at which time it was widely described as growing from a focus on the "corruption of morals" and, in 1970, Dickson (then serving on the Manitoba Court of Appeal) had defended this part of the statute in terms of "the right of the state to protect its moral fibre and well-being."[11] In *Butler*, however, with some apparent embarrassment, the majority worked its way around the earlier strictures against using a "shifting purpose" analysis for Charter purposes.[12] They did so by finding a "prevention of harm" purpose as the

---

9 *R. v. Butler*, [1992] 1 S.C.R. 452.

10 There was also an extended discussion of the "community standard of tolerance" test which I am omitting from consideration at this time.

11 *R. v. Great West News Ltd.*, [1970] 4 C.C.C. 307 p. 309.

12 "Purpose is a function of the intent of those who drafted and enacted the legislation at the time, and not of any shifting variable." *R. v. Big M Drug Mart Ltd.*, [1985] 1 S.C.R. 295 per Dickson, p. 335.

implicit core of the criminal law power, and then linking moral corruption with social harm; this may not really have moved things very far but it did allow the Court to deal with the pornography issue without the entanglement of historic phrases like "moral corruption" and "protection of moral fibre." It is disappointing, though, that the Court admitted that "a direct link between obscenity and harm to society may be difficult, if not impossible, to establish" but nonetheless concluded that "it is reasonable to presume" that these images have a negative effect on public attitudes— in the immediate case, we seem to have changed the name of the highway even though it is still capable of carrying the same traffic.[13]

I think there is a deeper subtext involved that goes beyond the Charter, and hints at a judicial project that would redefine the criminal law. In Canadian federalism, this matters because of the division of legislative authority between the two levels of government. Sections 91 and 92 of the Constitution Act, 1867 give the federal Parliament and the provincial legislatures, respectively, exclusive jurisdiction over "matters" coming with the "classes of subject" that are listed within those sections.[14] One of the items in the section 91 list is "the criminal law"—whatever that is, and whatever its boundaries, the federal Parliament has exclusive jurisdiction over it, even if its content or its target might otherwise be thought to infringe on the exclusive jurisdiction of the provinces. How do we define "the criminal law" for these purposes? A completely static definition is

---

13 This is, of course, one face of a very large question. Strictly speaking, the plaintiff must stand ready to prove every single aspect of a case. If I were to be charged with speeding through a Lethbridge school zone, the Crown would have to be ready to offer evidence that Lethbridge is actually in Alberta. Pushed too far, this becomes silly, so judges can take judicial notice of things that everybody knows (like the fact that it is darker before the sun comes up)—but this raises further problems because the things that "everybody knows" can be tainted by broadly accepted cultural stereotypes or unexplored assumptions. "Reasonable to presume" is of course a slightly fancier version of "everybody knows."

14 It is actually a bit trickier than this, because section 91 gives Parliament the power to legislate for the "peace, order, and good government" of Canada, and then "for greater specificity but not so as to limit the generality of the foregoing" it goes on to list 29 classes of subjects. Exactly how much, and in what ways, the "P.O.G.G." clause adds to that list is a question that has enjoyed an evolving answer that even today has flexible and debatable boundaries.

not attractive (e.g., "those matters that were the subject of the criminal law in 1867"[15]—before there was even a criminal code, and when much of our criminal law was judge-made common law); neither is a totally open definition attractive (e.g., "any prohibition accompanied by a penalty"— which actually was the constitutional definition for a while),[16] because provincial jurisdiction becomes completely permeable. For decades, the answer has been a Supreme Court decision from early 1949:[17] a criminal law is a prohibition accompanied by a penalty directed to an appropriate public purpose (although it jars a bit today to see that such purposes are unfolded to include public morality as well as public safety and public health).

Butler, as I read it, is working in a roundabout way towards a new definition. It is roundabout in that it does not deal up front with the definition or redefinition of the criminal law as such. Nonetheless, we are dealing with a specific criminal code provision; the offence in question leads us to the freedom of expression, and then to section 1's reasonable limits; and the finding is that the Criminal Code section survives because its purpose is the prevention of harm to society. This is the logical lever that the Court uses to create its three different categories of sexually oriented material, with varying levels of potential harm more easily triggering the use of more significant criminal penalties. "The prevention of harm" is, in the modern context, a much more palatable legislative purpose than the 60-year-old language of "the promotion of public morality," and although the Court is generally reluctant to save legislation by ascribing a shifting objective (different today from what it clearly was at the time of passage), they were willing to do so in *Butler*.

However, this shift to "prevention of harm," as the way to square Criminal Code prohibitions with the Charter, hit a serious speed bump during the McLachlin Chief Justiceship, when these same principles were invoked to mount a challenge against federal criminal legislation involving

---

15 This statement was, in all seriousness, the Judicial Committee's first answer to the question in *Re: Board of Commerce*, [1922] 1 A.C. 191.

16 The relevant case is *Proprietary Articles Trade Assn. v. A.-G. Canada*, [1931] A.C. 179.

17 The *Margarine Reference*, [1949] S.C.R. 1, per Rand at p. 50. This reasoning was adopted by the Judicial Committee on the subsequent appeal.

the possession and selling of marijuana. The case was *Malmo-Levine*, which was actually a pair of cases mounting slightly different attacks on the legislation.[18] (This was a section 7 challenge—the liberty interest—rather than a section 2 challenge regarding freedom of expression, so the "prevention of harm" element was being brought in as a "principle of fundamental justice" rather than a legitimate objective under section 1. Still, all the judges, majority and minority, accepted the *Butler* argument as directly relevant and requiring attention.) One argument, which sought to invoke Charter equality rights to protect the lifestyle choice of smoking marijuana, was put aside fairly easily—the equality protected by section 15 centres on "immutable personal characteristics," and lifestyle choices do not qualify. The other, which directly picked up on the "harm principle" approach to valid criminal law, was more difficult, because it has two different and powerful prongs: the first is the question of whether the criminal law really should prevent me from making choices that (might) harm only myself, and the second, which is even more pointed, is a challenge to identify the harm that the marijuana laws are targeted on preventing.[19] "Prevention of harm" is harder to demonstrate in the case of so-called victimless crimes. A minority of justices stayed with the point, but the majority denied that "prevention of harm" was a legal principle of sufficient clarity such that it could usefully operationalize the principles of fundamental justice. If there ever was a movement towards "prevention of harm" as a central focus for a constitutionally satisfactory criminal power, it had been set back, if not abandoned.

THE LAMER COURT AND JUDICIAL INDEPENDENCE

Perhaps not so much in the public spotlight, the Lamer Court expanded, even transformed, the notion of jurisprudence. On purely logical grounds,

18 *R. v. Malmo-Levine; R. v. Caine*, [2003] 3 S.C.R. 571, 2003 SCC 74.

19 As I read the reasons, several of the judges clearly did not think that current federal policy regarding marijuana is very sensible, but quite properly they were answering the question "Does government have the power to create the policy?" and not the tempting but line-crossing "Do we think it is a good policy?"

this was not unconnected with the whole issue of what a Charter is and how it is to have its impact—if the constitutional statement of rights as interpreted and invoked by the courts is to provide an effective constraint on government, then the courts that are doing the interpreting and invoking have to stand at an effective arm's length from the government that is being constrained, and it is not a small matter to ask what that "arm's length" should look like.

The Canadian notion of judicial independence that was in play at the time of the entrenchment of the Charter was essentially the set of English practices anchored in the Act of Settlement of 1701[20]—judges enjoy security of tenure (they are very hard to remove) and security of pay (generally operationalized as equal pay for all judges on the same bench, so as to prevent political manipulation of bonuses or penalties), and they are directly supervised only by other judges, not by bureaucrats or politicians.[21] These provisions are found today, as they always have been, in sections 96–100 of the Constitution Act, 1867. Our pre-1982 constitution provided these guarantees only for judges of the superior courts (there was some academic debate as to whether the federal courts or the Supreme Court itself fully qualified, but for practical purposes I think we should take it that they did); a string of provincial reforms through the 1970s had reorganized the provincial courts of inferior jurisdiction to provide legislative protection of the same principles for provincially appointed judges (including such offices and structures as the Chief Judge of Provincial Court and the provincial Judicial Councils). An early Charter decision (*Valente*[22] in 1984) had effectively read these reforms back into the constitution, by finding that the Charter's section 11 requirements for an "independent and impartial tribunal" could only be satisfied in a way that conformed with the English model.

---

20 For the classical statement of English style judicial independence coming into the Charter era, see W.R. Lederman "Judicial Independence," *Canadian Bar Review* 34 (1956): 1139.

21 The detail-chaser in me wants to add: and their status is grounded in a fiercely autonomous legal profession, of which they must at the time of their appointment be experienced members in good standing. See Martin Shapiro, *Courts: A Comparative and Political Analysis* (Chicago: University of Chicago Press, 1986).

22 *Valente v. The Queen*, [1985] 2 S.C.R. 673.

Fast-forward to the mid-1990s, and the issue of judicial independence was back before the Supreme Court. Budget concerns and financial constraints had led province after province to cut back dramatically on their spending, and one of the targets for these constraints was the level of compensation for all public employees. Down towards the end of this list (and it is worth emphasizing that it was towards the end of the list for every province, making it hardly credible to suggest that the judiciary was specially targeted and everything else was shallow pretense) were the provincially appointed and provincially paid judges of the "section 92 courts," who were expected and eventually required to share the pain of the other provincial employees, such as public servants, hospital staff, municipal government employees, teachers and professors, and police and firefighters. This involved some form of salary rollback, which in some provinces took the form of a cycle of days without pay ("Filmon Fridays" in Manitoba, "Rae Days" in Ontario). In several provinces, the judges went to court alleging that a unilateral cut in their pay compromised the Charter requirement of judicial independence; several of these challenges were combined in a single case that was decided by the Supreme Court in September of 1997.

The Lamer Court used this as the occasion for a dramatic ratcheting upwards of the Canadian notion of judicial independence. Even today, the ambitious nature of the decision is clear on the very face of it—the decision in the *Remuneration Reference*[23] is still the longest set of reasons for judgement ever delivered by the Supreme Court of Canada, clocking in at almost 40,000 words, which is to say about half the length of this book.[24] Because one doesn't usually fire off that much artillery without hitting something, it goes without saying that the pay cuts were found to be constitutionally impermissible; Lamer used the occasion, however,

---

23 *Reference re Remuneration of Judges of the Prov. Court of P.E.I.*, [1997] 3 S.C.R. 3.

24 As a total decision, *Gosselin v. Quebec (Attorney General)*, [2002] 4 S.C.R. 429, 2002 SCC 84 is slightly longer (67,000 words to *Remuneration*'s 55,000 words), but most of the length of *Gosselin* (53,000 words) is driven by the several sets of minority reasons; the reasons for judgement in *Gosselin* total only a relative modest 14,000 words. As far as I can determine, there has never been another set of reasons for judgement that has exceeded 30,000 words, and only 2 have come particularly close: *R. v. Finta*, [1993] 1 S.C.R. 1138, and *R. v. Advance Cutting and Coring Ltd.*, 2001 SCC 70.

to redefine judicial independence in Canada in a fashion which arguably makes us the world leader, or at least the global outlier, on this issue.[25]

For one thing, Lamer rediscovered the foundation of judicial independence not as lying within sections 96–100 of the Constitution Act, 1982, or within section 11 of the Charter, but rather as a foundational constitutional principle anchored in the famous preamble to the Constitution Act, 1982, which refers to "a constitution similar in principle to that of the United Kingdom." For another, he linked judicial independence to the Court's new role as a "guardian of the constitution," necessitating a strict principle of the separation of powers—an American constitutional notion that has never been applied by our Supreme Court in any context other than judicial independence, and this without any hint of the American obverse concept of cheques and balances. This means that there can be no bargaining, or appearance of negotiation, between the courts and the government of the day, as this would make the courts subordinate to the government in a way that is incompatible with independence, and therefore incompatible with public confidence in the role of the judiciary. On the question of salaries, it is therefore necessary to establish Judicial Compensation Commissions, and Lamer was quite specific on the terms of reference, the structures, the membership, and the procedures of such a body; any challenge to the recommendations of a compensation commission would itself have to come before a court.

For a time, the Court was exploring a broader concept of decision-maker autonomy, of which judicial independence was the most important but not the only example, and reading out some attenuated version of this independence into a variety of boards and agencies (although this seems to have run its course).[26] Curiously, one of the effects of the decision has been to separate judicial independence from the Charter. If you review the judge-written headnotes for any of the subsequent judicial independence decisions (and there have been several), you will look in vain for

---

25 For a treatment of the original elements in the *Remuneration Reference*, see Peter McCormick, "New Questions about an Old Concept: The Supreme Court of Canada's Judicial Independence Decisions," *Canadian Journal of Political Science* 37 (2004): 839.

26 See McCormick, "New Questions about an Old Concept."

any reference to the Charter, although all of the comparably numerous earlier cases did prominently include this designation.

It is probably true that in terms of public impact and public opinion, the judicial independence decisions hardly compare with blockbuster issues like abortion, gay rights, or kiddie porn. I have described the major decision that anchors this particular set of game-changers in some detail because it so nicely catches the Lamer Court in full flight, flamboyantly and confidently building an impressive new structure on rather shaky foundations. The decision was not unanimous; Justice La Forest wrote alone in dissent, and I am far from alone among court-watchers when I suggest that he very much had the better of the argument in terms of strict law and history.[27] How do you get from "a constitution similar in principle to that of the United Kingdom" to a new principle which extends beyond superior courts (as English-style judicial independence still does not) and mandates powerful commissions that have never enjoyed an English counterpart? No matter: Lamer's audacity is the precedent, La Forest's reticence the obscure footnote, and subsequent decisions of the Supreme Court have shown not the slightest trace of embarrassment, nor the smallest hint of reconsideration or retreat.[28] The lower courts have not been slow to get the message; there have been major confrontations between courts and governments about staffing levels and facilities in (for example) British Columbia and Alberta, with the government most definitely coming out of it second-best. The judicial independence cases show a Court with no doubts or hesitation about the fact that the Charter permits it—even requires it—to restructure in a fundamental way some of the country's major institutions, including

---

27 Goldsworthy's scathing commentary, in my opinion, makes all the relevant points without reticence or apology. See Jeffrey Goldsworthy, "The Preamble, Judicial Independence and Judicial Integrity," *Constitutional Forum* 11 (2000): 60; see also W.N. Renke, *Invoking Independence: Judicial Independence as a No-Cut Wage Guarantee* (Edmonton: Centre for Constitutional Studies, University of Alberta, 1994); and Tsvi Kahana, "The Constitution as a Collective Agreement: Remuneration of Provincial Court Judges in Canada," *Queen's Law Journal* 29 (2004): 487.

28 Most recently (at time of writing) in *Provincial Court Judges' Assn. of New Brunswick v. New Brunswick (Minister of Justice); Ontario Judges' Assn. v. Ontario (Management Board); Bodner v. Alberta; Conférence des juges du Québec v. Quebec (Attorney General); Minc v. Quebec (Attorney General)*, 2005 SCC 44.

the judiciary itself. The curious fact that judicial independence winds up slipping out of the Charter spotlight does not (paradoxically) take away from the fact that the judicial independence decisions reveal the Lamer Court at its most Charter-enthusiastic.

THE LAMER COURT AND CHARTER REMEDIES: THE EXPANDING REPERTOIRE

The first thing we focus on in any Charter decision is, of course, who won—that is to say, the outcome of the case, the appeal allowed or dismissed, and the litigant vindicated or frustrated. The equally obvious second thing that we focus on is why they won—that is to say, the reasons for the outcome—because these will tell us how other sets of actors may have used the immediate case to strengthen their own cases in the future. The third thing we need to know is what they won—that is to say, the remedies that are awarded (or refused), because this will tell us more clearly what is at stake for those other sets of actors in the future.

This is, if you like, the complete judicial package—outcome plus reasons plus remedy. That the Lamer Court greatly expanded the repertoire of remedies, even if that were all that it did (which is not the case), is still a very significant accomplishment. Let me invent the concept of "judicial Charter presence" to make the point.[29] Imagine a graph where the y-axis represents the Court's exploration and expounding of the rights that are protected by the Charter, with a higher value meaning a more robust, more generous, and more open-ended conception of the rights language, and a lower value meaning a narrower and more constricted interpretation. The x-axis represents the Court's exploration of the consequences and remedies that flow from the finding of a violation, with a higher value meaning more imaginative and intrusive remedies and a lower value meaning more modest or constrained measures.[30] "Judicial Charter presence" is the combination (more aptly, the product) of these two values.

---

29 I am deliberately not using the more obvious term "judicial activism" both because its notoriety has attracted such a voluminous literature and because attempts to achieve a rigorous definition are ongoing but highly contested.

30 If your imagination is so inclined, you could turn it into a three-dimensional figure, with not only height and width but also a depth reaching out from the page

An aggressive rights definition has an impact even if the remedies are constrained, and aggressive remedies have an impact even if the rights tend to be defined rather modestly; the greatest impact, however, comes when the Court is prepared in some non-trivial proportion of Charter cases to pursue and expand both dimensions simultaneously.

The most obvious remedy is the one found in section 52 of the Constitution Act, 1982, which declares, "The Constitution of Canada is the supreme law of Canada, and any law that is inconsistent with the provisions of the Constitution is, to the extent of the inconsistency, of no force or effect." If you are confronted by a law, and if you persuade the courts that the law is a violation of your Charter rights that cannot be saved as a reasonable limit, then the law is—to use the standard metaphor—"struck down," declared invalid, and rendered legally null and void.[31] It may only be a single section or even a single phrase that offends, such that the rest of the statute makes sense and accomplishes a useful purpose without it, in which case it is the offending section, and not the whole of the law, that is struck down. The point remains, however, that the Charter's emphatic "no" drowns out the statute's fainter "yes," like the orchestral brass section overwhelming the solo piccolo, and this no-saying drowning out is what the Charter is, at first glance, all about.

I describe this as the most obvious remedy because it is simply a continuation of what the courts used to do when legislation violated the federal–provincial division of legislative authority in sections 91–95 of

---

towards you, that third dimension reflecting how often the Court finds a Charter violation and imposes a remedy—crudely, in a measure that has been used a number of times to evaluate the impact of the Charter, the percentage of the time (or even just a count of the number of times) that the claimant against government is successful. Since I do not intend to turn these ideas into actual numbers, let alone map them against yet another dimension which is change over time coming forward from 1984, the notional picture is the point I want to make: "judicial Charter presence" is a two-dimensional product of rights interpretation and remedy application.

31 This is a slightly misleading phrase, because the court has no power actually to amend legislation. Should you look at the statute on a government website a year or two later, you are likely to find the legislation unchanged; what this really means in practice, then, is that when any court looks at any challenged government action, it will read the statute as if the words had actually been removed by amendment, or (if the whole act was struck down) as if the act had been repealed.

the Constitution Act, 1867. The logic was straightforward—the division of powers is like a fence, and if either a legislature or Parliament has appeared to pass a law that reaches impermissibly beyond that fence, then there is no legitimate authority to pass that law in the first place. The legal term that the courts used was *ultra vires*, meaning "beyond the limits," which perfectly captures the geographic metaphor. Such a finding means that there never was a law—what "looks like a statute" was actually invalid from the day it appeared to have been passed, because the legislature never had the legal authority to create it in the first place. By extension, the easiest first take on the Charter was to see it as a new fence (or perhaps a new pair of fences, one for each level of government), creating a new zone within which government action is prohibited; the finding of illegitimacy would draw on a different logic and generate a different language for the reasons, but the logic of "beyond the limits" remains, and the geographic metaphor of a fence, at least initially, frames our thinking. Laws are either valid or invalid the day they are passed; federalism sets the old (and the Charter, the new) fences that we use to define this validity and legitimacy.[32]

For the Dickson Court, this was pretty well what a finding of invalidity meant, and all of its major decisions worked on the assumption that the appropriate remedy was to immediately strike the law in whole or in part. Search warrant provisions in *Hunter v. Southam*, Criminal Code abortion sections under *Morgentaler*, the Lord's Day Act under *Big M*, refugee appeal procedures under *Singh*, the BC Law Society's membership rules under *Andrews*—all were effectively erased by the Court's decisions, leaving a legal void that the relevant authority could either attempt to refill or just leave open. Indeed, the only remedy that the Dickson Court ever provided for a finding that a statute violated a Charter right was the immediate and retroactive invalidation of that statute in whole or in part.[33] I do not recall anybody being particularly surprised by this remedy

---

32 This is not to say that the geographic metaphor of "fences" or "limits" perfectly captures either federalism or the logic of the Charter, because it does not, but merely to identify it as a metaphor so obvious as to be embedded in our language and therefore easily taken for granted without necessarily being carefully examined.

33 See Bruce Ryder, "Suspending the Charter," *Supreme Court Law Review* 21 (2003): 289.

(which is not to say that they were not sometimes surprised by the finding of a Charter violation in the first place). The Dickson Court may have been fairly robust in its conception and definition of many of the new Charter rights, but it was highly constrained in its conception of remedies and consequences.

One of the major contributions of the Lamer Court to the Charter revolution was to apply itself precisely to this question of remedies and consequences. This challenge was built into the Charter itself; section 52 may point us to the remedy—if you like, to the easy remedy—of invalidation, but it is not the only section of the Charter that suggests answers to the "What next?" that occurs after the finding of a Charter violation. Section 24(2) is a spectacularly wide-open invitation of a remedy-seeking Court, a strong hint—if anybody needed it—that the early and obvious answer did not end the discussion. It provides that "Anyone whose rights or freedoms, as guaranteed by this Charter, have been infringed or denied may apply to a court of competent jurisdiction to obtain such remedy as the court considers appropriate and just in the circumstances." This may be the invalidation of the law, or it may be something else. As Justice McIntyre rightly observed in *Mills*, "It is difficult to imagine language which could give the court a wider and less fettered discretion."[34]

To put it starkly, the Dickson Court spent most of its time parked in remedies that could be grounded in section 52, while the Lamer Court was much more engaged with exploring (with mixed results) the potential territories of section 24(2). The Dickson Court was like the Queen of Hearts in *Alice in Wonderland* who said that if the defendant is guilty then "Off with his head!" The Lamer Court was like the Lord High Executioner in Gilbert and Sullivan's *The Mikado*, trying "to make the punishment fit the crime" or, in this case, to make the remedy more precisely fit the right (purposively understood) and the specific context of the violation of that right. Manfredi has somewhat provocatively suggested that the Lamer Court's willingness to explore remedies is directly related to the receding legitimacy—and therefore the decreasing likelihood of the actual use—of the notwithstanding clause in section 33

---

34 *Mills v. The Queen*, [1986] 1 S.C.R. 863, at p. 965.

of the Charter; a Court less worried about an effective riposte from an unhappy government is a Court more willing to do things that might make governments unhappy.[35]

In terms of my notional "judicial Charter presence" table, the Dickson Court was high for rights definition but low for remedies, while the Lamer Court was slightly higher for rights definition, but much higher for remedies. I reserve for now any characterization of the McLachlin Court in these terms. The net result is that the Lamer Court had a much higher Charter presence, but this was arguably the product of its willingness to explore the question of remedies.[36]

CHARTER REMEDIES: RETROACTIVE INVALIDITY

What does the arsenal of remedies ultimately look like? As described above, the most obvious remedy from our constitutional tradition, and the only one used by the Dickson Court, was an immediate declaration of retroactive invalidity—since the challenge to the existing law had been sustained on a constitutional basis, there never was a valid law. Still, other remedies are entirely possible, and seem to be invited (indeed, demanded) by section 24(2).

CHARTER REMEDIES: DECLARATION

Perhaps the most politically innocuous remedy is a simple declaration of a constitutional violation without any ordered remedy, leaving the selection of an appropriate reaction entirely to the discretion of the relevant

---

35 Christopher Manfredi, "Strategic Behaviour and the Canadian Charter of Rights and Freedoms," in Patrick James, Donald E. Abelson, and Michael Lusztig, eds., *The Myth of the Sacred: The Charter, the Courts and the Politics of the Constitution in Canada* (Kingston: McGill-Queen's University Press, 2002).

36 Turning entire decades into single blocks—"the Dickson Court"; "the Lamer Court"; "the McLachlin Court"—is a distorting simplification that obscures more subtle shifts that are at work within these periods as shifting sets of judges interact and revisit ideas, and I intend all these generalizations to carry these invisible asterisks.

decision-maker.[37] Examples would be *Eldridge*[38] (the finding was that it violated Charter rights for a patient not to have access to interpretation services for emergency medical services, but it was left to the government to decide how to remedy the situation, since there were "myriad options" that could serve) and more recently *Khadr*[39] (constitutional rights had been violated in a way that implicated the Canadian government, but it was up to the government to decide how to deal with this violation). This remedy is much more appropriate in the case of a government action (or inaction) that violates the Charter than it is for a direct challenge to a statute, and it is presumably available to the Court only in those circumstances. To describe it as "politically innocuous" is a little disingenuous; especially in the *Khadr* case, the result was to embarrass a government that had no real sympathy for the individual in question, but without making a direct order that could result in a major confrontation. Accustomed as we are to the more robust status of the American Bill of Rights, this must strike many as incredibly tame (although this is still all that the New Zealand Bill of Rights provides for in that country). If we assume a public that will be upset, and a government that will be embarrassed, this is not necessarily as weak an option as it might appear.

CHARTER REMEDIES: ADJUSTING THE LEGISLATION THROUGH INTERPRETATION

A more intrusive but simultaneously more flexible remedy is to adjust the legislation through interpretation so as to "save" it from constitutional invalidity in circumstances where an alternative (and, on the face of it, most plausible) reading of the legislation would involve a constitutional violation.[40] This may be achieved through "reading down"—that is to

---

37 The question of how quickly and how responsively governments deal with these findings and remedies of various sorts is a whole literature of its own that I will not get into at this time.

38 *Eldridge v. British Columbia (Attorney General)*, [1997] 3 S.C.R. 624.

39 *Canada (Prime Minister) v. Khadr*, [2010] 1 S.C.R. 44, 2010 SCC 3.

40 Pinard objects to treating this as a "remedy" since it is really a way of interpreting the statute so as not to find a violation that needs a remedy at all; since courts interpret legislation all the time, and frequently do so to prevent conflicts with other

say, taking a more general word or phrase and interpreting it as carrying some contained but narrower and more specific meaning, this narrowing removing the constitutional problem—with the consequence that lower courts will henceforth read the statute in question as if it had been amended to intend these narrower meanings.

CHARTER REMEDIES: READING UP AND READING IN

Somewhat more controversially, the Court may save the legislation by "reading up"—which is to say, turning a narrowly specific word into a more general word. This is more controversial because it can involve committing the government to the financial implications of a measure that now becomes more expensive than it was intended to be on passage. For example, in *Schachter*[41], legislation that restricted a financial entitlement to adoptive mothers was expanded to mean adoptive parents (that is to say, including adoptive fathers as well).[42]

More controversially, the Court can save the legislation by "reading in"—which is to say, adding words through interpretation that the legislature, possibly deliberately and intentionally, omitted. The premier example of this is *Vriend v. Alberta*.[43] Delbert Vriend was an employee

---

pieces of legislation, this is a much less dramatic activity. It also makes simple sense: if there are two different plausible and defensible ways of reading a statute, one of which would make it unconstitutional while the other would not, it is surely the less destabilizing for the courts to adopt the principle of assuming that the legislature intended not to violate the constitution. See Danielle Pinard, "A Plea for Conceptual Consistency in Constitutional Remedies," *National Journal of Constitutional Law* 18 (2006): 105.

41 *Schachter v. Canada*, [1992] 2 S.C.R. 679

42 In the immediate case, the legislation in question having been amended to accomplish precisely this purpose while the case was working its way up through the courts, the actual impact was zero; and the fact that the Court chose to use a case where the remedy had already been supplied by legislative action to discuss the notion of remedies is in itself a fascinating display of judicial willingness to seize the opportunity to alter the playing field, the antithesis of a purely reactive Court waiting for specific consequential questions to answer.

43 *Vriend v. Alberta*, [1998] 1 S.C.R. 493.

of King's College in Edmonton, a religious college affiliated to the University of Alberta. After working for some time as a lab instructor, he was dismissed either because he was gay or because he openly presented himself as gay on the campus (accounts differ). His court case against the College was constrained by the fact that Alberta's Individual Rights Protection Act at the time did not identify sexual orientation as a prohibited ground of discrimination for private actors (such as employers) within the province, so his case became a challenge against that legislation for failing to include his situation; that is to say, he was challenging a legislative omission. (This is why the style of cause for the case is "Vriend v. Alberta" not "Vriend v. King's College.") Vriend was successful at trial but not in the Alberta Court of Appeal, leading to an appeal to the Supreme Court.

After *Egan*, the initial finding of a section 15 violation was straightforward (analogous grounds, immutable personal characteristics), and this time there was no fragmentation on the Court—no "functional realities" analytic detour. Nor was there any disagreement as to whether the legislation constituted a reasonable limit under the *Oakes* test—it is impossible to think of an objective for the omission except the discrimination itself—so the only remaining question was the remedy. It was obviously not possible to declare the offending section null and void, since the whole point of the case was that there was no section at all to protect gays from discrimination; nor did it make any sense to declare the entire piece of legislation null and void because of the omission, as this would have the undesirable effect of at least temporarily depriving all minorities of any legislative protection. The Court decided on the remedy of "reading in"—the legislation should henceforth be read as if it included the section that it should always have included, and therefore people in Vriend's situation who brought complaints under the IRPA were to be treated exactly as they would have been if the words were on the printed page. (Since Alberta did not actually amend the legislation for a considerable length of time, this meant that for many years you still would not find "sexual orientation" in the statute, but the courts would nonetheless act as if the words were there.) Only Justice Major dissented, and only on this single question of the remedy; he would have preferred a finding of invalidity for the employment-related sections of the statute, with a time-limited suspension of invalidity to allow the legislature to address the problem.

As remedies go, "reading in" is not unreasonable, especially compared with the extreme alternative of striking the entire piece of otherwise acceptable legislation. However, reasonable or not, it is still a more intrusive approach than uttering a Charter "no" over the top of an unacceptable legislative "yes" (which is rather closer to a judicial "yes" overriding a legislative "no") and clouding the logical boundary between legislating and litigating in the process. The Court's rather strained argument (that the Alberta legislature had shown that they were waiting for the Court to make the decision as to how to deal with the problem) implicitly acknowledges this awkward role-blending without completely or satisfactorily resolving it.

CHARTER REMEDIES: TEMPORARY SUSPENSION OF INVALIDITY

The Lamer Court's most frequent remedy for a Charter violation was the temporary suspension of invalidity for a stated time period (which was often extended upon subsequent application of the offending government). This was not completely novel—it had been used before, as I will describe below—but its extension to the Charter context, and the frequency of its use, are definitely worth noting.

The logic of this remedy is straightforward: the invalidation of a statute creates a legislative void, along with a period of uncertainty and confusion as governments scrambled to fill it, as various groups and organizations struggle to work out their immediate rights and obligations, and as many try to anticipate (indeed, to have some influence on) the replacement legislation. A temporary suspension of invalidity puts the same pressure on government for action (unless it is simply willing to live with the void, which is sometimes the case) and provides the same opportunity for public involvement in the process of designing the new legislation, although it does so without creating the intervening period of uncertainty.[44]

---

44 Actually, things are slightly more complicated than this. Assuming a Charter-violating statute and a decision to invalidate it, there are not two but three choices: immediate retroactive invalidation; invalidation that operates from the present moment but is not retroactive; and invalidation with a suspension of that finding for a

The *Morgentaler* abortion case illustrates both horns of the dilemma. Recall that the challenged legislation was, if you will allow the phrase, just barely unconstitutional—two of the judges would have upheld it in its entirety, and two others thought it needed modest procedural tweaking. Had the Dickson Court practised "reading in" as a remedy, we might still have laws regulating abortion. Instead, that Court used the only remedy it thought was available, striking that part of the statute down and leaving the government to deal with the unexpected mess. Our current situation, with a complete absence of legislation on the subject is not what the Court directly wanted or ordered, but it is a direct consequence of its ruling. On the other hand, a temporary suspension of invalidity would have changed nothing: the repeated efforts to legislate would have failed anyway, still leaving a legislative void.

To be sure, the temporary suspension of invalidity has its own logical problems—after having found that a statute violates Charter rights, this measure simply leaves the law in place and in full effect for a specific (but usually expandable) period of time. It is not just that people whose rights were violated before the decision are left without any remedy except the knowledge that the law is being revised, but that people may continue to be subject to the legislation and suffer its negative consequences during the intervening period; if they go to Court on their own behalf, it is the suspension, and not the finding of invalidity, that will be cited against them. Indeed, even the immediate litigant whose success has invalidated the statute (some time in the future) may not be granted any relief other than the knowledge that the relevant law is being changed to respond to their complaint.[45]

---

specific period, with or without special treatment for the immediate litigant. See Sujit Choudhry and Kent Roach, "Putting the Past Behind Us? Prospective Judicial and Legislative Remedies," *Supreme Court Law Review* 21 (2003): 205. The recent case in which the Court has attempted to provide a framework for this triple choice is *Canada (Attorney General) v. Hislop*, [2007] 1 S.C.R. 429, 2007 SCC 10; for a discussion of this case, see Daniel Guttman, "*Hislop v. Canada*: A Retroactive Look," *Supreme Court Law Review* 42 (2008): 547.

45 This is probably not as big a problem as it can be made to appear. Some Charter cases involve solitary individuals invoking Charter rights in response to the immediate impact of a law on them in their own particular circumstances; but others represent the more concerted action of organized groups to use the Charter as a means

The decision in which the Lamer Court laid out its new framework for remedies in general, and for the suspended finding of invalidity in particular, was *Schachter*.[46] It invoked a judicial precedent for the remedy of the temporary suspension in a decision of the Dickson Court, which seems to invalidate my earlier suggestion that the Dickson Court limited its remedial speculations to immediate findings of retroactive validity. The case in question, though, was not a Charter case but the Manitoba language reference,[47] in which the Supreme Court found that, although Manitoba thought it had rendered itself unilingual English in 1899, the constitutional requirements for bilingualism in the legislature and the courts had never been removed. The rather astonishing result was that every piece of legislation passed in the province of Manitoba since the beginning of the twentieth century was invalid, and would have to be repassed in both official languages in order to become valid. Such an outcome would have been catastrophic,[48] to put it mildly, so the Court "discovered" a doctrine of constitutional necessity that would prevent such an unacceptable result. Under that doctrine, it suspended the finding of invalidity against the entire corpus of Manitoba statute law and gave the province five years

---

of leverage that will generate more suitable legislation and government policy. For the second group, the remedy of suspended invalidity may well be completely (or almost completely) satisfactory; it is only the first type that may feel they have been handed an empty box. Presumably the Court takes this into account before it invokes a remedy.

46 *Schachter v. Canada*, [1992] 2 S.C.R. 679. The remedy in the immediate case was, as it happens, a temporary suspension of the finding of invalidity, but since the government had already amended the offending legislation in a way that anticipated and satisfied the Court's Charter concerns, this had no immediate impact and caused no immediate problems. This is, of course, how the Court would presumably prefer to insert its ideas into the public debate—but since the remedy had already been accomplished, the Court could just as easily have declined to consider the case at all. In one sense, then, the remedy is unobtrusive—it requires no change. In another sense, the decision is massively intrusive, because it injects a very abstract consideration of a range of possible remedies into a situation that strictly speaking called for no action at all.

47 *Re: Manitoba Language Rights*, [1985] 1 S.C.R. 721.

48 If only because it is not clear that a provincial legislature elected within a legislative framework that had been retroactively annulled would have any legitimate authority to do the repassing.

(subsequently extended) to accomplish the translation and repassage of every single statute; by this means, it avoided creating a "legal vacuum" and the "legal chaos" that would have resulted. It seems to me a bit of a stretch to use this as a precedent for dealing with issues like whether an adoptive father is entitled to unemployment benefits; Lamer did lay out some restrictions on the use of the remedy that he thought would make it a very unusual recourse for the Court, but this expectation has been completely left behind by subsequent developments.

As Ryder notes, the temporary suspension of the finding of invalidity has become the Charter remedy of choice of the Supreme Court, and the frequency of its use (both on actual count, and on a proportional basis) steadily increased through the following dozen years.[49] The period of suspension has varied from 6 months (the most common) to 18 months. Arguably, six months is often a very short time for a government to come up with legislation that satisfies the continuum of affected actors as effectively as the about-to-be-invalidated statute, especially when it represents a new item inserted into what may already be a crowded legislative schedule; on the other hand, 18 months may be a regrettably long time to be suspending the rights of a group of people if, in the end, the government lets things drift and, at the last moment, introduces the absolute minimal adjustment that would take care of the immediate case. More to the point, the Court has been criticized for not fully explaining why the temporary suspension (rather than the immediate invalidation, retroactive or not, that would really provide a governmental incentive for action) is the best remedy, or why a particular time span (6 months, 1 year, 14 months, 18 months, etc.) has been selected.

In one sense, the suspended invalidity device is a less intrusive measure than the immediate retroactive finding of invalidity that previously predominated. There is no legislative void and therefore no prospect of having created immediate uncertainty as to what the law "really" is while the legislature regroups, and this non-crisis gives the opportunity for a period of more measured reflection while government canvasses opinions and consolidates a consensus before proceeding (or not) with new legislation. It also permits the government in question to consider of a full

---

49 Ryder, "Suspending the Charter."

range of alternative responses rather than being obliged to act more precipitately to close a void. Lamer specifically defends the device in terms of a Charter violation that could be resolved in a variety of ways, such that it is not appropriate for the Court to impose its own specific "fix" for the problem, but rather to give the government time for this reflection before making its legislative choice. There is a logic here that works very much like that suggested by Manfredi for the Court's response to the dwindling prospects of a legislative override—an apparently less intrusive or disruptive remedy is actually an invitation to be bolder in finding violations to be remedied, because the potentially negative consequences seem to have been so largely contained.

In another sense, however, the suspended invalidity declaration can be a much more intrusive mechanism if the Court decides to use this opportunity to give focused advice on the optimal legislative regime to replace the not-yet-invalid measures. To some extent, the Court always has to give such advice—it does not just say, "this legislation is unconstitutional," but rather explains at some considerable length why it is unconstitutional, and in the process, necessarily puts down a lot of markers as to the tracks that a constitutionally acceptable replacement must follow. It was characteristic of the Lamer Court to tend towards the enthusiastic in its desire to help the offending legislature get it right next time. The *O'Connor*[50] case is a prime example: in this case, the Court dealt with the conditions for the production of private records relating to a complainant in a sexual assault case, and found that the challenged provisions of the existing law did not pass constitutional muster. Not only did Lamer and Sopinka provide an itemized list of factors that needed to be considered, but L'Heureux-Dubé, in minority reasons, provided her own slightly different and slightly longer list, which appears in the amended statute that was again challenged (but upheld) in *Mills*.[51] Giving reasons for invalidation are one thing, making some suggestions as to how to remedy the cause of the invalidation is another, but providing a prescription so detailed as to amount to rewriting the offending legislation shifts the process to a different level altogether.

---

50 *R. v. O'Connor*, [1995] 4 S.C.R. 411.
51 *R. v. Mills*, [1999] 3 S.C.R. 668.

The suspended finding of invalidity plays into another idea, namely, that of the constitutional dialogue.[52] Introduced into a Canadian context by Hogg and Bushell in 1995,[53] this argument suggests that a Supreme Court decision finding a statute or policy unconstitutional is not (or at least not necessarily) the end of the matter, because the legislature[54] can always come back with an alternative means of accomplishing much the same set of policy objectives (designed to accommodate the Supreme Court's new strictures) without abandoning the project altogether; they will attempt (through the preamble, through the legislative history, and through the arguments presented to the Court when and if this new law is itself challenged) to persuade the Court that this is accommodation enough. Played well, this option means that neither the Court nor the legislature simply get their own way in any complete sense, and the final outcome is (or sometimes can be) somewhere in between these two extremes.

For a time, the Supreme Court itself was quite taken with this metaphor, most particularly by Iacobucci and most explicitly in *Vriend*, where Iacobucci cited Hogg and Bushell while describing the Charter as redefining Canadian democracy so as to establish a "more dynamic interaction among the branches of governance" (para. 25). If there was a heyday for the dialogue theory, however, it is over now, and McLachlin rang down the curtain abruptly in *Sauvé 2*—dialogue theory, she said tartly, is not

---

52 I am not suggesting that Hogg and Bushell made this connection to suspended validity, only that it makes a little more sense to think of the conversation as coming, not in the wreckage of a totally invalidated policy as the government scrambles to clean up the rubble, but rather with the clock ticking as the government tries to come up with an acceptable compromise solution that will make the threatened demolition unnecessary.

53 Peter Hogg and Alison Bushell, "The Charter Dialogue between Courts and Legislatures (Or Perhaps the Charter Isn't Such a Bad Thing After All)," *Osgoode Hall Law Journal* 35 (1997): 75.

54 It is curious how we always say "the legislature" when we really mean "the cabinet" which initiates and drafts legislation subject to its possible amendment or, more rarely, defeat by the legislature. We do ourselves little good by presenting the Charter challenge as "Court versus legislature" when it is really "Court versus government" with the legislature, if anything, the completely sidelined minor player in the whole drama. See James Kelly, *Governing with the Charter: Legislative and Judicial Activism and Framers' Intent* (Vancouver: UBC Press, 2005).

simply another way of saying "try, try again"[55] (para. 17). There always was an asymmetry involved in the supposed dialogue, because although the legislature (more correctly, the government, which is not quite the same thing) was expected to accept the fact that it had been wrong, the Court never would—indeed, it never could, because it wasn't that kind of dialogue. McLachlin's closing retort is the clearest demonstration of this asymmetry, making the point almost as well as Mark Tushnet in his delightfully succinct article title, "'Shut Up' He Explained."[56]

CHARTER REMEDIES: THE CONSTITUTIONAL EXEMPTION

It is also worth mentioning the "remedy that wasn't," namely, a possible constitutional remedy that the Lamer Court mulled over for most of the decade without fully committing to it. This is the notion of the "constitutional exemption."[57] The idea is that we might find an unusual circumstance in which a general rule or law violates the Charter rights of a specific individual or a small set of individuals, but we can have our cake and eat it too if we uphold the general rule while allowing the relevant individual (and the small set of other people who are relevantly similar) a nongeneralizable exemption from the effect of that rule.

The case that provoked the most extensive media consideration of the argument for a constitutional exemption was the *Latimer* case, involving the Saskatchewan farmer who took the life of his severely disabled daughter. There was a considerable degree of public sympathy for Mr. Latimer, despite the fact that there is no "mercy killing" provision in our criminal law on homicide; the jury that found him guilty (since the basic

---

55 To be fair: her tartness may follow from the fact that she found no "rational connection" between the purpose of the legislation and the violation of the right, usually one of the easier parts of the *Oakes* test for governments to satisfy, and I may be reading a little too much into it.

56 Mark Tushnet, "'Shut Up' He Explained," *Northwestern University Law Review* 95 (2001): 907.

57 For a more extended discussion, see Morris Rosenberg and Stephan Perreault, "Ifs and Buts in Charter Adjudication: The Unruly Emergence of Constitutional Exemptions in Canada," *Supreme Court Law Review* 16 (2002): 375.

facts involving his actions were hardly in dispute) not only recommended leniency but suggested that they might not have found him guilty had they realized that leniency was not available for a crime with a minimum sentence of 10 years in prison. The trial judge, after an exchange with the jury, went so far as to invoke the principle of a constitutional exemption and to sentence the accused to a single year in prison, well below the mandatory minimum. The Saskatchewan Court of Appeal, however, allowed the Crown's appeal and imposed the mandatory minimum. When this case arrived in front of the Supreme Court on appeal,[58] one would have thought this the perfect opportunity to explore the concept of a constitutional exemption, either by embracing it in the immediate case while carefully delineating the circumstances in which it could be invoked, or by rejecting it outright and thereby ending the speculation. In fact, they did neither: after listing the concept of a "constitutional exemption" as one of the six issues before the Court, they ultimately concluded that it was "not necessary" to answer this question.[59]

The idea was clearly under consideration by the Lamer Court right through the 1990s.[60] In 1991, Sopinka observed that "the Court has not decided yet" whether this is an appropriate Charter remedy,[61] with Wilson (with L'Heureux-Dubé) writing short separate reasons to oppose the idea.[62] I take this as a clear indication that the justices were talking about the idea among themselves, but had not yet reached a firm

---

58 *R. v. Latimer*, 2001 SCC 1, [2001] 1 S.C.R. 3.

59 Strictly speaking, the "not necessary" treatment is justified, but there is a considerable amount of Supreme Court case law that has dealt with side issues that it was not strictly necessary to answer at that time. To be sure, this was more true of the Lamer Court than it has been so far of the McLachlin Court.

60 For simplicity's sake, I am limiting my consideration to Supreme Court decisions. It is certainly the case that constitutional exemptions were considered and sometimes granted by trial courts, especially in the late 1980s and early 1990s but continuing into this new century, and often in relation to mandatory minimum sentences. When not appealed, these decisions of course stood, although when they were appealed they were often reversed by the provincial court of appeal. I am focusing on the slightly different story of this remedy at the Supreme Court level.

61 In *Osborne v. Canada*, [1991] 2 S.C.R. 69.

62 Although half a dozen years later, in *R. v. Rose*, [1998] 3 S.C.R. 262, L'Heureux-Dubé in separate reasons simply asserts, without citation or further comment, that a constitutional exemption is an available remedy.

conclusion. Later the same year, in the highly controversial *Seaboyer* case,[63] McLachlin in her majority reasons, once again "assuming, without deciding" that the remedy was available, provided fairly extended reasons why it would not be appropriate for the case at hand; again, this was not quite an endorsement of the idea, but the fact that its non-use was justified in such specific terms does hint at a formal Court position firming up behind the scenes. A year later, in a short oral decision,[64] Lamer touched on the matter again in similar terms but only in passing, once again "assuming without deciding" that the remedy existed before concluding that it would not, in any event, be appropriate in the immediate case. (This is a fascinating literary device—that is, bracketing an idea from direct consideration and analysis in the immediate case, neither adopting it nor rejecting it, and thereby keeping it "alive" so as to invite persuasive arguments from future litigants; searching for the terms "assuming without deciding" on the Supreme Court decision website at LexUM yields more than 150 examples of this device in the last 75 years.)

The high-water mark for the constitutional exemption idea was arguably the *Rodriguez*[65] case in 1993. The case involved the issue of assisted suicide; under the Criminal Law it is not a crime to commit (or, more meaningfully, to attempt to commit) suicide, but it is a crime to counsel or to assist someone in committing suicide. Sue Rodriguez suffered from ALS, a condition which involves gradual progressive muscular atrophy such that the person usually eventually dies of respiratory failure. Well short of that point, however, they have lost the physical capacity to act in such a way as to take their own life, and could only commit suicide—that is, could only act on their decision that the suffering had reached the point where it was no longer tolerable—with the assistance of someone else. She asked the courts to declare that the Criminal Code sections on assisted suicide violated her Charter rights (using a number of different arguments, which are not necessary for me to list or describe) and should therefore be declared invalid. She lost her case at trial, lost again in the British Columbia Court of Appeal (with an extensive and vigorous dissent by the Chief Justice), and then lost yet again in the Supreme Court of

63 *R. v. Seaboyer; R. v. Gayme*, [1991] 2 S.C.R. 577.

64 In *R. v. Sawyer*, [1992] 3 S.C.R. 809.

65 *Rodriguez v. British Columbia (Attorney General)*, [1993] 3 S.C.R. 519.

Canada by the narrowest of margins (a 5–4 split, rather unusual on our Court), again with an extensive and vigorous dissent by the Chief Justice. Lamer's dissent, which was a single judicial signature away from being a majority decision, found a Charter violation and built a remedy around the constitutional exemption; following McEachern CJBC he went so far as to lay out in detail the language that would be included in the court order, with the understanding that it would serve as a guideline for future petitioners making an application in similar circumstances.

The implication of a term like "high-water mark" is that, having once risen this high, the water then receded—and that is indeed what happened. At the end of the Lamer decade, the Court was still suggesting in *Corbiere* that "The remedy of constitutional exemption has been recognized in a very limited way in this Court"[66] but in language that now linked the option in an ancillary way to the temporary suspension of invalidity—a remedy that I considered separately above.[67] It was left to the McLachlin Court to close this option off more definitively. McLachlin does mention it as a "live" possibility in *Sharpe*, but only in passing;[68] furthermore, when Bastarache picks up the theme in *Kingstreet*,[69] he does so in flatly negative terms. He suggests that a constitutional exemption raises problems of "horizontal equity" and concludes instead that "In my view, constitutional law should apply fairly and evenly, so that all similarly situated persons are treated the same" (para. 56). Technically, this is *obiter* rather than *dicta* (that is to say, not part of the analysis such that its removal would not make it possible to reach the conclusion), and therefore not as binding on a future Court as it might have been; I am more impressed, however, that this was a unanimous decision, and the digression firmly states an unambiguous conclusion. Were I a lawyer, thinking about asking for the remedy of constitutional exemption for a Charter violation, I think those reasons would tell me that the hill just got a whole

---

66 *Corbiere v. Canada (Minister of Indian and Northern Affairs)*, [1999] 2 S.C.R. 203.

67 Curiously, the *Corbiere* reasons cite the *Schachter* case of 1992 as a basis for the remedy of constitutional exemption, although that particular remedy is in fact not mentioned at all in that case.

68 *R. v. Sharpe*, [2001] 1 S.C.R. 45, 2001 SCC 2, at para 113.

69 *Kingstreet Investments Ltd. v. New Brunswick (Finance)*, 2007 SCC 1, [2007] 1 S.C.R. 3.

lot steeper. McLachlin slams the door, in even more emphatic language, in *Ferguson*[70] in 2008: "constitutional exemptions buy flexibility at the cost of undermining the rule of law" (para. 67). Coughlan concludes that this marks "the end of constitutional exemptions," not just under section 12 of the Charter but more generally[71] (although, curiously, three years later a unanimous Court would only say, somewhat more weakly, that "constitutional exemptions are to be avoided"[72]). When the Court now talks about a constitutional exemption these days, they are usually wondering whether the immediate litigant should get special relief when the general remedy is a suspended declaration of invalidity—or, in a curious inversion, whether there is enough indication that the official in question was attempting to act conscientiously for there to be a "good faith" exemption of the action from the constitutional ban.

CONCLUSION

These are, of course, only the highlights of the Lamer Court's Charter jurisprudence. A fuller account would mention the string of cases in which Sopinka dramatically expanded the requirements for the Crown to disclose to the defence all the information it gathered in the case (starting with *Stinchcombe*), as well as the string of cases in which Lamer expanded the notion of a "right to counsel" in terms of both the contexts in which it could be invoked (see *G v. New Brunswick*[73]) and the obligations of government to make legal advice available. Even that, however, would understate the cheerful imperialism of the Lamer Court, with its willingness to answer questions much wider than anything it had actually been asked.[74]

---

70 *R. v. Ferguson*, 2008 SCC 6, [2008] 1 S.C.R. 96.

71 Steve Coughlan, "The End of Constitutional Exemptions," *Criminal Reports* 54 (2008): 220.

72 *Canada (Attorney General) v. PHS Community Services Society*, 2011 SCC 44, [2011] 3 S.C.R. 134, at para. 149.

73 *New Brunswick (Minister of Health and Community Services) v. G.(J.)*, [1999] 3 S.C.R. 46.

74 Not only in the *Remuneration Reference* described above but also and most famously in the *Secession Reference*, which turned the "soft" question on whether Quebec had a constitutional right to unilateral secession into the much "harder" question of Canada's obligations to negotiate in good faith a serious and democratically supported

Lamer's decade, the 1990s, saw a constant string of Charter decisions—some major and some minor, some stand-alone decisions and some part of a clearly demarcated developing string, some within a package of companion cases where the leading decision enunciated a clear principle and the accompanying cases spelled out the implications for variant circumstances. When the Court stumbled—as it famously did in *Askov*, on the meaning of "trial within a reasonable time"—it recovered blithely and without embarrassment (in *Morin*), while wondering out loud how people could possibly have misunderstood. Whatever one might have thought about the details of the emerging doctrine on specific issues, or even about the Court's general direction, there is no denying that it was a truly splendid performance—national jurisprudence as a grand showcase, with various judges taking turns in the spotlight. The Supreme Court's place in national politics has been altered, if not forever then certainly for decades to come, by the period of Lamer's leadership.

Petter points out the problem, however, in the Court's bold exploration of the remedy spectrum.[75] It was not that the Dickson Court was too blinkered to see these options, but rather that it had chosen to define its Charter role in different terms. Limiting the Court's response to the single option of (immediate and complete) invalidity allows it to remain within the framework of liberal legalism, and to maintain a credible divide between politics (which governments do) and law (which courts do). All the Court does, on this model, is lay the statute alongside the constitution and see if it fits,[76] renouncing any judicial duty to stretch the statute to fit or to reframe the statute by reading it "as if it said

---

demand from Quebec; and also, even more blatantly, in the mandatory retirement quartet (*McKinney* was the lead decision), where the Court decided that there was no Charter case because universities and hospitals and colleges were not "government" in the Charter sense—but proceeded to deal with the issue of mandatory retirement under the Charter anyway.

75 Andrew Petter, "Twenty Years of Charter Justification: From Liberal Legalism to Dubious Dialogue," *University of New Brunswick Law Journal* 52 (2003): 187.

76 As Dickson put it in *Morgentaler*: "Simply put, assuming Parliament can act, it must do so properly. For the reasons given earlier, the deprivation of security of the person caused by s. 251 as a whole is not in accordance with the second clause of s. 7" (73).

(whatever)."[77] Only this allows the Court to minimize, even to avoid, an appearance of a political role; any other action involves the political engagement of saving a government measure by restructuring it, demanding both a decision regarding what pieces of legislation deserve the saving, and the choice among a (possibly modest, possibly extensive) range of alternative accommodations of the Charter problem, ultimately begging the question as to whether the legislature would rather have the Court-adjusted statute on this question than no statute at all. It is hard to maintain the stance that the Court is not concerned about policy, but only about law, when it is effectively rewriting the policy to make it good law; any remedy set other than simple invalidation necessarily involves the Court in a political policy role. The Dickson Court explicitly and consistently renounced this role; the Lamer Court embraced it.

---

77 As Dickson said in *Hunter v. Southam*: "While the courts are guardians of the Constitution and of individuals' rights under it, it is the legislature's responsibility to enact legislation that embodies appropriate safeguards to comply with the Constitution's requirements. It should not fall to the courts to fill in the details that will render legislative lacunae constitutional" (169).

CHAPTER FIVE

THE MCLACHLIN COURT: THE CHARTER CONTAINED

Justice Beverley McLachlin became Chief Justice of the Supreme Court of Canada on January 7, 2000, with just short of 11 years of service on the Court. This made her one of the most senior judges on the Court,[1] and it is therefore not particularly surprising that she became Chief Justice; the only other likely candidate was Iacobucci, two years her junior in service. Unlike Lamer, who had consistently voted on divided panels with the Chief Justice to whom he was the successor, McLachlin had been something of an outlier on the Lamer Court. This suggested an intriguing possible storyline to the succession ("Outlier Becomes Chief Justice! Deepening Divisions on the Court!"), but the truth was quite the opposite: McLachlin came to the centre chair with a strong feeling that the Lamer Court had often been too divided and delivered too many separate sets of reasons on too many cases. As she has indicated in public comments,[2] she attached some real importance to leading a more unified

---

1 L'Heureux-Dubé (appointed two years before McLachlin) and Gonthier (appointed two months earlier) were senior, but both were within three years of mandatory retirement.

2 See, for example, Beverley McLachlin, "The First Decade of the 21st Century: The Supreme Court of Canada in Context," foreword in Adam Dodek and David A. Wright, eds., *Public Law at the McLachlin Court: The First Decade* (Toronto: Irwin Law, 2011).

Court, and in general she has succeeded, although this is somewhat less true since 2010.[3]

THE MCLACHLIN COURT: SUBSTANTIVE ISSUES UNDER THE CHARTER

The McLachlin Court began with every appearance that the Charter revolution was still well under way, extending its influence into aspects of governmental activity that had previously been largely untouched, but I will suggest that these indications, which are from the first few years of the Court, have not been sustained. My commentary below acknowledges these early signs, but will then seek to locate them within a broader trajectory of the Court's performance in relation to the Charter. I will first look at the performance of the McLachlin Court with respect to substantive areas of Charter law—such as election rights, equality rights, and freedom of association—to track the Court's trajectory in this regard. Of necessity, I will only be discussing about a dozen out of the hundreds of McLachlin Court decisions in total, including several dozen significant decisions that have been delivered. Readers will rightly be asking themselves if my selection is fair; as a general rule, if you let the other side pick the examples, you will not win many arguments. Nonetheless, I think my selection provides a meaningful highlight reel, and I will in the next chapter point to some empirical data that supports my story of a trajectory of Charter jurisprudence.

SUBSTANTIVE ISSUES: VOTING RIGHTS

On substantive issues, the McLachlin Court started with some decisions that marked out important new boundaries for the application of the Charter. Perhaps the set of decisions with the most potential future

---

3 I am on record as pointing out that her leadership was not the only factor in this shift in performance, because the sharp drop in non-unanimous decisions and the frequency of dissents and separate concurrences actually occurred about two and half years earlier. It is certainly true that her Court was, in general, less divided and dissensual and, even if a Chief Justice does not deserve all the credit for this, she certainly deserves some.

impact were the election cases—I would call them a trio, except that they were not companion cases but were rather spaced out over three years—which applied Charter principles to a series of election-related issues with rather surprising results.

VOTING RIGHTS AND *SAUVÉ*

The first case was *Sauvé*[4] in 2002, and the issue was voting rights for prisoners. (This case is usually referred to as "*Sauvé* 2" because there had been a "*Sauvé* 1"[5] in 1993, which raised similar issues but was dealt with in a terse and somewhat cryptic way that left untouched as many questions as it answered. Although I have complained about the Court giving legislatures rather too specific advice as to how to redraft legislation, *Sauvé* 1 clearly displays the problem with giving no real advice at all; Parliament followed what it thought was the advice in *Sauvé* 1 to amend the Elections Act, but still had the new legislation disallowed in *Sauvé* 2.)[6] The new Elections Act had denied the vote to prisoners in correctional institutions serving sentences of two years or more, an adjustment of the previous version of the legislation which had drawn Supreme Court disapproval for denying the vote to all prisoners. Since this is without question an infringement of a Charter right (section 3 declares that "every citizen has the right to vote in an election of a member of the House of Commons or a provincial legislature"), this immediately becomes a question of reasonable limits under section 1 of the Charter.[7]

Under the *Oakes* test, once a prima facie violation has been established, the government must present an argument establishing pressing and substantial objectives, a rational connection of the infringement to

---

4 *Sauvé v. Canada (Chief Electoral Officer)*, [2002] 3 S.C.R. 519, 2002 SCC 68.

5 *Sauvé v. Canada (Attorney General)*, [1993] 2 S.C.R. 438.

6 For a closer investigation of the Court's movement from *Sauvé* 1 to *Sauvé* 2, see Rainer Knopff, Dennis Baker, and Sylvia LeRoy, "Courting Controversy: Strategic Judicial Decision Making," in James B. Kelly and Christopher Manfredi, eds., *Contested Constitutionalism: Reflections on the Canadian Charter of Rights and Freedoms* (Vancouver: UBC Press, 2009).

7 The case was also argued as a possible violation of section 15 equality rights, but this was not a central feature of the decision.

the objectives, minimum impairment of the right, and proportionality between the violation of the right and the ends achieved. Governments almost never fail the first step, rarely fail the second, and suffer most of their defeats on the third, but this is one of the unusual cases where the Court's objections included both the first and second steps. With the objective of the exclusion of such prisoners, the government suggested enhancing civic responsibility and respect for law, and enhancing the general purposes of the criminal sanction. Not only did the majority of the Court reject these arguments, but it did so with unusual incivility, complaining about "vague and symbolic" objectives, a complete failure to establish any rational connection, and the government's "novel political theory" that was said to have no place in a constitutional democratic order. My favourite is McLachlin's biting sentence: "At the end of the day, people should not be left guessing about why their *Charter* rights have been infringed" (para. 23). This was closely followed by, "The rhetorical nature of the government objectives advanced in this case renders them suspect" (para. 24).

This incivility is all the more striking in that the legislation had already been amended to respond to a Supreme Court decision a decade earlier complaining about over-breadth, which could quite plausibly be taken as a suggestion that the issue was with the precise calibration of means, not with categorical principles. In the United States, it is worth noting, many states disenfranchise convicted felons not just for the term of their incarceration but for life. This is also the decision in which McLachlin put paid to the more robust versions of constitutional "dialogue theory" (which I have discussed elsewhere in this book), declaring with equal acerbity that the notion of dialogue "should not be debased to a rule of 'if at first you don't succeed, try, try again'" (para. 17). That is rather like saying, "Of course we can argue about things, but don't you ever dare to disagree with me!" So much for dialogue theory.

It is also striking that the majority's biting broadsides hit not only the government (still the Chrétien Liberal government and not yet the Conservatives) but also its own dissenters—this was a very narrow 5–4 decision, and the four were fully supportive of the government's position and of the theory of citizenship and democratic rights that it advanced. Move a single vote, and this important question goes the other way. It is one thing for a reasonably solid Court to set aside a significant piece of government legislation as unconstitutional (and the Elections Act would surely qualify as significant); it is a little more problematic when a single vote on the panel would transform the outcome. In this context, one must feel some sympathy for Baker and Knopff's suggestion that the legislation-annulling decisions of bare majorities should perhaps be subject to a simple legislative override without the need to resort to the Charter's section 33 notwithstanding clause.[8]

VOTING RIGHTS AND *FIGUEROA*

The second case in this sequence was *Figueroa*,[9] and what was at issue here was the differential treatment of political parties under the Canada Elections Act. In order to become a "registered" party, the Act required that a political party field candidates in at least 50 different ridings; registered parties did, and nonregistered parties did not, enjoy benefits such as an entitlement to issue tax receipts outside of the election period, the capacity of candidates to transfer unspent election funds to the party (rather than to the government), and the right to have their candidates list their party affiliation on the ballot papers.[10] (The Act also entitled registered parties to free broadcast time, to purchase reserved broadcast time, and to partial reimbursement of election expenses, but these were not directly at issue in the case.)

The argument for a two-tier system for political parties is fairly obvious: it works (perhaps only modestly) to reduce the proliferation of political parties, and (at least slightly) to enhance the opportunity for the larger

---

8 Dennis Baker and Rainer Knopff, "Minority Retort: A Parliamentary Power to Resolve Judicial Disagreement in Close Cases," *Windsor Yearbook of Access to Justice* 21 (2002): 347.

9 *Figueroa v. Canada (Attorney General)*, [2003] 1 S.C.R. 912, 2003 SCC 37.

10 Many readers may feel that knowing the name of your favoured party's local candidate is not a great deal to ask of voters, but many people make their electoral choice not in terms of the local candidate but in terms of what the party stands for in a broader sense (or who its national leader is). Smaller parties are already less able to undertake the extensive advertising and publicity that will ensure that potential voters know which local name to connect to which party—while the parties most able to do this don't have to give it a high priority because the party affiliation will be on the ballot in any event.

political parties to win representation in Parliament, where higher degrees of fragmentation are liable to prove problematic. The Ontario Court of Appeal accepted that it was appropriate to see effective representation in terms of contributing to the likelihood of a stable majority government, which representative fragmentation undermines. The argument against it, however, is equally obvious: it constrains the capacity of Canadian voters to make an effective choice from the full range of political points of view that could be represented by candidates in federal elections.

At first glance, the Charter does not seem to help us very much—section 3 only says that citizens have the right to vote in federal and provincial elections,[11] and whether or not the legislature can establish a modest two-tier party system seems rather a different question. The Supreme Court decision finesses this observation with a delightfully succinct demonstration of the interpretive implications of "broad and liberal" interpretations driven by the purposive method. It is conceded that, "on its face," the wording of the Charter is "rather narrow," but this means that "Charter analysis requires courts to look beyond the words" (para. 19), and the way to look beyond the words is to "ascertain their purpose" (para. 20). The result of this "looking beyond" is to find that section 3 actually involves "the right of each citizen to meaningful participation in the electoral process" (para. 27). It follows from this that the democratic process is best served by "the free flow of diverse opinions and ideas" (para. 28) and that democratic participation has an intrinsic value completely independent of the question of whether or not it contributes to stable (by which we mean majority) governments. Framed this way, it is difficult not to conclude that a two-tier electoral system, which gives some political parties a modestly steeper hill to climb than others, violates the Charter; furthermore, since the government's section 1 arguments were couched in terms of facilitating stable outcomes, it did not fare well either. A minority of judges on the Court agreed with the outcome but fashioned a slightly more government-friendly analytic method, which, in the end, the legislation did not satisfy either.

---

11 And, of course, the right to be qualified for membership therein—somewhat opaque wording which I take to mean that citizens also have the right to run for office, although it seems to me they need to win before they are fully qualified for such membership.

VOTING RIGHTS AND *HARPER*

Both *Sauvé* and *Figueroa* point in the same direction: they open up the election process first to a wider set of voters, and then to a wider set of political parties,[12] but the third case in the sequence rounds off this process in a slightly unexpected way. The case was *Harper v. Canada*[13] (the "Harper" in question being our present prime minister in his earlier capacity as leader of the National Citizens Coalition), which challenged the Election Act for the way that it limited election spending, and especially election spending by non-party entities[14] such as the National Citizens Coalition, which wished to impact the voting outcome without running candidates.[15]

This is obviously not a small matter; as most readers are undoubtedly aware, the United States Supreme Court has recently intervened in the American electoral process on this very issue, and in a very dramatic way, when it struck down relatively modest election spending restrictions in *Citizens United*.[16] This contributed to the fact that the 2012 US Presidential and Congressional elections were by far the most expensive set of elections in American history.[17] That decision was couched in terms of the US prime constitutional value—namely, freedom of speech as enshrined in the First Amendment—but given the language of my

---

12 For an excellent discussion of three different ways that political parties could be understood as fitting into the idea of the right to vote, and a placing of the Court's recent decisions within that framework, see Heather MacIvor, "Judicial Review and Electoral Democracy: The Contested Status of Political Parties under the Charter," *Windsor Yearbook of Access to Justice* 21 (2002): 479.

13 *Harper v. Canada (Attorney General)*, [2004] 1 S.C.R. 827, 2004 SCC 33.

14 Which, somewhat confusingly, the legislation and the court decision both refer to as "third parties," a label which Canadian political scientists through the twentieth century tended to use to describe political parties which had no reasonable prospect of winning the election by forming a majority government.

15 I hasten to add that the legislation also limited spending by the political parties themselves—for example, by advertising on the day of the election—but this is not the focus of my discussion here.

16 *Citizens United v. Federal Election Commission*, 558 U.S. 310 (2010).

17 Although it does seem that every Presidential election cycle in the United States sets new records in this regard.

preceding paragraph, it would be very easy to get there from section 3 premises as well, and three of the judges from the *Figueroa* majority (McLachlin, Major, and Binnie) did so. However, they wound up writing a dissent, and the majority upheld the legislation.

This was not really much of a surprise, because the Court had considered the same issue in *Libman v. Quebec*,[18] which resulted from a challenge against the very strict spending rules that the province of Quebec had framed around its 1995 referendum—creating two "umbrella" groups (one for groups supporting the "yes," the other for the "no") and defining their money-raising and money-spending operations very narrowly. In that case, the Court had found that although those particular restrictions were excessive to the point of violating Charter norms, the notion of spending restrictions was not itself objectionable. The Court's description of what sort of restrictive measures would satisfy Charter requirements was transparently similar to precisely the measures challenged in *Harper*. Although the National Citizens Coalition had fared well at the trial level on two previous occasions in challenging similar types of restrictions[19] (decisions that, surprisingly, were left unappealed by the government of the day), *Libman* seemed the better predictor.

In *Harper*, all the members of the Court agreed that there was a violation of the Charter right to freedom of expression, which was all the more significant because it involved political speech, and all the more important because it occurred in the context of a federal election. Although the majority identified the right of citizens to a full range of information to direct their voting choice, they also found that the right to vote (in the expanded *Figueroa* form of a right to effective participation) provided a strong off-setting consideration. Their concern was that removing the restriction on "third party" spending would unbalance the political debate. The danger is that "those having access to the most resources" might be able "to monopolize the election discourse," and this "unequal dissemination of points of view undermines the voter's ability to be adequately informed of all views" (para. 72). Because the restrictions on third-party

---

18 *Libman v. Quebec (Attorney General)*, [1997] 3 S.C.R. 569.

19 For example, *Somerville v. Canada (Attorney General)* (1996), 184 A.R. 241 (C.A.).

spending enhanced the possibility of "equality in the political discourse," they served, and were rationally connected to, a significant public purpose in such a way as to satisfy the "reasonable limits" of section 1. The majority rejected the idea that the information implications of the right to vote could simply be folded into the right to freedom of speech—in the terminology of the contemporary US discourse, they denied that "money is speech" such that more is always better. The minority, on the other hand, was concerned that the effect of the measures was to limit election debate to the issues that the political parties wanted to campaign on, and to facilitate the screening out of other issues and ideas; they were also concerned that the government had offered no evidence to support the proposition that unlimited spending skewed the debate towards monied interests.

The result is that the contemporary electoral process is nicely framed by three non-unanimous Supreme Court Charter decisions on controversial matters. The trio of issues—who can vote, who can compete, and who can spend—are central and important; on two occasions, the Court overrode the legislative choice, and on one occasion, they affirmed it, which somewhat qualifies any suggestions of an imperial judiciary.

Canada's *Harper* versus the Americans' *Citizens United*: it is quite surprising how two sets of entrenched rights could go such different directions, the more so as both documents give prominent place to freedom of speech. They provide a solid demonstration that the words in the constitutional text do not do the work directly or on their own, but only as they are processed through the interpretation styles and rules and expectations of a particular set of judges working within and responding to a particular social and political and historical context. We in Canada have votes for prisoners, a level playing field for even smaller parties, and strict limits on what non-party actors can do during campaigns; they in the United States prevent convicts in many states from ever voting again, have a remarkably effective and deeply entrenched two-party lock on politics, and set the PACs free to spend and say what they like. Yet, ironically, if our Charter sought to emulate any existing model (which is not inconsistent with wanting to improve and expand it), it was unquestionably the American Bill of Rights.

On the other hand, the trio of decisions seems to me to be vaguely off-target—fewer people bother voting every cycle, and political parties no longer seem to be the vehicle of choice for the expression of popular demands (although it is far from clear what may have replaced it). I do not claim to know where the political inclinations of the average young Canadian are taking us, but I am not sure that the Charter has the court even facing in the right direction. The right to vote and the right to participate in democratic discourse about important issues are somehow pulling apart, and limiting non-party speech during election campaigns may not be an unalloyed good.

SUBSTANTIVE MATTERS: EXTRADITION AND THE DEATH PENALTY

Before I argue that the McLachlin Court's net Charter score has been modest, I should deal with the slightly curious outlier case of *Burns*.[20] At issue was the extradition of two young men who were accused of having committed gruesome murders in the United States before fleeing across the border to Canada. Prosecutors in Washington state had applied to have the two returned to the United States for trial. There is an extradition treaty between the United States and Canada, but because the United States has the death penalty and Canada does not, the treaty stipulates that the Canadian government has the right, where it believes that the circumstances warrant, to insist that the extraditing authorities guarantee that they will not seek the death penalty in the immediate case. This right is sometimes, but not always, exercised and, to the best of my knowledge, the Americans might grumble but they always acquiesce.

Because the guarantee was not sought in the case of Burns and his colleague, and because it seemed very likely that the prosecutors would be seeking the death penalty (given the gruesome circumstances of the multiple murders), extradition was resisted through appeals all the way up to the Supreme Court. In the Supreme Court, the attention was entirely upon the death penalty issue; although the treaty gave the federal minister of justice discretion regarding the seeking of assurances about the death penalty, the Court insisted that this discretion (like all governmental activities) was constrained by Charter values, and the fact that

---

20 *United States v. Burns*, [2001] 1 S.C.R. 283, 2001 SCC 7.

the United States had a judicial system that was, in general, very similar to our own was not conclusive either. These were not "fair trial" issues but more narrowly and specifically "death penalty" issues; this was not a mobility rights case under section 6 of the Charter (the right to remain in Canada), nor a "cruel and unusual punishment" case under section 12, but rather a "right to life, liberty and security of the person" case under section 7.

The case was unusual in that it was heard by the nine-judge Lamer Court in 1999, and then reheard (that is to say, re-argued) in front of a nine-judge McLachlin Court just over a year later.[21] It was unusual again in that it was a "by the Court" decision (i.e., unanimous, and anonymous in the sense that its authorship was not attributed to any specific judge or judges on the panel)—something that only happens about once in every 20 cases. By the Court decisions are normally taken as indicating an unusually resolute and unified decision—not just unanimity but, if you will, "unanimity plus."[22] It has also been suggested that the "by the Court" device might sometimes be used precisely because the Court is about to directly reverse some significant aspect of an earlier precedential decision.[23]

The decision emphasized several relevant considerations:

- Canada's rejection of the death penalty
- Canada's leadership in international efforts to eliminate the death penalty
- the youth of the offenders as a mitigating factor

---

21 This sometimes signals that the Court is strongly considering basing its decision on some factor that was not emphasized or not fully addressed in the oral arguments at the initial hearing; and sometimes it indicates that too many judges from the initial hearing panel are no longer available to participate in the decision. The latter clearly was not the case here.

22 Bzdera suggests that the "By the Court" device has the purpose of making constitutional decisions more emphatic. See Andre Bzdera, "Comparative Analysis of Federal High Courts: A Political Theory of Judicial Review," *Canadian Journal of Political Science* 26 (1993): 3.

23 See Rainer Knopff, "Charter Reconsiderations," *National Magazine* 21 (2012): 38.

- accelerating concerns in Canada and elsewhere about the possibility of false convictions, which are, for obvious reasons, particularly critical in death penalty cases (to put it crudely, you can't say "sorry" to a corpse)
- the "death row phenomenon" of very protracted appeal procedures that lead to psychological trauma

The outcome was a finding that the extradition could not be supported without the seeking of assurances that the death penalty would not be sought, and that, in general, the presumption of the treaty should be reversed: rather than providing that there was an extradition process in which assurances would be sought only on government discretion when circumstances warranted, the extradition process should routinely include the request for such assurances except in unusual circumstances. Since extradition involves a judicial process, of course, this meant that the final judgement as to whether circumstances were sufficiently unusual would be up to the courts, but the tone of *Burns* makes it clear that the standards would be high.

This is a remarkable rhetorical device—a weakness of courts is used to justify the Court doing something very powerful indeed. The potential fallibility of judges in death penalty cases means that the judges of the Supreme Court have to take the dramatic step of sternly lecturing our southern neighbour, doing an end-run on a minister of the Crown for making a discretionary decision that was completely consistent with prior jurisprudence, and overriding the clear terms of a deliberately negotiated international treaty. (Just think what they might have done if judges were not fallible!) Furthermore, I read the decision in *Burns*, with its lengthy expansion of the right to life, liberty, and the security of the person, as being inconsistent with the possible imposition of the death penalty— that is, as meaning that although the abolition of the death penalty was a Parliamentary decision in 1976, it would violate the Charter for any future Parliament to attempt to reinstate it—although my colleagues point out that the Court did not (quite) say this in so many words.[24]

---

24 I should also point out a story in the *Globe and Mail* from 2007 that reports on Ontario Court of Appeal Justice Rosenberg giving a speech in which he says that Burns

It is therefore hard to know in the end what to make of *Burns*. On the one hand, given that Canada has done away with the death penalty decades ago and there is not a trace of a movement to restore it, it is a bit like boarding over a door that is already solidly locked. On the other hand, it did effectively rewrite an international treaty with a global superpower; even if the death penalty is not now an issue in Canada, a basic lesson of politics is never to say something could never happen, and formally shutting down an option before it gathers momentum is often an effective way of making it more likely that it never will. The Court's apparent willingness to answer a question they were not even asked (that is, about the constitutionality of a death penalty in Canada) is profoundly reminiscent of the Lamer Court at its most enthusiastic.

In general terms, then it was "so far so good," and "more of the same," as the Supreme Court continued to move with the Charter into new areas—the electoral arena, and death penalty matters (at least as they impinge on extradition practices, and possibly more generally). These are not small issues, and the Court remained willing to confront legislatures and governments, and to answer questions in much broader ways than might have been expected. These are early decisions, though—"momentum" decisions if you will—for the McLachlin Court, and this momentum was not sustained in several important respects. I will point to one very important area—namely, equality rights under section 15—in which the Court signalled a major rethink of the most ambitious decisions of the Lamer Court and (arguably) a step back towards the major precedents of the Dickson Court. Then I will indicate two very important areas—namely, freedom of religion and freedom of association—in which the McLachlin Court led a clear and embarrassing retreat from its own very ambitious and enthusiastic opening statements.

---

means "we can never have the death penalty" in Canada. See Kirk Makin, "Ruling Ensures Death Penalty Won't Return, Conference Told," *Globe and Mail*, April 13, 2007, retrieved June 16, 2014 from http://www.theglobeandmail.com/news/national/ruling-ensures-death-penalty-wont-return-conference-told/article4259388/. See also *Withler v. Canada (Attorney General)*, 2011 SCC 12.

SUBSTANTIVE MATTERS: EQUALITY RIGHTS

I have suggested earlier that the Dickson Court decision in *Andrews* was the initial landmark decision on section 15 equality rights, setting a basic framework within which the meaning of section 15 could be expanded, and in terms of which section 15 claims were to be evaluated. This led to several different lines of interpretation, however, because of fragmentation within the Court, and the result was the Lamer Court's ambitious decision in *Law*, intended to pull together the divergent trends and establish a new framework that was more comprehensive and robust. All indications were that this attempt was, at least initially, largely successful; *Law* quickly became one of the most frequently cited of the Lamer Court's decisions—the obligatory "go-to" case in all section 15 jurisprudence, not so much supplementing or complementing *Andrews* as (on the indication of relative citation frequency) largely displacing it.

Not all was well in Charterland, however, and there was considerable and growing dissatisfaction with the complexities of the *Law* framework. Less than a decade after *Law* was handed down, it was gently but firmly revisited in a McLachlin Court decision; the case was *Kapp*.[25]

The immediate context of the case was an exploration of the relationship between the two parts of section 15 of the Charter. Subsection 1 says that every individual is equal, and is entitled to be treated "without discrimination" by the law with respect to a range of attributes, enumerated and analogous; subsection 2 states that this does not preclude laws or programs whose object is "the amelioration of the conditions of disadvantaged individuals or groups," including those identified in subsection 1. In other words, crudely, discrimination is okay if the target is right and the purposes are righteous. In the immediate case the categories were straightforward enough—it involved 24 hours of preferential fishing access for three aboriginal bands—so the basic question of "Is this the right kind of group?" was not particularly problematic. Nonetheless, the Chief Justice used the occasion to revisit *Law* in a very direct and critical way.

---

25 *R. v. Kapp*, [2008] 2 S.C.R. 483, 2008 SCC 41.

She identified *Andrews* ("twenty years past") as having established the basic template for the treatment of section 15 in terms of substantive, rather than formal, equality, a template that has been "enriched but never abandoned" (para. 14). "A decade later," *Law* took the further step of placing the focus of the Court's attention on the impact of a law or program on the "human dignity of the complainant group," having regard to a number of contextual factors (para. 19). The great achievement of *Law*, she said, was to have unified what was becoming a seriously divided approach to the matter by the Court (para. 20), but it soon became clear that there were serious "difficulties" in using human dignity as a "legal test" (para. 21); there were growing complaints that the new test or set of tests was "confusing and difficult to apply" and, moreover, that because of the use of the test, the case law was tending towards "formalism" (para. 22). The modern Supreme Court does refer to the academic literature, although sparingly and (since a brief heyday in the early 1990s) decreasingly often; unlike the United States Supreme Court, the Supreme Court of Canada does not have a decision presentation format that makes use of substantive footnotes. In *Kapp*, however, McLachlin took the unprecedented step of appending two substantive footnotes to paragraph 22 that included references to no fewer than 20 different articles in academic journals or edited collections of articles.

As a result, McLachlin suggested, we need to see *Law* simply as an alternative way of focusing on the central concern of *Andrews*—that is to say, combating discrimination by pursuing substantive equality—and for the rest of her reasons, she focused on, and referred only to, *Andrews*, and not once to the more complex and detailed steps and factors of *Law*. A minor statistical confirmation of the actual impact of this decision is evident: before *Kapp*, the judges of the McLachlin Court had cited *Law* 39 times, and *Andrews* 20 times, but since *Kapp*, *Andrews* has been cited six times to *Law*'s two.[26]

---

26 These counts also make another useful point about the frequency of equality rights cases—in the eight years before *Kapp*, the McLachlin Court cited the two leading section 15 cases a total of 39 times, or five times a year. In the four years since *Kapp*, it has cited the same two leading cases only eight times, or twice a year.

SUBSTANTIVE MATTERS: FREEDOM OF RELIGION

Freedom of religion was, for a surprisingly long time, one of the great unexplored corners of the Charter. To be sure, there was an early decision—*Big M*—which, in typical Dickson fashion, sketched the general outlines of the idea. The case itself, however, had to count as a very easy decision—how hard can it be to find a focused religious purpose in a statute which calls itself "The Lord's Day Act"?—and somehow the Court took a long time to find it necessary or convenient to expand on those ideas.[27]

FREEDOM OF RELIGION AND *AMSELEM*

The McLachlin Court was the one that grasped the nettle, and the case was *Amselem*.[28] Amselem (and his three co-litigants) were tenants in an upscale Montreal condominium building. They erected temporary structures on the balconies of their units to permit them to observe the annual nine-day Jewish festival of Succot, but this violated the condominium bylaw (included in the contract which the litigants had signed but, according to the record, had not read) which prohibited decorations, alterations, or constructions on the balconies. They brought an action to have the bylaw declared to be a violation of their right to freedom of religion under the Quebec Charter of Rights; after losing on both trial and appeal in the Quebec courts, they appealed to the Supreme Court. Although the case was initially framed in terms of the Quebec Charter, which has different terminology and employs an intriguingly different conceptual framework, the Supreme Court decision used the case to tackle the definition of religion for the purposes of the Canadian Charter as well, this logical slide occurring very casually at paragraph 40 of the majority reasons.

---

27 Not that it didn't have the opportunity—many court-watchers expected the *Trinity Western* case (*Trinity Western University v. College of Teachers*, [2001] 1 S.C.R. 772, 2001 SCC 31) to be the second shoe to drop, but only the dissenting minority rose to that challenge, and the majority treated it as an administrative law case with no Charter overtones.

28 *Syndicat Northcrest v. Amselem*, 2004 SCC 47.

What makes this case interesting from a constitutional-law viewpoint is the dissent—not only does Bastarache differ from Iacobucci's conclusion for the majority, but he does so in a set of reasons which, most unusually, are directly parallel and of almost identical length to those of the majority. The core of the disagreement is, precisely, the definition of religion—as Iacobucci says, "In order to define religious freedom, we must first ask ourselves what we mean by 'religion'" (para. 39). Iacobucci would define religion in terms of the sincerity of a set of "personal convictions or beliefs connected to an individual's spiritual faith [that are] integrally linked to one's self-definition and spiritual fulfilment, the practices of which allow individuals to foster a connection with the divine or with the subject or object of that spiritual faith" (para. 39). Bastarache, on the other hand, would anchor the freedom of religion in a concept of "orthodoxy": "a religion is a system of beliefs and practices based on certain religious precepts. A nexus between personal beliefs and the religion's precepts must therefore be established" (para. 135). It is not enough that an individual has sincere beliefs; in order to trigger the Charter right, those beliefs must match up with the central precepts and requirements of an established religious organization. In the immediate case, they did not; inhabiting a *succah* during the nine-day festival of Succot was, on the testimony of Jewish religious experts, an optional, rather than a central, tenet of the Jewish faith, and this is why Bastarache dissented.[29]

The choice between these two definitions is profoundly important. Iacobucci's is clearly the most open and expansive, with both "sincerity" and "connection with the spiritual" being potentially problematic. On the one hand, it is vulnerable to very new and very small (even single-person) affirmations of religious conviction; taking a real-life example from American experience, consider a group of college students who declare themselves members of the "Temple of the Holy Brew," with services every Friday and Saturday evening. On the other hand, it is so wide-open that it invites trivialization; Ogilvie worries that it is actually a subtle attack on religion because it reduces religion to "nonsense" that is

---

29 I had the occasion to speak with Justice Bastarache after he retired from the Supreme Court, and when asked about the sets of reasons that he was proudest of having written, he identified his dissent in *Amselem* as being at the top of that list.

undeserving of legal or constitutional protection.[30] Bastarache's approach is considerably more restrictive, hinting at the need for a Court-approved list of religions whose tenets of orthodoxy provide protection for their followers, with all other sets of self-designated religious beliefs treated differently. Both are problematic, but in different ways, which simply demonstrates the pitfalls in the allegedly "easy" constitutional right of freedom of religion.

For myself, I very much share Justice Binnie's bewilderment, expressed in his solo dissent, that this wound up as a Charter case in the first place, not only because there is nothing in the reasons of the lower courts that dealt with the Canadian Charter, but also because there is no sign of the "government nexus" that is the logical focus of the Canadian (but not of the Quebec) Charter—the major issue here is one of private contract, not government regulation. Crudely put, no government has violated any rights because no government has done anything at all. Nonetheless (and notwithstanding the preferences of Justice Binnie and myself), this is the Supreme Court's great and glorious entry into the question of freedom of religion, and because the Quebec Charter is built around a notion of balancing of rights, an element of that has been injected in the Supreme Court's Charter jurisprudence.

FREEDOM OF RELIGION AND *MULTANI*

The critical questions about "freedom of religion" in the Charter ultimately have to be the following: What does it add? Under what circumstances can it be used as a "get out of jail free" card? What is it that I can do (or refuse to do) because of my religious convictions or connections, that other people without such convictions or connections cannot do (or refuse to do)? Given some of the practices that have historically been associated with religious beliefs, there has to be some hedging about the answer—cannibalism and child sacrifice could not possibly be on the agenda—but unless freedom of religion is some kind of "get out of jail free card" under at least some circumstances, then the constitutional

---

30 Margaret H. Ogilvie, "And Then There Was One: Freedom of Religion in Canada—the Incredible Shrinking Concept," *Ecclesiastical Law Journal* 10 (2008): 197.

inclusion of the phrase was an empty gesture. The answer in *Amselem*—building a temporary structure on a condominium balcony—can only be a beginning; *Multani*[31] carries it into more controversial territory.

Multani was a Sikh, whose religion requires him (among other things) to wear a kirpan—a religious object that resembles a dagger and must be made of metal—at all times. The school's code of conduct, however, included an absolute prohibition on weapons, and once the authorities were aware of his kirpan (when he accidentally dropped it in the school-yard) they ordered that he cease wearing it in favour of either a symbolic kirpan (a pin or some such) or one that was made of a material that would render it harmless. Multani's parents went to court for an order setting aside the school board's ruling; at trial, they were successful, but this was reversed by the Court of Appeal, bringing the appeal to the Supreme Court of Canada.

Although four judges on the nine-judge panel would have preferred not to treat the matter as a constitutional issue, but rather as a question of administrative law and procedural issues, the five-judge majority saw it as a clear matter of freedom of religion, and the background case was *Amselem*. The *Amselem* hurdle is easily cleared; the appellant "genuinely believes," the school board order undoubtedly violates his freedom of religion, and the infringement is neither trivial nor insignificant. Although the action has both a valid purpose, and the infringement is rationally connected to that purpose, it does not satisfy the other elements of the *Oakes* test; in particular, a total prohibition on wearing the kirpan is not a minimal impairment of the right. It also sends a message to other students and to the broader society that certain religious beliefs are not as deserving of respect as others.

Given the cogency of an issue such as school safety in the face of possible violence, this would have to count as a modest but significant enhancement of the Court's treatment of freedom of religion, invoking freedom of religion in a context where it traded off against a higher profile concern or value. In terms of my question—What difference does it make to be able to invoke a constitutional right to freedom of religion?—the

---

31 *Multani v. Commission scolaire Marguerite-Bourgeoys*, [2006] 1 S.C.R. 256, 2006 SCC 6.

answer would have to be, "more than it had meant two years earlier." The flipside of that question—How far can the right to religious freedom take you in terms of behaviour that is at least tangentially at odds with the authorities and broader society?—the answer would have to be: "We haven't found that yet."

There are intriguing dimensions to the decision. Although I have presented it as a 5–4 decision, it was not a 5–4 result; the minority judges concurred with the outcome, and would also have set aside the total prohibition and directed that there be an arrangement that would allow the appellant to wear a kirpan. The 5–4 split was not on outcome but rather on reasons; more particularly, it was about whether or not the case should be handled as a Charter case engaging freedom of religion.[32] That, in turn, suggests an uneasiness within the Court on where the logic of freedom of religion seemed to be taking them, on a journey that some judges would rather not be taking—at least not yet. One distinct possibility, which turned out to be correct, was that the journey might therefore wind up not taking the Court much further at all.

FREEDOM OF RELIGION AND *HUTTERIAN BRETHREN*

There is a familiar slogan from the court reform movement, If you pave a road, you get more traffic. In Charter terms, if you ceremoniously unlock a door, more people will knock on it. The next knock on the door was *Hutterian Brethren*,[33] a case whose origins are in my part of the country— not just my province, but my part of the province, namely, southern

---

32 In this it resembles *Congrégation des témoins de Jéhovah de St.-Jérôme-Lafontaine v. Lafontaine (Village)*, [2004] S.C.R. 650, 2004 SCC 48—a companion case (same panel, same basic issues, decided on the same day) to *Amselem*, involving a complaint by a Jehovah's Witnesses congregation that zoning regulations had prevented them from building a new church. In that case, it was four judges in the minority that wanted to treat the case as engaging Charter freedom of religion issues, and a five-judge majority that decided instead to handle it as a question of municipal law. In the American literature, the capacity of an appeal court to alter the nature of the question it is answering is referred to as "issue fluidity." See, for example, Kevin T. McGuire and Barbara Palmer, "Issue Fluidity in the U.S. Supreme Court," *American Political Science Review* 89 (1995): 691.

33 *Alberta v. Hutterian Brethren of Wilson Colony*, 2009 SCC 37.

Alberta (about 30 kilometres down the road). Considering the recency of *Multani*, with its modest demonstration of the expanding potential of freedom of religion, the outcome in *Hutterian Brethren* must be considered a distinct surprise.

The Hutterian Brethren are a religious group whose usually prosperous and expanding communal farms stud the southern Alberta landscape, sometimes to the disquiet of the family farmers who surround them; a Hutterite colony grows, or generates a new colony, only by absorbing some of the neighbouring family farms, which in turn diminishes the villages and small towns that are the other side of Western Canadian rural existence. They dress distinctively, and on their go-to-town day (which used to be Thursday, although the practice seems to have loosened up a bit), you can see them in the towns and cities in the area.

The issue in the case at hand was drivers' licenses, and in particular, the requirement for photographs on those drivers' licenses. A long-standing tenet of Hutterite belief is that personal photographs violate the Biblical prohibition on graven images—not the most common reading of that particular passage, to be sure, but one that has long been important to the Hutterites, and has for years been accommodated by the Alberta government, which was willing to issue drivers' licenses to members of the community without the usual photographs. Recently, worried about the possible (but not actual) problems that photograph-free government ID might pose for identity theft or impersonation, the government adopted new procedures which ended this accommodation, and the Hutterites went to court for a ruling that the new policy violated their freedom of religion. The lower courts agreed with them, and agreed as well that the policy was not a reasonable limit; the Supreme Court agreed on the first, but not on the second. By the narrowest of margins (4–3 on a seven-judge panel) the Court declared itself satisfied that the *Oakes* test had been met.[34] Enhanced protection against identity theft

---

34 It is striking how cheerfully, even casually, the Court accepted the government's arguments on this score, and this is a comment that can be generalized to earlier significant cases (like *Gosselin*) and more recent ones (like *Whatcott*). If the now-discredited option of the section 33 "notwithstanding clause" was potentially a way that governments to eviscerate the Charter if they are so minded, the "reasonable limits" clause in section 1 is the comparable opportunity for the courts to do so.

by maintaining a province-wide database of drivers' photos was a valid objective; allowing no exemptions for the license photo requirement was rationally connected, because it neither prevented the complainants from following their preferred worship or from making alternative transportation arrangements. Furthermore, there was minimal impairment, and the balance between enhanced province-wide protection from identify theft and minority religious inconvenience was easily struck in favour of the province.

I admit to having been surprised by the tone of the decision, and in particular the comment that being unable to have a driver's license was not a real hardship because the community could always hire drivers or taxis to provide them with the mobility that they needed. "Let them hire taxis" resonates more than a little of Marie Antoinette's famous quip, "Let them eat cake." On a deeper level, it resembles the new mood of the United States Supreme Court regarding freedom of religion—since *Smith*, the First Amendment "free practice" is not a minority-religion exemption from government measures of broad and general application, but only a shield against specifically targeted repression. We have come a long way from Wilson's defiant comments in *Singh*—that mere governmental convenience was not in itself grounds for finding a policy to be a reasonable limit on a right.

FREEDOM OF RELIGION AND *N.S.*

The even more recent case of *N.S.*[35] continues the ambivalence. The question was whether the complainant in a sexual assault case could wear a face-concealing niqab while giving testimony. This is the sort of question that frequently arises in Charter litigation—not a straightforward case of a government policy running rough-shod over a Charter right (as we might characterize *Hutterian Brethren*), but two different rights sending us different directions on a policy question. On the one hand, many Muslim women believe that their religious convictions require them, or at least strongly incline them, to conceal their faces in public; on the other hand, the right of the accused to a fair trial implies a right of

---

35 *R. v. N.S.*, 2012 SCC 72.

confrontation, and historically we have tended to believe that the judge (and the jury, should there be one) take a lot of cues about the reliability of a witness or of a particular piece of testimony from that person's facial expressions and demeanour, which is made much more difficult when the face is concealed.

For my purposes, the decision in *N.S.* is even more frustrating than the one in *Hutterian Brethren,* because it is not so much dismissive as inconclusive. Caught between these two Charter rights, both of which have some jurisprudential track record, the Court ultimately can do nothing more than say that both rights are important and the matter has to be handled by trial judges on a case-by-case basis. On the one hand, freedom of religion is important (and although the trial judge was chided for commenting on the "strength" of the complainant's beliefs, the majority still wants judges, among other things, to assess the "importance" of the belief), but the right to a fair trial is also important and "there is a strong connection between the ability to see the face of a witness and a fair trial" (para. 27). In the immediate case, then, the question is remanded to the original judge, where things started four years earlier; every time the issue re-emerges in the lower courts, the losing side has an incentive to appeal in search of a clearer statement (or a slight shifting) of the balance.

Freedom of religion allows adherents of a major traditional religion to erect temporary structures on their balcony despite condominium regulations to the contrary, but it does not exempt Hutterites from having photographs on their drivers' licenses despite long-established "graven image" prohibitions on such photographs (reasonable limit), while the Court equivocates on whether it allows Muslims to wear the niqab while testifying in court (case-by-case basis). The deeper problem, of course, is that it is considerably easier to observe the freedom of religious belief and speech than it is to provide the policy space for the freedom of religious practice, which helps to explain why American doctrine so enthusiastically endorses the former but virtually strangles the latter. We have not, after all, progressed very far from the striking down of the easy-target Lord's Day Act. The freedom of religion cases are a bit of a boomerang—that is, we seem to have taken a big step forward, only to wind up very much where we started—just as equality rights jurisprudence boomeranged from *Andrews* through *Law* to *Kapp* and back to (or at least towards) *Andrews.*

SUBSTANTIVE MATTERS: FREEDOM OF ASSOCIATION

The same could be said (only more so) of the freedom of association decisions of the McLachlin Court, which, to understand properly, we should unfold as the "freedom of collective bargaining" issue, because this is the section of the Charter where the unions have been engaged in highly frustrating action ever since the *Labour Trilogy* of 1987.

FREEDOM OF ASSOCIATION AND *DUNMORE*

The process starts with *Dunmore*,[36] in December 2001, an early indication of a reconsideration of the rather unwelcoming position on trade unions that the Court had taken in the Dickson Court's *Labour Trilogy* and stayed with thereafter. The case was slightly complicated; for one thing, it involved a challenge not to a legislative initiative but rather to an attempt to repeal a previous action. One would think that if the legislature had the power to pass the previous act, it must have the power to repeal that act in whole or in part, and this logic is all the more compelling if we think of the Charter as primarily intended to prevent governments from taking actions that violate Charter rights, such that "stopping acting" (or "not acting at all") are generally Charter-invisible.

Nonetheless, as is often the case with life, the situation was a bit more complicated than that. The issue involved agricultural workers, a sector of the economy which is distinctly different from industrial concerns, government offices, or large retail outlets where, generally speaking, a larger proportion of the workforce is involved. Governments in Canada have routinely treated this sector as different enough that in most provinces it is excluded (completely or largely) from the labour laws that provide the legal framework for workers who wish to organize for the purpose of unionizing or (not precisely the same thing) engaging in collective bargaining; it is not unfair to say that the effect of this exclusion is to make such organizing more difficult. In 1994, Bob Rae's NDP government in Ontario amended that province's labour laws to end the exclusion

---

36 *Dunmore v. Ontario (Attorney General)*, [2001] 3 S.C.R. 1016, 2001 SCC 94.

of agricultural workers, and then in 1995, Mike Harris's Conservative government wanted to repeal the NDP amendment, which is to say that it wanted to restore the status quo (*ante* Rae) and once again exclude agricultural workers.

The workers lost at trial and in the provincial court of appeal, which was not altogether surprising given the firmness of the *Labour Trilogy* and the consistency of the outcomes in subsequent cases in the Supreme Court; surprisingly, however, they won their case in the Supreme Court itself, and by a substantial margin with Major alone dissenting. Intriguingly, though, Bastarache for the majority did not directly overrule the earlier *Labour Trilogy*—the Supreme Court definitely can "change its mind" and has done so from time to time, but does not do so casually. Conceding the earlier precedents, Bastarache nonetheless wove his way through dicta[37] from the earlier cases to find a narrow path through the quicksand: there are certain kinds of legitimate activity, he suggested, that can only be pursued as a collective activity, and for government to act so as to prevent collective action in such circumstances is a violation of individual rights. Pushing agricultural workers back out from under the "normal" regime for organizing themselves for collective bargaining activities fell within this unusual category.

Bastarache, however, went a good deal further in his arguments. Where the earlier Court had casually dismissed collective bargaining and other labour rights as different from the historic core of human rights, and the "mere" product of legislation, Bastarache drew a connection between the pursuit of human dignity and the protection of a degree

---

37 Legal doctrine makes a distinction between various parts of the reasons for the Court's judgement; *ratio decidendi* is that part of the reasons that is logically necessary for the Court's reasoning to get to its conclusion; but *obiter dicta* are the other comments or arguments or suggestions that the judges might make along the way. Strictly speaking, it is the *ratio* that constitutes binding precedent, and while the *obiter* may be of some interest—as suggesting where those judges might like the Court to go in the future, and inviting litigation to prompt this movement—it does not bind future and lower courts in the same way. My own feeling is that the boundary between *obiter* and *ratio* is (to put it politely) a little flexible, and also that "binding" precedent is not what it once was, but this is not to deny that there are distinctions to be made between the various elements in a judgement.

of autonomy in the workplace and in the activity of labour—as I have suggested above, "human dignity" emerged under the Lamer Court as a touchstone of particular significance, and it is a positive thing for a litigant to see the Court link their cause to such a purpose.[38] He alluded as well to the historic realities of labour–management relations, which the labour legislation framework was designed to channel and contain; absent government involvement, workers who attempted to organize were subject not only to a range of unfair labour practices, but also to the many unfriendly-to-labour presumptions built into many surviving elements of the common law (para. 20). "The evidence is that the ability of agricultural workers to associate is only as great as their access to legal protection, and such protection exists neither in statutory nor constitutional form" (para. 45).

Of course, if the Ontario government could not amend the legislation to re-exclude agricultural workers without violating the constitutional rights of those workers, this raised the question of whether the legislation excluding workers had been (to this extent) constitutional in the first place; furthermore, if the first question was one for Ontario alone, the other, definitely, was not, because all the other provinces were doing something similar. The *Dunmore* decision does (tentatively) speak to this, and in a highly interesting way that I will discuss below when I deal with the McLachlin Court and the question of remedies.

FREEDOM OF ASSOCIATION AND *HEALTH SERVICE WORKERS*

Three years later, the Court went considerably further, and in much less cautiously couched terms. The case similarly involved a swing from an NDP government to one that was much more concerned with controlling expenses and reducing taxes, and this similarly involved legislation to undo what the previous government had done. This time, it involved British Columbia, where Gordon Campbell's provincial Liberal government came within two seats of a clean sweep of

---

38 The corresponding negative term, especially for the McLachlin Court, is "arbitrary."

the legislature, and proceeded to pass legislation to undo the results of collective bargaining with a number of public sector unions. Salary increases were rolled back, and other elements of the negotiated agreements were annulled and unilaterally replaced with the government's own strict conditions. Not too surprisingly, the unions went to court over the matter—several different sets of unions, in fact, relating to the frustrations of several different sectors of public service employees. The first set to make it to the Supreme Court was the health service workers, although, in a real sense, it would not have mattered which of them won that particular race, because the factual circumstances were so similar that a decision made with respect to one would, by implication, apply to the others.

I will refer to the case as *Health Service Worker*s (the way it is actually indexed by the Supreme Court is a much more awkward mouthful).[39] The majority reasons (there was a single dissenter) include a paragraph that is so remarkable that I will quote it in its entirety:

> In earlier decisions, the majority view in the Supreme Court of Canada was that the guarantee of freedom of association did not extend to collective bargaining. *Dunmore* opened the door to reconsideration of that view. We conclude that the grounds advanced in the earlier decisions for the exclusion of collective bargaining from the *Charter*'s protection of freedom of association do not withstand principled scrutiny and should be rejected. (para. 22)

It is not that the Supreme Court never changes its mind—it does, sometimes incrementally and sometimes dramatically—but it very seldom points to an earlier decision and says, "We blew it completely."[40] To say that the grounds of an earlier decision "do not withstand principled

---

39 *Health Services and Support—Facilities Subsector Bargaining Assn. v. British Columbia*, 2007 SCC 27.

40 The preferred mode is either to shift to a new direction without actually pointing out that it is a new direction, or to suggest that the current decision is simply correcting a curious but widespread misunderstanding of the earlier decision—as witness the *Askov/Morin* sequence, or the *Marshall 1/Marshall 2* package.

scrutiny" is a remarkable repudiation of an earlier Court,[41] and it turns the Dickson dissent in that 20-year-old case into what American scholarship would call a "canonic dissent"—a set of minority reasons that is so totally vindicated by later reflection and experience that the former judgement simply vanishes.[42]

I have earlier suggested that the Dickson Court—mostly through the written words of Dickson himself—laid the basic framework for most of the major sets of rights in the Charter, making a bold initial statement, but in such a way as to leave the refinement of details to subsequent Courts as experience with the Charter developed. I also suggested, however, that the freedom of association cases—the *Labour Trilogy*—were the major exception to that, with Dickson in dissent while the Court handed down a very restrictive interpretation that, at least for the union movement, suggested that the section had no growth potential whatever. What McLachlin's judgement in *Health Service Workers* seems to do is to push the reset button, to magically jump us back 20 years to the moment when Dickson's last-major-part-of-the-package sketch was turned into a dissent as first McIntyre and then Le Dain "stole" his majority; suddenly it was as if we were back in 1987, and the unfolding of freedom of association doctrine could now begin, 20 years later, to undergo the same expansion and clarification that had applied to the other fundamental freedoms and to equality rights. The deliberate exclusion of the right to strike from the immediate decision ("the present case does not include the right to strike," para. 19) is not particularly problematic in that regard—it neither includes nor specifically excludes that right from the broader freedom of association, leaving the consideration to future cases that will draw on this much more union-friendly foundation.

It was, however, a matter of some concern that there was considerable rhetoric, but not a great deal of detail, contained within the *Health Service* decision—clearly, Premier Campbell had overstepped the Charter limits,

---

41 Although it was perhaps made easier by the fact that not a single judge who served on the panel that handed down the *Labour Trilogy* remained on the Court for the *Health Service Workers* decision.

42 See, for example, Richard A. Primus, "Canon, Anti-Canon and Judicial Dissent," *Duke Law Journal* 48 (1998): 243; and Anita S. Krishnakumar, "On the Evolution of the Canonical Dissent," *Rutgers Law Review* 52 (2000): 781.

and clearly the Court wanted to make its disapproval unmistakable, but apart from that, there was considerably more bark than bite. In the interests of complete disclosure, I should add that I was at that time active in the university's Faculty Association (sort of Alberta-speak for "faculty union") in my province. After such a resounding judicial vindication for the labour movement, we thought, there had to be something in it that we could use in a province that is far from the most labour-friendly jurisdiction in the country, and has the labour legislation to prove it. Not finding anything much ourselves, we commissioned a formal report from a legal expert who could not find very much either; when we put on a bold face by sending a package of proposals to the government anyway, they casually brushed us off. Maybe not such a bold new day after all—maybe just a hint of sunshine on the horizon, although even that was more than the unions had seen up to that point.

FREEDOM OF ASSOCIATION AND *FRASER*

But even that modest hope is frustrated by a later decision, namely *Fraser*[43]—or, as we might better label it, "the return to *Dunmore*," in more senses than one. When we left Ontario a few pages ago, the Supreme Court had struck down as unconstitutional the Harris government's repeal of the New Democrat legislation including agricultural workers in the coverage of provincial labour legislation. New legislation was passed in 2002, and shortly afterward the agricultural workers were back in the courts again, arguing that the new act, while less egregious than the previous one, did not fully follow through on what *Dunmore* had required. This time the Court did not accept their arguments (although the Ontario Court of Appeal had done so); there was only a single dissenter (Abella), but the eight judges supporting the outcome were (for our Supreme Court) unusually fragmented.

McLachlin and LeBel co-authored the judgement, just as they had previously co-authored *Health Service Workers*. This is already slightly curious; co-authorship is a relatively new development on the Supreme Court of Canada, so we are still learning how to decode the message that

---

43 *Ontario (Attorney General) v. Fraser,* 2011 SCC 20.

this device sends, either in general or in the case of particular pairings.[44] Sometimes, it seems to be used by pairs of judges that are unusually solid allies as revealed by their voting; Cory and Iacobucci, who effectively invented the practice, are the most obvious example. On other occasions, when the co-authorship links judges who do not regularly vote together, it hints at a different implicit message, namely, compromise. If the pair "compromised up" in *Health Service Workers*, they clearly "compromised down" in *Fraser*.

The majority reasons revisited *Dunmore* (and the intervening *Health Service Workers*) to discern a basic set of instructions that should have guided the new legislation, and although they could not find a legislative entrenchment of several of the more important ideas and concepts that they had suggested, in the end they found enough of an improvement over the previous legislation that the workers' challenge was rejected. Just how hard the Court was willing to reach for a compromise that would save the legislation is the most clear at paragraph 101; although the workers had complained that there was not even a requirement that employers must negotiate in good faith, the Court offered them a disappointing half-loaf:

> Sections 5(6) and (7) are critical. They provide that the employer shall listen to oral representations, and read written representations, and acknowledge having read them. They do not expressly refer to a requirement that the employer consider employee representations in good faith. Nor do they rule it out. By implication, they include such a requirement.

Given the centrality of "bargaining in good faith" to any vigorous system of labour relations, this is curiously weak; it looks like a salvage effort, a saving of face—in short, it looks like a compromise.

By contrast, the concurring judgements were energetic and precise. Deschamps stood firm with the position that led her to dissent in *Health Service Workers*, which was that the Court should be very cautious in using

---

44 See Peter McCormick, "Sharing the Spotlight: Co-Authored Reasons on the Modern Supreme Court of Canada," *Dalhousie Law Journal* 34 (2011): 165.

the freedom of association to intrude upon legislative determinations of an appropriate labour relations regime, and that it was unfortunate that the Court unnecessarily used language in that case that suggested it was imposing a duty to negotiate in good faith. Rothstein (with Charron) was even more emphatic, "respectfully disagreeing" that collective bargaining deserves any protection whatever under the Charter's freedom of association (para. 124), and flatly preferring that the Court directly and explicitly overrule the decision in *Health Service Workers*; a substantial part of his reasons (which were, very unusually, longer than those of the majority) directly focused on the question of when and how Courts should, or should not, overturn their own precedent.

Abella's solo dissent was openly critical of the majority's strategy, but from the other side; she began her remarks with the following:

> I have great difficulty with stretching the interpretive process in a way that converts clear statutory language and express legislative intention into a completely different scheme. The *AEPA* does not protect, and was never intended to protect, collective bargaining rights. (para. 322)

Her reasons condemned the "formalism" of the *Labour Trilogy*, and celebrated the Court's decision in *Dunmore* and *Health Service Workers* to enhance the content of freedom of association by including protection for the process of collective bargaining. Nonetheless, she was writing in dissent—alone.

The fact that the judges who disagreed with the *Health Service Workers* precedent (to the point of openly suggesting the repudiation a precedent that was not a half-dozen years old)[45] concurred with the outcome, while the most outspoken supporter of that four-year-old case dissented, makes the point clear: the McLachlin Court's bold initiative on freedom of association was in tatters immediately, its majority fragmenting even for an unusually direct follow-up to the case that really signalled the beginning

---

45 Particularly ironic since the *Health Service Workers* decision itself was such an unusual candid and categorical repudiation of the 20-year-old precedent of the *Labour Trilogy*.

of the turnaround, namely *Dunmore*. I see this as another boomerang—another occasion when an escalating interpretation of a Charter section turned into a retreat; the turnaround is all the more striking both because the two cases occurred so closely together and because the movement towards a more vigorous and union-friendly interpretation of the freedom of association was so clearly something that the McLachlin Court itself had initiated, rather than building on momentum from previous decisions. That is to say, it was another demonstration that the Charter revolution was over.

SUBSTANTIVE MATTERS: HEALTH CARE

And then there was *Chaoulli*.[46]

Two people in Quebec—a patient who had had to wait a long time for hip surgery, and a doctor who wanted to work outside the public system—brought an action before the Court seeking a declaration that their rights were violated by medicare, or more specifically, by preventing them from purchasing the private health insurance that would permit people to afford to seek alternatives should there be unacceptable delays in accessing the public system. They lost at trial and in the provincial court of appeal, but in the Supreme Court they were successful.

Well, sort of successful—it was one of the Supreme Court's less lucid expressions of constitutional meaning. The seven-judge panel split three ways: three judges (Binnie, LeBel, and Fish) found no violation of the Charter in the Quebec legislation implementing medicare; three judges (McLachlin, Major, and Bastarache) found a violation of the Canadian Charter that could not be saved as a reasonable limit, as well as a violation of the Quebec Charter; and the seventh judge (Deschamps) found a violation of the Quebec Charter but declined to extend her analysis to the Canadian Charter as well. As a result, the Quebec government was obliged to amend its legislation to accommodate private health care insurance (which, after a time extension, it eventually did), but the message

---

46 *Chaoulli v. Quebec (Attorney General)*, [2005] 1 S.C.R. 791; 2005 SCC 35.

for the other provinces was much less clear.[47] Technically, Deschamps's solo reasons mean that it was a three-to-three tie on whether medicare without private health care insurance violates the Charter, so the question is not yet answered, but it remains surprising that such a critical issue was fought to a draw—and then just left there.

For me, this raises the broader question of the grand framing of the Charter, a problem raised by its intriguing timing. The 1960s and 1970s were the era of positive government, of grand social programs and major intervention, and of crown corporations playing a major economic role; the 1990s and this new century clearly reflected a neo-conservative mood, with less confidence in the capacity of governments, a major shift to free enterprise rather than bureaucrats, and the winding up of most of the crown corporations. Is the Charter, then, the last gasp of our social democratic decades, or the first dawning of the neo-conservative period? The truth is probably that entrenched Charters are not firmly, narrowly, and specifically directive of very much, and they are amenable to being read and interpreted in a number of different ways—which is to say that it could be either (or something else entirely), depending on how the courts, and the Supreme Court in particular, decide to handle it. Either way, *Chaoulli* is important because it brings together in confrontation the two great legacies of the 1970s. To overdramatize: you can have the Charter or you can have medicare: take your pick. The outcome is particularly ironic in Alberta, where our maverick premier was widely vilified for wanting changes to the health care system that would have accommodated private health care facilities and private health care insurance. I find it hard not to read *Chaoulli* as saying that Ralph Klein was right all along—not a wrecker and a rebel at all, but rather someone who correctly identified the kind of medicare that was consistent with the Charter.[48]

---

47 I say "the other provinces" and do not speak directly about the federal legislation, because formally medicare is a set of 10 provincial and three territorial programs under a general federal umbrella—all the operational aspects are within the provincial and territorial acts, not the federal one. And although we speak about "Canadian medicare," there is actually a considerable diversity between the various provinces and territories, both with respect to the range of services that are covered and the public/private mix that can be used to deliver those services.

48 Not that he ever defended his ideas in quite these terms.

I cannot help asking myself the following: What would Lamer, and the Lamer Court of (say) 1995, have done? How would he have handled this question had it surfaced a decade or so earlier? I think he and his Court would have found a more robust constitutional grounding for medicare, not (to be sure) in the strong sense of a "right to medicare," but rather the slightly more oblique but still effective sense expressed by saying, "If government chooses to regulate, then it takes the Charter with it." The problem, of course, is that down this track, you may wind up ordering governments to spend more money—and in the case of medicare, a *lot* more money—on a specific program, and this is something the courts have been very reluctant to do (and even more so for this, the most expensive of modern governmental services). As the dissenters pointed out, though, if you permit a growing private health care system alongside the public one, and if you insist that people can purchase insurance so that they are able to access it within containable costs, then you have a two-tier system where the wealthier classes no longer have any personal investment in the public system and will not invest any political capital in sustaining it at a robust level.

This is a tough choice either way, to be sure—maybe even just a "choose how to lose" corner—but this still lets me see *Chaoulli* as another "top of the hill" occasion followed by a failure to advance. It has always baffled me that the decision did not have a more direct public impact; certainly academics went into a minor frenzy over it, and there have been conferences and article collections on what it means and where it is taking us, but this never really seemed to carry over to the broader public. When I mention it in public talks, I just get blank looks. Perhaps it was the fragmented nature of the decision—a plurality decision, such that the tie-breaker that was (most plausibly) the judgement of the Court[49] was a solo set of reasons focused on the Quebec, not the Canadian, Charter—which in turn made it harder for the mass media to convey quickly and easily what had just happened. In terms of the broader framing above, this strongly suggests that the Charter cannot be seen in any sense as a way of

---

49 In the Supreme Court Reports, *Chaoulli* is one of the very rare cases where there is no set of reasons that is designated as the "judgement of the Court"—this is something that does not happen as often as once per year.

entrenching the socially progressive government programs of the 1970s, and even if it was not a neo-conservative document in any strong sense, its individualistic premises and its dominant protection-against-government trope can certainly take on that kind of spin. It is perhaps too much to say that *Chaoulli* amounted to nothing more than, "Medicare or the Charter: take your pick" (with the Court's pick being an individualist Charter), but it was still an important moment and it still had some of those overtones. If the good ship medicare is in trouble (as it clearly is), the Court's message is that the government should not get in the way of people maintaining their own lifeboats.

SUBSTANTIVE MATTERS: FREEDOM OF EXPRESSION

I have earlier suggested that *Irwin Toy* in 1989 was the landmark decision on the meaning of freedom of expression under the Charter, and is still the major reference point two and a half decades later; this was done by establishing a very expanded notion of what was included under the right, which in turn had the effect of pushing any of the collateral issues of free speech (such as pornography, hate speech, and soliciting for the purposes of prostitution) to be dealt with in terms of section 1 and its notion of reasonable limits. Such issues continued to come before the Court well into the twenty-first century; one such case was *Saskatchewan Human Rights Commission v. Whatcott*.[50]

Mr. Whatcott had published and distributed a number of flyers vehemently expressing his concerns about homosexuality and the way that it was being talked about in the school curriculum. Several complaints were filed with the Saskatchewan Human Rights Commission, which conducted hearings and determined that the flyers were a violation of provincial legislation prohibiting the exposing of individuals to hatred and ridicule on the basis of their sexual orientation. Upon appeal, this order was upheld; when further appealed to the Saskatchewan Court of Appeal, the decision was that the legislation was constitutionally valid, but that it did not apply to Mr. Whatcott's actions since they had been directed

---

50 *Saskatchewan Human Rights Commission v. Whatcott*, 2013 SCC 1.

to a matter of public policy. That decision was in turn appealed to the Supreme Court of Canada, which deliberated for 16 months (rather longer than usual) after oral argument before handing down its decisions.

I think we can agree that most people would not be entirely comfortable with the things that Mr. Whatcott was saying, especially considering the angry flamboyance of the rhetoric, but in a very important sense, that is precisely what is at stake in the notion of "freedom of expression." If freedom of expression only means the right to say in public (politely) the things that everybody agrees with, it would hardly be worth including it in the constitution; the saying of some highly objectionable things, even in highly objectionable ways, that annoys at least some people absolutely has to be part of the protection. The question, of course, has to do with how much protection different kinds of speech enjoy, and what sorts of considerations justify real limitations.

Rothstein, for a unanimous Court, signalled his answer in the first sentence: "All rights guaranteed under the Canadian Charter of Rights and Freedoms are subject to reasonable limitations." This was different to the earlier positioning in cases like *Oakes*, where a vigorous celebration of the "guaranteeing" was grudgingly qualified by noticing the heavily hedged limitations (limits that are reasonable, that are not only justified but are demonstrated to be justified, and that are fully consistent with a free and democratic society). It therefore came as little surprise when Rothstein sided vigorously with the Human Rights Tribunal that found against Whatcott, and was very critical of the Saskatchewan Court of Appeal's reservations about that action.

For Rothstein and his unanimous colleagues, it did not matter whether the expression at issue was religiously motivated or not; freedom of religion had nothing to do with the matter (para. 163).[51] He was willing to concede that simply quoting selectively from Scripture cannot be problematic, but this did not apply to any commentary or expansion that is wrapped around those simple quotations. Unlike the Saskatchewan

---

51 To be sure, I am just as annoyed by La Forest's casual acceptance in *Ross v. New Brunswick School District No. 15* ([1996] 1 S.C.R. 825) that anti-Semitism is entitled to be considered as a religious belief within the Christian tradition, which seems to go too far in the other direction.

Court of Appeal, Rothstein did not believe that it made any difference if the expression was directed (however intemperately) towards a discussion of real issues of current public policy;[52] he criticized them as well for having suggested that the inflammatory nature of the language used was a matter secondary to the issues and the ideas being presented (para. 172). Indeed, he suggested that even "one phrase or one sentence" in a considerably longer publication would be enough to violate the Code and preclude publication, regardless of the broader context (para. 175). It did not matter that there was no defence of truth in the legislation, because "not all truthful statements must be free from restriction" (para. 141)—a comment that I still find rather startling. To be sure, this was building on suggestions from Dickson in *Keegstra*[53] and *Taylor*,[54] but those reasons expressed the idea much more hypothetically, hedged in by being presented with "some doubt" and defensible only in circumstances that were "difficult to accept." There is no comparable reservation in Rothstein.

It is also worth noting that when the hard-to-object-to proposition was advanced that restricting speech can be justified in the interest of preventing harm to other individuals, Rothstein's argument was entirely of the "everybody knows" variety. There was no suggestion that the government was obliged to present any evidence that this particular speech, or speech like it, had actually caused demonstrable harm to particular

---

52 This is relevant because the Court has begun to distinguish between different types of speech, in terms of how closely they connect to the fundamental purposes of freedom of expression; for example, discussions of public policy issues better serves those purposes, and therefore must be less subject to limits and restrictions.

53 *R. v. Keegstra*, [1990] 3 S.C.R. 892 was a case in which a school teacher from rural Alberta was charged under a rarely used "disseminating hatred" provision of the Criminal Code for having worked his own ideas on Jewish conspiracy into the official curriculum. Dickson, for a 5–4 Court, upheld the conviction on the grounds that other elements of the Charter validated the Criminal Code provision as a reasonable limit.

54 *Canada (Human Rights Commission) v. Taylor*, [1990] 3 S.C.R. 892, a companion case (same panel, same general issues, decision handed down the same day) to *Keegstra*, involved an individual whose recorded telephone messages were found by the CHRC to denigrate the Jewish race and religion, and who further ignored both the CHRC's order to withdraw them and a "cease and desist" order from the Federal Court. The same 5–4 majority upheld the CHRC's finding and order.

individuals in circumstances like then present-day Saskatchewan, or that it was likely to do so in the immediate future. Indeed, one could hypothesize that perhaps this particular speech was so intemperate that it turned people off and undermined support or sympathy for the ideas supported in it. The relevant phrase in the Charter, however, is "demonstrably justified," not "plausibly hypothesized." Completely contrary to what I said in an earlier chapter about the whole point of generating the *Oakes* test, it would seem that the Court was very close to returning to a view of limits that approximates saying, "Yes, this legislation violates Charter rights, but the limits feel reasonable to me."

Perhaps the most surprising feature of the decision is the fact that it was unanimous. *Keegstra* was a one-vote majority on a divided Court, as was *Taylor*; two years later, *Zundel*[55] was a one-vote majority the other way, striking as too vague a "false news" statute used against a Holocaust denier. It was (then justice and now Chief Justice) McLachlin who wrote the dissent in both *Keegstra* and *Taylor*, as well as the decision in *Zundel*; in *Whatcott*, however, she signed on to a unanimous judgement that took the hypothetical claim that "even truthful statements might have to be limited, although the circumstances under which this would be appropriate seem very unlikely," and turned it into a more definite claim, namely that "the truthfulness of a statement doesn't matter if it is worded inappropriately or used for the wrong purposes." Whether or not one approves of the result in this particular case, there is definitely a change of mood that is quite striking.

REMEDIES UNDER THE CHARTER

I have suggested above that the remedy issue impacts directly the real meaning of the Charter, and the political role of the Court in relation to that document. The Dickson Court had been highly constrained as to its remedy options, while the Lamer Court availed itself of a considerably more ambitious and imaginative set. The early McLachlin Court extended this exploration in several ways, boldly exploring (or publicly

---

55 *R. v. Zundel*, [1992] 2 S.C.R. 731.

thinking about) some novel extensions of the doctrine on remedies that it inherited, but eventually fell back to the basic style of the Lamer Court (although most definitely not to the even more constrained remedial imagination of the Dickson Court).

REMEDIES: THE SUPERVISORY ORDER OPTION

The critical case in this regard was *Doucet-Boudreau*,[56] which involved a delay in building French-language schools in Nova Scotia, which—it was alleged, and the trial court had agreed—violated the minority language education rights of the litigants. Indeed, the provincial government had conceded as much, having earlier promised to deliver the facilities in question but having, for various reasons, failed to follow through. The controversial part of the decision was not the finding that a Charter right had been violated, but the fact that the trial judge ordered the provincial government to report directly to him on a regular basis about the progress of the project, resulting in a number of hearings for which the government was required to submit material. The provincial government appealed the reporting requirement, and the provincial court of appeal upheld that appeal; the litigants then appealed that decision to the Supreme Court, which (in a sharply divided 5–4 decision) restored the requirement.

The controversial element in the decision was the supervisory order, which is (to put it mildly) not normal practice in Canadian courts. It is, however, something that has happened more often in the United States, and the two most obvious and high profile examples of judicial activism in that country—the extensive busing of school students to overcome desegregation, and the judicial supervision of state prisons and prison budgets to deal with the deplorable conditions in many southern states[57]—both operated through the mechanism of these supervisory orders. *Doucet-Boudreau* is, at the least, a first tentative step in that direction—a "first"

---

56 *Doucet-Boudreau v. Nova Scotia (Minister of Education)*, [2003] 3 S.C.R. 3.

57 See, for example, Malcolm M. Feeley and Edward L. Rubin, *Judicial Policy Making and the Modern State: How the Courts Reformed America's Prisons* (New York: Cambridge University Press, 1998).

which arguably makes a "second" easier. Manfredi and Kelly put it in precisely this context, suggesting that "the Court has systematically enhanced the scope of remedial powers under the *Charter* from *Schachter v. Canada* (1992) to *Doucet-Boudreau v. Nova Scotia* (2003)."[58] Minor and Wilson similarly suggested that "the majority took the opportunity that presented itself to plant a 'stake in the ground.'"[59]

If the purpose was to put a stake in the ground, then the Court has subsequently been satisfied to look at that stake from a considerable distance rather than permanently take up occupation there. There has been no real follow-up on this, largely because, as Minor and Wilson conclude, Canadian governments comply with court orders, such that the supervisory order is unnecessary overkill, and the only reason to engage the courts again is if one of the parties believes it is necessary to alter the order. The point remains that the supervisory order was (for Canada) an unusual innovation, that it was applied in a Charter context, and that a sharply divided Supreme Court upheld it as a legitimate and appropriate move, establishing a precedent (unused, but theoretically available) for future reference.

REMEDIES UNDER THE CHARTER: DAMAGES AND MONETARY REMEDIES

Pre-Charter, the Court had considered the idea of creating a "tort" for the violation of a human right; the case leading to this consideration had arisen in Ontario and was supported by an Ontario Court of Appeal decision authored by then appeal court justice (later Supreme Court justice) Bertha Wilson. The Supreme Court unanimously rejected this at the time,[60] but the McLachlin Court has (sort of)[61] revisited the idea in the

---

58 Christopher Manfredi and James B. Kelly, "Misrepresenting the Supreme Court's Record?" *McGill Law Journal* 49 (2004): 741.

59 Janet E. Minor and James S.F. Wilson, "Reflections of a Supervisory Order Sceptic: Ten Years after *Doucet-Boudreau*," in Kent Roach and Robert A. Sharpe, eds., *Taking Remedies Seriously* (Ottawa: Canadian Institute for the Administration of Justice, 2009), 321.

60 *Seneca College v. Bhadauria*, [1981] 2 S.C.R. 181.

61 "However, it should always be borne in mind that these are not private law damages, but the distinct remedy of constitutional damages." *Vancouver (City) v. Ward*, 2010 SCC 27, per McLachlin CJ, para. 22.

quite different context of an entrenched Charter, and has (sort of) come out with a different result.[62]

The case was *Ward v. Vancouver*, 2010 (SCC 27), and it involved a political tactic that has become popular of late, namely, the "pie-ing" of prominent politicians—that is to say, embarrassing a politician by delivering a pie (preferably loaded with whipped cream or something of similar appearance) to his or her face in public. Mr. Ward was mistakenly identified as a person who was thought to have this activity in mind during a visit to Vancouver by Prime Minister Chrétien; consequently, he was apprehended and arrested by Vancouver City Police, subjected to a strip search (I am baffled as to where the police thought he might be hiding the pie), and had his car impounded. When the police applied for a search warrant to search the car (a much more plausible hiding place), their application was dismissed for lack of grounds. Mr. Ward subsequently sued the police for improper behaviour, including the violation of his section 8 right to freedom from unreasonable search and seizure, succeeding in both the trial court and the provincial court of appeal. The City of Vancouver appealed to the Supreme Court of Canada—and lost.

McLachlin, writing for a unanimous nine-judge panel, acknowledged that the case law on financial compensation for a Charter violation was "light"—indeed, she did not cite a single case, from either her own or any lower court, that dealt directly with this matter—but she observed the undesirability of unduly constraining the broad generality of section 24(1), and found that the remedy was appropriate in the immediate case[63] because it met the triple-function of such an award: compensation, vindication of the right, and/or deterrence of future breaches.

This is self-consciously new ground with respect to Charter remedies, and as befits such a "first time" statement of principle, we are dealing

---

62 For a more focused consideration of this idea, see David Stratas, "Damages as a Remedy against Administrative Authorities: An Area Needing Clarification," in Robert J. Sharpe and Kent Roach, eds., *Taking Remedies Seriously* (Ottawa: Canadian Institute for the Administration of Justice, 2009), 374.

63 Interestingly, the case she cites most directly for authority is *Doucet-Boudreau:* "The general considerations governing what constitutes an appropriate and just remedy under s. 24(1) were set out by Iacobucci and Arbour JJ. in *Doucet-Boudreau v. Nova Scotia (Minister of Education)*, 2003 SCC 62, [2003] 3 S.C.R. 3" (para. 20).

with very small stakes but accompanying it with a careful laying out of the test that is to be applied: a prima facie breach such that damages are appropriate, the lack of countervailing circumstances established by the offending officials, and the establishment of an appropriate level of damages in terms of either "making the victim whole" (in the case of compensation), or providing an appropriate vindication and deterrence. The novelty is well worth noting, but one should take note that this is (so far) an unusual and isolated case rather than a new trend; also important to remember is that the amount involved was small enough ($5,000, far below the court costs for either party) that it was little more than a "declaration with emphasis." Just as with a simple declaration (e.g., "This violates the Charter and we leave it to the offending official to decide on the remedy"), the point was primarily (or perhaps even more so) to embarrass the public officials involved and discourage such action in the future.

These were hints rather than major changes of direction—isolated exploratory hints rather than the new "business as usual." The main remedy mechanism was still to "suspended invalidity" with advice as to a legislative fix. These brief gestures aside—and lacking follow-up cases, they really are only gestures—the McLachlin Court stayed within the tracks for remedies.

REMEDIES UNDER THE CHARTER: THE NOTION OF POSITIVE RIGHTS

But there is a remedies issue that is more significant by far—something that was implicitly a potential from the beginning, and that I included in my "ladder" of Charter meanings in Chapter 3. The McLachlin Court had a tentative early look over this particular wall without, in the end, doing anything conclusive.

The basic logic of the Charter, as the Court laid it out in earlier decisions, is that the Charter is a limit on what government can do. This is implicit in the geographic metaphor, which it is difficult not to import from federalism jurisprudence (where it doesn't work particularly well, but no matter): the Charter lays out a strict line over which governments should not, must not, or are not allowed to step. The basic process in a Charter case is therefore a government action, after which somebody argues that their Charter rights are violated in such a way that government is not allowed to commit that action. The Court either agrees with the challenge or not; if it finds a prima facie violation, it either accepts the government's argument that it was a reasonable limit or not. Government action triggers a Charter challenge; a successful Charter challenge erases or blocks the government action. Simple enough.

There is always another question, however, hovering at the edge of the debate. Consider section 7: everyone has the right to life, liberty, and security of the person, and the right not be deprived thereof except in accordance with the principles of fundamental justice. The straight-up meaning is easy enough: government cannot act in a way that interferes with my right to life, liberty, and security of the person, and if they do act in such a way (and if I can persuade the courts that they have), then the action is annulled. But can I flip it over? Can I argue that governments have a duty to act in such a way as to promote my life, liberty, and security of the person?—perhaps not all the time and in such sweeping circumstances, but maybe just for certain kinds of rights for certain kinds of people in certain circumstances? Somewhere in the "duty not to act" in certain ways, is there a "duty to act" such that inaction, rather than action, is the Charter violation? Are there commands to government buried somewhere within the prohibitions to government?[64]

POSITIVE RIGHTS AND *DUNMORE*

Bastarache, in *Dunmore*,[65] addressed this question with remarkable carefulness. He observed that in an earlier case, the Court's judgement suggested that "a situation might arise in which, in order to make a

---

64 It is of course the case that the Language Rights in section 16 to 22 of the Charter, and the Minority Language Education Rights in section 23, do create a strong positive obligation on the part of government to provide a certain kind of services to a certain set of citizens; my comments should be taken as raising the question as to whether the earlier parts of the Charter, the sections 2 through 15 that lay out the basic rights and freedoms that apply to all citizens, can be taken as carrying a similar implication, and I think the general assumption has been that they do not—although, as Justice Arbour said in *Gosselin* (discussed below) this is "a view that is commonly expressed but seldom examined" (para. 319).

65 *Dunmore v. Ontario (Attorney General)*, [2001] 3 S.C.R. 1016, 2001 SCC 94.

fundamental freedom meaningful, a posture of restraint would not be enough, and positive governmental action might be required,"[66] although they did not find that case to meet the requirements for this move. It would take very solid and specific evidence to justify the Court's picking upon these ideas, and Bastarache never quite said that these are the circumstances or that this is the necessary evidence trail. He did observe, however, that "under-inclusive state action" was problematic not only to the extent to which it was itself discriminatory, but also to the extent to which it "substantially orchestrates, encourages or sustains the violation of fundamental freedoms," even by private actors (para. 26). He then took still another step back, by insisting that this doctrine "does not, on its own, oblige the state to act where it has not already legislated in respect of a certain area," although "once the state has chosen to regulate" an activity, Charter values are carried into that regulation (para. 29). In the end, though, he was "not prepared to say" that the employee–employer relationship of agricultural workers fell within that zone; still, it was not the Court's fault if investigation into the immediate situation should lead to imposing a positive obligation on the state. Perhaps, in the end, there is not much fire under all that smoke—but there is some.

POSITIVE RIGHTS AND *GOSSELIN*

The matter is raised even more directly in *Gosselin*,[67] a case which involved social assistance programs in Quebec, and can in some sense be seen as raising (but ultimately rejecting) the possibility of a "right to welfare." The central point of the case was that, under Quebec's policies, full social assistance payments were made available to young adults only if they met specific conditions that applied to them and not to others, including enrollment in job training programs to better prepare themselves for the workforce; failing to meet this condition meant that the not-particularly-generous social assistance programs were sharply

---

66 *Haig v. Canada (Chief Electoral Officer)*, [1993] 2 S.C.R. 995; judgement for the Court by L'Heureux-Dubé, at 1039; quoted in *Dunmore* at para. 23. The fact that Bastarache found nothing more to cite or quote on this question speaks for itself.

67 *Gosselin v. Quebec (Attorney General)*, [2002] 4 S.C.R. 429, 2002 SCC 84.

reduced, to the point where they would not cover even the minimal costs of subsistence. This was challenged on a number of grounds, with interveners from many public interest groups concerned with poverty issues. The major outcome was that the policies were upheld by a majority of the Court—although a minority of judges would have found that they violated the Charter right to security of the person, and a slightly overlapping minority would have found that they violated equality rights.

Arbour was the most outspoken on the section 7 issue, flatly asserting in the second paragraph of her solo dissenting reasons that she "would allow this appeal" because she concluded "that the s. 7 rights to 'life, liberty and security of the person' include a positive dimension" (para. 308); she cited *Dunmore* in her favour as "finding that the state has a positive obligation" in relation to the freedom of association (para. 320). To be sure, these were only solo minority reasons, and even L'Heureux-Dubé seemed a bit discomfited by the assertion, joining in the proposition that section 7 was violated, but not for these particular reasons. McLachlin felt obliged to respond to the idea in her own majority reasons. "One day," she says, "s. 7 may be interpreted to include positive obligations," but the real question before them was "whether the present circumstances warrant a novel application of s. 7 as the basis for a positive state obligation to guarantee adequate living standards" (para. 82). On this question, and "with due respect for the views of my colleague Arbour J," she concluded that they did not. I cannot help reading the overtones of "one day, it may" as subtly but firmly negative—the sound of a door sliding shut.[68]

This is not a small question; I will go further and say that it is the biggest question with respect to the Charter, the one with the greatest long-term implications for the future balance between judicial power on the one hand, and legislative power and executive discretion on the other. Which side of this choice we find ourselves on will make a profound difference to what kind of a Charter we have and where that Charter

---

68 As distinct from a superficially similar wording that the Court uses from time to time, when it says "it may well be" that a right may extend to something or the other—I take this as more of an invitation, a suggestion that the Court would not mind some litigant framing an argument that leads in that direction, although it may be a considerable time before the "it may well be" turns into anything.

is going to take us. Just for a moment, Bastarache stuck his foot ever so delicately over this line in *Dunmore*. Just for a moment, Arbour argued strongly for it, and McLachlin, in her majority judgement, granted the general principle without following through in the immediate case. I suppose one could argue that once the dike is genuinely breached, it is no longer a question as to whether the water will flow through, but only a question of when—I think the better reading, however, is that the Court looked over that particular fence, and decided not to cross it after all. In a profound sense, this was the high point of the Charter, the high-water mark for what was until then an evolving and expanding story; everything after this is condemned to be mere afterthought and detail.

CONCLUSION

I suggested that the central notion in Charter interpretation for the Dickson Court was purposivism, and for the Lamer Court it was dignity. For the McLachlin Court, it is balancing and proportionality—not in the sense that those previous emphases have been repudiated, nor in the sense that there was never any balancing/proportionality talk earlier, but in the sense that it reflected a new emphasis and a higher profile for the ideas. Balancing of elements within rights, balancing within ideas like fundamental justice, and balancing between rights: "balance" is a powerful metaphor. Still, it involves the Supreme Court in much more complex exercises than finding clear-cut rights violations resulting in invalidity, or in "bright-line" standards that unambiguously signal what the court will be doing in similar or related cases.

The purest example of this is perhaps *N.S.*, where the Court was so caught up with the need to balance freedom of religion against the right to a fair trial (in the context of a sexual assault complainant wanting to wear the face-obscuring niqab) that it could only conclude that both needed to be taken into consideration, such that decisions would have to be made on a case-by-case basis, while the immediate case was remanded to the trial judge. I always tell students that one of the virtues of a litigation route as against a political pressure route is that, ultimately, judges have to give answers to even difficult questions, unlike politicians (for whom evasion is often a more functional response) or even professors (who sometimes may just admit that it is a very difficult question and promise to get back to you next class). In *N.S.*, the Court stopped well back from this particular hurdle.[69]

Emmett Macfarlane has suggested that this gambit is emerging as the typical style of the McLachlin Court: "Her *modus operandi* in difficult Charter of Rights cases," he suggests, "has usually consisted of avoiding one-sided proclamations of principle in favour of meting out compromise and getting her colleagues to join her on a moderate, often minimalist, judicial path."[70] I would put it a little differently; I would say that her style is to forge this compromise by salvaging a formal commitment to a vigorous constitutional principle at the cost of minimalist or even empty practical outcomes. Freedom of religion is affirmed, but the Hutterians are turned down, and *N.S.* returns to the lower courts for case-by-case handling; collective bargaining remains notionally under the umbrella of freedom of association, but Ontario's farm workers are more or less back where they started.[71] To be sure, compromise is better than surrender, and these particular compromises may have been hard-won, but by no means do they imply any forward momentum in Charter interpretation. And that is precisely my point.

Allow me to describe the Charter revolution in a nutshell (which may be reductionist but not, I think, unfair):

The "typical four" Charter cases for the Dickson Court were *Oakes*, *Morgentaler*, *Irwin Toy*, and *Andrews*. Each decision sketched a vigorous but deliberately open-ended approach to an important element of the new Charter (section 1's reasonable limits, section 7's security of the person, section 2's freedom of expression, and section 15's equality rights); two of them

---

69 To be fair to the Court, I think we are catching it just now in a major recalibration as the balance swings from Liberal (Chrétien and Martin) appointees to Conservative (Harper) appointees. Such a swing does not (necessarily) mean the repudiation of large bodies of jurisprudence, but it can certainly involve a change in priorities and emphasis and tone.

70 See Emmett Macfarlane, "Supreme Court Splits in Messy Decision on Face Veils," *Maclean's*, December 20, 2012, retrieved February 13, 2013, from http://www.macleans.ca/news/canada/supreme-court-splits-in-messy-decision-on-face-veils/.

71 Or an alternative tactic: a vigorous statement of the general principles, linked to a remedy so narrowly crafted that it is difficult to see how any other litigants could draw upon it for their own non-identical circumstances. *Health Service Workers*, as I have already suggested, is one example; the Vancouver *Insite* decision—*Canada (Attorney-General) v. PHS Community Services Society*, 2011 SCC 44—is arguably another. In the American literature, this is sometimes referred to as a "golden ticket"—good for one ride only.

struck down part of a piece of federal legislation in the process, and although the impugned legislation survived the challenge in *Irwin Toy*, it arguably established the most expansive operational definition of a Charter right—not just out of the four cases, but "most expansive" in a more general sense.

The typical four Charter cases for the Lamer were *Remuneration Reference, Law, Butler*, and *Vriend*. All of them were big and ambitious, settling the immediate case in a confident and expansive way, which opened up wider issues for future resolution. Three of them were effectively reconsidered and blunted within a decade—*Law's* elaborate framework for section 15 has been set aside in *Kapp, Butler's* harm principle was trimmed back in *Malmo-Levine*, and *Vriend's* remedial creativity has not been continued. Only the *Remuneration Reference* (and how could one possibly exclude the case with the longest set of reasons for judgement in the history of the Court) survives unscathed.

The typical four Charter cases for the McLachlin Court were *Gosselin, Kapp, Fraser*, and *Hutterian Brethren*. All four represent a containment of ideas carried over from an earlier period of Charter enthusiasm, even when (for two of them) that period was the early years of the McLachlin Court itself. *Gosselin* flirted with, but put off to a vague and indefinite future, the idea of positive obligations in the Charter, *Kapp* stepped back from the bold ambitions of *Law, Fraser* eviscerated the union-friendly pretensions of *Dunmore* and *Health Service Workers*, and *Hutterian Brethren* sidelined the ambitious freedom of religion doctrine first revealed in *Amselem* and ratcheted upwards in *Multani*. Line up all the dates, and the forward-pushing indications are all 2007 and earlier, whereas the pull-backs and hesitations are all 2008 and later. I will not emulate Bishop Usher—who thought he could assign an exact date to the Lord's creation of the universe—by pushing this to the extreme of announcing the day when the Charter revolution ended, but I will suggest that "some time in 2007" is not an unrealistic suggestion.

Put simply, the forward motion of Charter interpretation is at an end, and I have chosen to call this the end of the Charter revolution. For the Dickson Court, for the Lamer Court, and even for the very early years of the McLachlin Court, we could be justified in seeing the Court's interpretation of the Charter as something that was on the move and wondering: Where is the Charter going to take us? Today, I think we can acknowledge that we are now there, and the question is whether we will stay where we are or slide backwards.

CHAPTER SIX

THE CHARTER BY THE NUMBERS

I have told a story about an end to the Charter revolution—about a major disruption to the status quo that was gradually contained and absorbed and turned into a new normal. This new state of affairs differs from what existed before—it is after all a "new normal," not a return to the "old normal"—but it involves something rather different from a "permanent revolution" of long-sustained and continuous major change. I have argued that it is in the nature of the legal system and the judicial system to periodically generate change and uncertainty, but then to contain it, to "normalize" it in the interests of stability and predictability; and I have suggested that although the Charter may be a spectacular example of the "generate change" idea, this by no means makes it an exception from that general tendency towards containment and normalization.

But a story is just a story. Alternative narratives are entirely possible, and they still tend to be the dominant theme in the academic discussion of the Charter today. I constantly read about more big Charter-driven changes down the road, of more hints in today's decisions of dramatic new steps sometime in the future, of more big things to come that will send governments and legislatures scrambling to accommodate them, or of the Court's disappointing reluctance or timidity or narrowness of vision that is selling short the Charter's true potential. That is quite a different story about the Charter; so, which should you believe?

Think of me as the woodsman trying to tell the incredulous towns-people that a mighty creature called a judicial revolution has passed through the nearby woods, but that it has now wandered off. There are many other woodsmen who agreed that there was indeed such a beast in the area, but I am the only one saying that it has gone away. You would ask for some proof, something clear and objective that you could hang on to in order to justify accepting my claim, all the more so because from time to time you have been hearing loud crashes in the forest as some big trees come down (*Morgentaler* on abortion, *Seaboyer* on the rape shield law, *Sharpe* on kiddie porn), although this has not happened lately. You would rightly ask me to show you the clear footprints in the ground that provide solid evidence that the beast has indeed moved off down the hill. In this chapter, I will draw on my own empirical research of the Supreme Court of Canada over several decades to show you those footprints.

The beast is not, of course, the Charter itself; that is firmly in place, presumably forever, and much of the change it has accomplished will last for just as long—those big trees are well and truly knocked down, and they won't grow back. The beast is the legal and judicial uncer-tainty created by the insertion of the Charter into the Canadian con-stitutional framework, and the period of disruption and destabilization that resulted. The really big trees falling are the decisions that both caused major change and came as something of a surprise, an impact that had not been anticipated (even if, sometimes, we can see in retro-spect that we should not have been quite so surprised). It is that capacity for surprise, that possibility that another big tree might unexpectedly go down with profound legal and policy implications, that is rapidly fading as the activities of the Court become more routine and more predictable—which is, of course, what courts always try over the long run to become, for very good reasons. It is in this sense that the beast has wandered off.

To frame this chapter in less picturesque terms: as the Supreme Court goes about its business, it is constantly transmitting all kinds of informa-tion to us beyond the actual content of the decisions. The way it handles its business—indeed, the way that it chooses what business to handle in the first place—sends signals about what is going on, and how this is changing over time. I will try to convince you that these indicators all point in the same direction: they all tell us that the time of really big change is over, and that the Supreme Court has gone "steady state." I mean this as description, not criticism; if anything, it is praise, because courts are not supposed to be in the business of surprising people.

A number of the things that I describe in this chapter have been noted in other contexts, but they have usually been attributed to the particular character and the particular leadership style of the current Chief Justice. I am reluctant to accept personality-driven explanations or single-person causes for broader phenomena; I have no problem with people speaking of "the McLachlin Court" as behaving in a certain way that is somewhat different from "the Lamer Court" or "the Dickson Court," but this is always just a convenient shorthand for a more complex reality. It is not that individual judges (and particularly the Chief Justice) don't matter; it is just that they don't matter so much as to be the whole story. The changes I describe began to show up in 1997–98, and sometimes as early as 1995, well before McLachlin moved into the centre chair in January 2000. Chief Justiceships provide convenient organizing labels for talking about the performance of the Supreme Court over time, but we should never simply assume that these are necessarily the major change-of-direction moments for the Court.

It is a basic principle of modern architecture that "form follows function" (the real meaning of the aphorism is the much stronger idea that function *drives* form), and the same is true of the way that the Supreme Court does its work. Henderson suggests that changes to the Court do not "just happen" but rather reflect a changing social, legal, and political context within which the Court is trying to perform an evolving function[1]—the new behaviour "makes sense" (and more sense than the old one) once we decode this story. Similarly, a recent note in the *Harvard Law Review* observes that "there exists a demonstrable nexus between institutional *practice* ... and institutional *purpose*."[2] The important thing,

---

1 M. Todd Henderson, "From *Seriatim* to Consensus and Back Again: A Theory of Dissent," *Supreme Court Review* 1 (2007): 283.

2 Note: "From Consensus to Collegiality: The Origins of the 'Respectful' Consent," *Harvard Law Review* 124 (2011): 1305.

then, is to pay close attention to that practice as a guide to the change in purpose that lies behind it.

In this chapter, I will consider eight objective indicators of how the Supreme Court's performance has changed in recent years, and use them to support my notion that we have passed through an exceptional period of doctrinal uncertainty and entered a time of relative stability—that is to say, that we have moved from revolutionary instability to status quo normalcy. No one of these indicators is necessarily conclusive in itself, but they all provide objective support for the narrative that I have presented in earlier chapters. My eight indicators are:

1. Caseload size and its components
2. Frequency of disagreement: Minority reasons in Charter cases
3. Size and content of decisions
4. "Swing" and "contest" judgements
5. Judicial citations, age, and precedential replacement
6. Citations of dissents and concurrences
7. "Foreign" citations
8. Academic citations

Together, these provide the footsteps leading off down the hill that allow me to say with some confidence that the beast has gone, and normal times are back—which is not to deny for a moment that it is a "new normal" and that (to stretch my metaphor again) the forest will never look quite the same.

1. CASELOAD SIZE AND ITS COMPONENTS

Theoretically, any judicial decision (and almost any quasi-judicial decision) in Canada can be appealed to the Supreme Court of Canada. This is unlike the United States, where questions of state law (even state constitutional law) cannot be taken to the United States Supreme Court unless they also raise questions of federal law or national constitutional law. But in practice, only a vanishingly small percentage of Canadian cases actually get that far; if we think of the Supreme Court as being able to deal substantively with a maximum of about 100 cases per year, this is a little high for current practice but it sets a reasonable frame.[3]

An important feature of the modern Supreme Court of Canada is that it has a large degree of control over its own docket—most cases come before the Supreme Court only if the Supreme Court has decided that it wants to hear them, using an "application for leave to appeal" process whereby three-judge panels screen the applications. There are 500 or more applications for leave each year, and perhaps one in every eight succeeds; the total count is trending up and the success rate is trending down. This was a major procedural reform accomplished in 1974–75 by an amendment to the Supreme Court Act, important because docket control significantly alters the role of a Supreme Court: for one thing, it can control the number of cases it hears each year to focus its energy and resources on a smaller number of cases steered by the Court's own assessment of importance; and for another, it can control the timing of the consideration of controversial issues either on a legal/professional basis (letting the issue mature through a wider spectrum of relevant cases in the courts below) or more tactically (waiting for public opinion to develop). This falls short of the total docket control that the United States Supreme Court has enjoyed since 1927; in Canada, there has always been a category of appeals by right. This was narrowed (by further amendment to the Supreme Court Act) in 1999, but it still accounts for one case in every six for the McLachlin Court; it was even higher (about one in every three) for the Lamer Court.[4]

But I will focus on a second largely overlapping differentiation within the caseload that happens slightly further down the decision track. Most Supreme Court decisions are reserved judgements—after oral argument, the Court "reserves judgement," which means that the parties will have

---

3 I hasten to add that my rule of thumb of "one hundred decisions on the merits" applies only to national high courts in common law systems; the French Court that is the most comparable to our Supreme Court, their "Court of Cassation" or "Supreme Court of Appeal," has an annual caseload in the thousands.

4 See Peter McCormick, "Compulsory Audience: Appeals by Right and the Lamer Court 1990–1999" (paper presented at CPSA Annual General Meeting, Congress of the Social Sciences and Humanities, Toronto, ON, June 2002).

to wait several months for the Court to deliver its decision (outcome plus reasons) in the case.[5] However, a certain number of cases are delivered as oral "from the bench" decisions on the same day as the oral argument. Many of these are indeed the "appeals by right" that still occupy a corner of the caseload, although the correlation is less than perfect in both directions. For one thing, a certain number of appeals by right raise issues that would almost certainly have gained them leave to appeal in any event; for another thing, from time to time cases that have been granted leave will (sometimes surprisingly) end their trajectory as abrupt from-the-bench decisions. And "abrupt" is no exaggeration; many contain nothing more than the single sentence "The appeal is dismissed for the reasons given in the court below" (or, less often, "The appeal is allowed for the reasons given in the dissent in the court below").

I am told by some that such a decision necessarily incorporates all of the reasons from the court below, and therefore I am wrong to make a distinction between these summary oral decisions on the one hand, and the more discursive reasoning in reserved judgements on the other. I am not convinced; if the Supreme Court really wants to firmly place its imprimatur on a lower court decision, it does so much more explicitly. The reasons might (or might not) be shorter than average, but the Court writes a full discursive judgement even when its main point is simply that "the Court of Appeal got it right." I think instead that the terseness is the message, intriguing and cryptic in its own right, and I therefore treat the "reserved for judgement" hurdle as important. My case count below is based on reserved judgements, not total ones.

Within these parameters, how have Charter cases fit into the Supreme Court caseload? Figure 6.1 shows the count for these cases, as well as the count for all reserved judgements for each calendar year of the Charter era. A frequent comment about the McLachlin Court is that its caseload has been much smaller than that of its predecessors, but because Figure 6.1 counts only reserved judgements, it conveys a somewhat different message. After a dramatic spike in 1990, echoed in 1994, the caseload has been moving downward for almost 20 years, long before McLachlin

---

5 More unusually, the Court will give the outcome (allowing or dismissing the appeal) immediately but reserve the delivery of reasons.

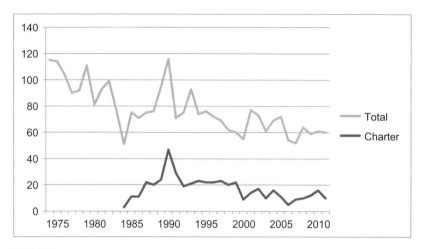

FIGURE 6.1 Count of total cases and Charter cases by year

became Chief Justice. There is still a reduction in the reserved caseload (from about 75 a year in the 1990s to about 65 a year more recently), and this is still worth noting, but it is not the major factor that the "total caseload" numbers misleadingly suggest. For one thing, it suggests that concerns about the "incredible shrinking caseload" of the sort that has shown up in the American literature[6] are an overreaction to the Canadian trend. But more importantly for present purposes, we seem to be directed to a change that was already well under way in the middle of the Lamer decade. This is something that cannot be attributed to a single leader's personality or style—indeed, it cannot be attributed to judicial personalities at all because it seems to occur right in the middle of the five-year "natural court" that centres the Lamer decade.[7]

---

6 See, for example, Arthur D. Hellman, "The Shrunken Docket of the Rehnquist Court," *Supreme Court Review* (1996): 403; David O'Brien, "A Diminished Plenary Docket," *Judicature* 89 (2005): 134; Kenneth Starr, "The Supreme Court and Its Shrinking Docket," *Minnesota Law Review* 90 (2006): 1363.

7 The term "natural court" is used to describe any period during which the membership of the Court remains absolutely constant, without any retirements and replacements. The "middle half" of the Lamer decade was such a period; it was one of the longest in the history of the Supreme Court of Canada.

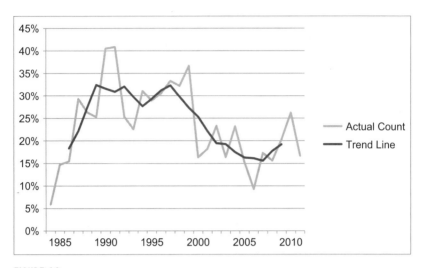

FIGURE 6.2 Charter cases as a proportion of all reserved decisions

The lines in Figure 6.1 do not quite make my point; the count of Charter cases is trending downward within a total caseload that is also trending downward. Figure 6.2 shows Charter cases as a proportion of the total caseload; the jagged line is the precise figure for each calendar year, the smoother line reflects five-year running averages (the two before and the two after as well as the specific year) to soften the lines and reveal the longer-term trends. These trends are clear: Charter cases as a proportion of the total caseload rose from the obvious standing start in the second half of the 1980s, hovered just over 30 per cent of the total caseload for about a decade, and then shortly after 1995 began a steady decline to their current level of something below 20 per cent. Charter cases are not a steady share of a slightly declining caseload, but instead a steadily decreasing share of a slightly declining total. In 2006, the first time since 1985 (2007 was the second time), the total count for Charter cases for a calendar year was in the single digits. In the single amazing year of 1990, the Court handed down five Charter decisions every month, and for the rest of that decade the number was just over two. For the last dozen years (since roughly 2002), it has averaged barely one. Whether it is because fewer Charter cases are knocking on the door or because the Court is more reluctant to let them in, there simply are fewer Charter cases for the court to deal with, and therefore fewer opportunities for surprises. These are the caseload figures of a Court that has moved on, a Court for whom the Charter is no longer so clearly the pre-emptively primary focus of its attention.

2. FREQUENCY OF DISAGREEMENT: MINORITY REASONS IN CHARTER CASES

Most of the Supreme Court's decisions of the last 25 years have been unanimous—that is to say, there is a single set of reasons explaining the outcome, and those reasons have been joined by every member of the panel. However, "most" is not a particularly strong word in this context, because there have also been a considerable number of decisions that included one or more dissenting opinions, meaning that one or more judges think that the majority got the decision wrong by awarding success to the wrong set of litigants and they want to tell a wider world about this error.[8]

Although this is not true of some other systems and some other countries, in Canada as in the other common law countries in the English tradition, dissents are clearly established as a legitimate option for judges serving on panel appellate courts, and judges who think the majority is mistaken have every right to say so. However, this does not take away from the fact that there is something inherently confrontational and challenging about the public action of a member of the Court who says that the judgement of the Court is wrong about something so important, something that is unavoidably subversive in that it undermines the Court's duty not only to declare with finality which side deserves to win but also to provide a clear statement of the law for the guidance of the lower courts. Dissents do nothing to disturb the finality in the immediate case, but they do create some doubt about the clarity and certainty of the law, especially if there is more than one dissenting judge. The Supreme Court of Canada has developed intriguing conventions for its

---

8 That is to say: it is one thing to disagree with a colleague, perhaps to the extent of sending him or her a memo during or after the deliberation process as something he or she might consider for the future; but it is another thing altogether to make a reasoned disagreement part of the official record. The important thing about judicial dissents is that not only do they indicate disagreement but they also do so publicly.

dissents[9]—it softens the disagreement by acknowledging the majority reasons, by indicating respect, and by focusing on a specific part of those reasons—but this simply acknowledges that there are rough edges to be softened. Bergman's title—"discord in the service of harmony"[10]—nicely catches the paradox of the dissenting opinion.

It is not very helpful to ask "when do judges dissent?" because the answer is simply "when they think the majority got it wrong."[11] The more useful question, then, is "in what circumstances are judges more likely to dissent?" and the answer surely is when they are dealing with new issues or with older issues that have been transformed by changing social circumstances and expectations, or when they are developing new law, or when they are attempting rigorously to complete answers to questions that have previously been handled in a more preliminary or ad hoc fashion. It is not that there is disagreement *only* on novel matters and *never* on more established matters, but rather that as a general rule there is more disagreement on novel matters and much more limited disagreement relating to generally settled issues. Anticipating my general argument, this implies that there will be a decreasing frequency of disagreement as the novel matters cease to be novel—as they generate their own landmark cases and become settled law.

THE FREQUENCY OF DISSENT

The standard way of measuring the frequency of disagreement is simply to count the number of those cases that include a dissent.[12] Figure 6.3 considers the year-by-year caseload of the Supreme Court in these terms,

---

9 See Peter McCormick, "Structures of Judgment: How the Modern Supreme Court of Canada Organizes Its Reasons," *Dalhousie Law Journal* 32 (2009): 35.

10 Matthew P. Bergman, "Dissent in the Judicial Process: Discord in the Service of Harmony," *Denver University Law Review* 68 (1991): 79.

11 Even this answer assumes—without proving that all judges are always totally candid—that the convention is that *all* disagreements must be publicly declared in full, and this is profoundly unlikely. See, for example, Scott Idleman, "A Prudential Theory of Judicial Candor," *Texas Law Review* 73 (1995): 307.

12 See, for example, Lee Epstein, William M. Landes, and Richard A. Posner, "Why (and When) Judges Dissent: A Theoretical and Empirical Analysis," John M. Olin Law and Economics Working Paper No. 510 (January 2010), retrieved February 13, 2010, from the Social Science Research Network http://ssrn.com/en/.

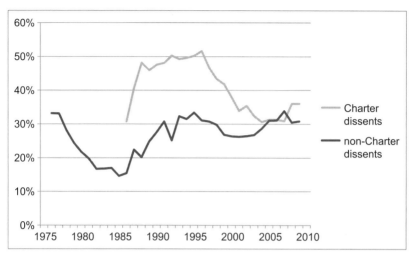

FIGURE 6.3 Percentage of cases with dissent, Charter and non-Charter

dividing the cases into Charter and non-Charter categories for this purpose. The figure works with five-year running averages to soften the graph lines so as to allow more general patterns to emerge from the year-on-year fluctuations. The general message is that for most of the last 25 years, Charter decisions have been much more dissensual than the other parts of the caseload, such that for the first decade, almost half of all Charter cases involved one or more dissents. Disagreement rates for other cases have generally been lower, although they track steadily upward over the 1985–95 period and the gap between the two narrows. After the middle of the 1990s, however, both frequencies fall significantly—for Charter cases, it is down from "almost half" to "less than a third"—and, just as significantly, the dissent frequencies for the two types of cases converge. For the last few years, Charter dissent frequencies have been lower than they ever have before, and (briefly and slightly) lower than non-Charter dissent frequencies.

But measuring disagreement solely in terms of the number of non-unanimous decisions has its limitations. For one thing, it simply ignores the question of whether the dissents are lonely solo voices, or several judges disagreeing for somewhat different reasons (disagreeing on why they disagree), or a solid bloc of three or four judges joining to fall just short of being a majority themselves. For another, it cannot reflect the shifting panel sizes of recent decades—the seven-judge panels that became standard for and after Dickson; the five-judge panels used by the Lamer Court to clear the large numbers of appeals by right; the nine-judge panels that have become the norm for McLachlin—but simply counts non-unanimous cases.

For this reason, it is more useful to measure dissent behaviour from a different angle. The relevant unit is not "the case" but rather "the panel appearance," and the question is not how many cases include at least one dissent but rather how many times individual judges wrote or joined a dissent. If a nine-judge panel registers a solo dissent, there have been eight opportunities to dissent (only eight, because it makes no sense to think of the judge delivering the majority decisions as declining an opportunity to dissent), and one judge has taken advantage of it. If a seven-judge panel splits 4–3, then this represents three judges choosing to dissent out of six on the panel who had that opportunity; and so on.[13] This can be calculated for individual judges and used to identify persisting blocs within the Court, but that is not the point here; rather, this can be calculated for every calendar year, measuring writing-and-joining dissent behaviour as a percentage of total opportunities. In practice, the total number of panel appearances per year varies rather little, the gradual decline in caseload being balanced by the gradual rise in average panel size; the long-term average for reserved decisions is about 540 panel appearances per year. The figure shows this as a percentage rather than an actual count; and again, the numbers presented are running five-year averages to soften the fluctuations and reveal general patterns.

The picture here is slightly different from Figure 6.3, but not so much as to change the basic message. Charter cases initially generated dissenting

---

13 Just to confuse things further, there is a third way of measuring disagreement, and that is to look at the number of sets of minority reasons without worrying about how many judges have signed on. Consider a panel with a five judge majority and two dissents, one a solo and one signed onto by the other three judges. On the first measure I have presented above, this is (obviously and easily) a non-unanimous decision; on the "opinion count" procedure there are two sets of minority reasons; but on the approach I am now suggesting, there are four judges who do not agree with the majority judgement.

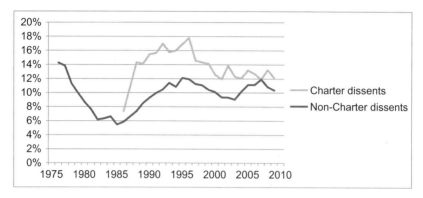

FIGURE 6.4 Participation in dissenting reasons as per cent of panel appearances

behaviour (writing or joining) much more often than non-Charter cases, but after about a decade this difference largely disappears and the two lines converge. More recently, on Charter and non-Charter cases alike, the judges of the Supreme Court participate in dissenting behaviour about one time in every nine panel appearances. The absence in this figure of the upward hook from the previous figure reflects the fact that, although dissents are beginning to occur in slightly more cases, they have in recent years tended to involve smaller groups of judges.[14]

THE FREQUENCY OF SEPARATE CONCURRENCE

Dissents are not the only form of judicial disagreement. Judges can also express themselves through separate concurrences, which means that they write their own reasons agreeing with the outcome but not agreeing

---

14 The limitation of this approach is that it cannot tell if the dissents represent the behaviour of the Court in a general sense or just that of a small group of its members—a perpetual minority dissenting much more often than its majority colleagues. As it turns out, there is a spread in the numbers for individual judges but it is not particularly large, and the behaviour displayed is appropriately attributed to the Court as a whole. Today we cannot, although earlier we could, identify a "gang of five" that tends to prevail when the Court divides; this is an interesting observation in itself.

(or at least not agreeing completely) with the reasons. Separate concurrences are easily undervalued, if only because they do not challenge the outcome. Indeed, the Supreme Court itself keeps its statistics in terms of whether or not decisions are "unanimous as to outcome," which carries with it the clear message that dissents do, but concurrences do not, undermine the solid unanimity of the decision.[15]

I do not agree with this practice because it prematurely relegates the often-important arguments in these concurrences to an inappropriately low status. As USSC Justice Antonin Scalia has eloquently said, a decision that gets the reasons wrong gets everything wrong that it is the business of a judicial decision to accomplish.[16] That is to say, for appellate courts, the reasons always matter far more than the outcome,[17] because it is the reasons that constitute precedent and thereby constrain the future decisions and direction of its own and lower courts. Nor is it the case that the disagreements contained within separate concurrences always or even usually represent small concerns about minor elements within larger agreement. Many separate concurrences involve a considerable level of disagreement indeed, which is typically signalled by the deceptively innocuous self-description of reaching the same outcome "but by a different route."[18] Far from being qualified support to a majority position, reasons like this can so undermine those other reasons as to provide no precedentially binding "judgement of the court" at all.[19] Given slightly different fact situations, many separate concurrences can easily become

---

15 For that matter, the new United Kingdom Supreme Court presents its decisions in a similar style.

16 Antonin Scalia, "The Dissenting Opinion," *Journal of Supreme Court History* 19 (1994): 33.

17 Except, perhaps, for the immediate parties, but often not even for them.

18 See Peter McCormick, "Standing Apart: Separate Concurrence and the Supreme Court of Canada, 1984–2006," *McGill Law Journal* 53 (2008): 137; and Peter McCormick "The Choral Court: Separate Concurrences on the McLachlin Court 2000–2004," *Ottawa Law Review* 37 (2005–06): 1.

19 See, for example, *Euro-Excellence v. Kraft Canada*, 2007 SCC 37, which has four sets of "reasons" but no "judgement of the court" because three members of the panel are pointedly concurring (only) with the results (which is to say, not with the reasons).

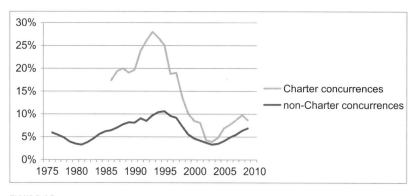

FIGURE 6.5 Participation in separate concurring reasons, as per cent of panel appearances

dissents without any changes to the argument they are making;[20] it is therefore entirely inappropriate to create too large a gap between the two kinds of disagreement. It may be tempting to think about dissents as a "big disagreement" and concurrences as a "little disagreement" (and I blush to admit that at an earlier time I sometimes scored concurrences as "half dissents" in some of my calculations), but this is a mistake. Consider, for example, Wilson's soaring concurrence in *Morgentaler*, which is remembered far more often and much more clearly than the more pedestrian and closely focused reasons it accompanied.

Figure 6.5 traces separate concurrences in the same way that Figure 6.4 traced dissents, again calculating wrote-or-joined concurrence behaviour in reserved judgements as a percentage of all opportunities, and running separate graph lines for Charter and non-Charter cases (again with five-year running averages). The pattern is much the same as for dissents, only much more pronounced. Again, concurrences are much more frequent for Charter cases than they are for the rest of the caseload—but rather

---

20 For example, consider that the companion cases of *Pecore v. Pecore*, 2007 SCC 17 and *Madsen Estate v. Saylor*, 2007 SCC 18, both of which deal with the issue of presumption of advancement, fall just short of unanimity with a solo concurrence in the first and a solo dissent in the second, and both by Abella. More to the point, she begins her dissent by saying "In *Pecore*, the difference in our legal approach did not lead me to a different result. In this appeal, it does" (para. 33).

than peaking at half again the rest-of-the-caseload figures, they rise to almost triple. Again, the pronounced surge through the Charter decade trails off sharply in the second half of the 1990s, although this too is much more exaggerated—instead of falling from 18 per cent to 12 per cent, it falls from almost 30 per cent to less than 5 per cent before rebounding somewhat. And again the last decade has shown a considerable convergence of the frequency of concurring behaviour, although it still remains slightly higher for Charter cases.

For separate concurrences as for dissents, then, the patterns clearly support the idea of a period of a prolific blossoming of ideas through the expression of separate opinions that flourishes briefly and, then, after some point toward the middle of the 1990s, begins to fade, with minority reasons becoming much less common. Since the critical change point happened in the middle of the 1990s and not at the very end of it, this is clearly not the "McLachlin factor" promoting greater collegiality, as some accounts have it, but rather a change that is driven by something other than changes in personnel. My suggestion is that it represents the gradual and inexorable establishment of a new constitutional doctrinal orthodoxy that limits and constrains the presentation of alternative tracks of interpretation.

THE FREQUENCY OF DISAGREEMENT

One might ask, why does this matter? Surely it is decisions (which is to say, majority judgements and reasons) that drive judicial precedent, such that minority reasons—especially, perhaps, dissents—are just the loser's history that matters only to the archivists and to bean counters like me. But as I will describe and expand upon below, this is not as strictly true as one might think. For one thing, minority reasons have over the last four decades been cited reasonably often, certainly often enough for the writers of minority reasons to have much more than lottery-ticket hopes that their ideas may survive to have some influence. For another, the incorporation of ideas from minority reasons seldom takes the form of "how could we have been so wrong" repentance followed by a sharp reversal;[21]

---

21 Which is not to deny that there are some reversals dramatic enough to satisfy any reader; it would be hard to find a mea culpa more complete and explicit than

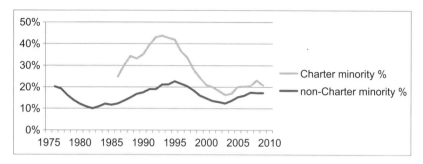

FIGURE 6.6 Participation in minority reasons, as per cent of panel appearances

rather, it is a more subtle and gradual incorporation of ideas. Minority reasons are better thought of as providing nuanced alternate tracks to the line of reasoning laid down by the majority, tracks that can later be partially incorporated without repudiating the initial judgement—"spin" rather than direction, to draw on Terrell's famous metaphor.

This being the case, I think it is a mistake to leave the two different types of minority reasons as if they should be put in different categories, as if they are being written for different motives and aiming at different consequences. Rather, both are attempts by a minority of the panel to put "on the record" a set of alternate ideas about the issue at hand, in the hope (and not a forlorn hope at that) that these ideas might yet be drawn upon by a future majority. Figure 6.6 therefore combines both categories of minority reasons participation, dissents as well as concurrences and joining as well as writing, expressed as a percentage of opportunities and softened to five-year running averages.

Charter cases start with a minority reasons participation rate double that of non-Charter cases, a rate that almost doubles again before a downward slide that starts just before 1995 and bottoms out at a level comparable to the long-term average for non-Charter cases before rebounding slightly at the end of the decade. At its peak, just short of one-half of all

---

that which leads off McLachlin's majority reasons in *Health Service Workers*, which completely vindicate Dickson's dissent in the 1987 *Labour Trilogy*. The point is that this is not the typical, and certainly not the most common, way to use ideas from minority reasons.

the judges on a Charter panel, other than the one delivering the judgement of the Court, are participating in minority reasons of one kind or the other. This is indeed a "let many flowers blossom" period, a profusion of ideas and counter-ideas and alternatives to an extraordinary extent. But it does not last: Charter cases are still somewhat more likely to draw minority reasons than non-Charter cases, but not much more often; and even non-Charter minority reason frequencies are lower than they were at the peak of the Charter era. This pattern is completely consistent with my revolution/normalization argument: a major change in the Court's circumstances generates an explosion of ideas, which is gradually replaced by a more unified Court.

To clarify why I think this is such a powerful indicator: it seems to me that the nature of minority opinions is somewhat different when the Court is dealing with a suddenly new set of issues rather than with much more established matters. To make the point metaphorically: suppose we are in Calgary and we want to drive to Edmonton. There really is only one choice for us, and that is Highway 2, the Queen Elizabeth II Highway. If I am driving and you pipe up from the back seat, "You have missed the turn, you are on the wrong road!" then we have quite a serious situation— if you are right, we aren't going to wind up in Edmonton after all.

But suppose we are in Calgary, and we want to drive to Miami, Florida. Given that the US interstate system is basically a criss-cross of east-west and north-south highways, and our trip will take us diagonally from one corner to another, there is no single best answer to the question of which route to take—of how far east to go before crossing the border into the US, of how far south to go before turning east again, and then how far east before turning south, and so on. There are many different answers to that question; we could make the trip 50 times and never take exactly the same route twice. In those circumstances, if I were to turn east on Interstate 70 and you would rather have waited to take Interstate 40 instead, you might still say "I think you have taken the wrong turn," but it would not carry any of the same weight (unless, of course, I have really messed up and we are actually heading north).

To extend the metaphor: if we are not just two people in a car but nine people in a van, things get more complicated and the arguments become more complex every time we approach a major intersection. The immediate choice will always be "Do we turn east (or south, as the case might be) or do we keep going straight ahead?" One or two might still want us to go back and remake our previous choice—but there is no real reason to think that the group voting to go east *this* time will all hold together for the next choice. And maybe we have oversimplified by assuming we all want to go to Miami; maybe some of us really think we should be going to New Orleans or Atlanta and, without knowing it, we are all working towards *that* argument.

Over time, if enough people were driving from Calgary to Miami, new highways might be built or existing non-interstate highways might be upgraded to provide a more direct route, and one day we might be able to say that there really is just one best route between the two cities such that it would be a mistake to wander off it. During the ferment of new ideas during a judicial revolution, the give and take contained in disagreements is like trying to find the best way to get from Calgary to Miami. During the period of normalcy, where there already is a single clearly marked road, it is either an argument about how to read road signs or a challenge to making the trip in the first place.

3. SIZE AND CONTENT OF DECISIONS

The discussion above suffers the inherent limitation of simply counting cases, such that every reserved decision is treated as being equal to every other decision. But this is not really realistic. Some cases are much more important than others and are much more likely to be picked up in the later decisions of the Supreme Court and other courts, and thus will have a much greater impact on government policy, police behaviour, and the scope of private obligations. If we think back over the last 40 years, we can see that there have been quite a number of important Charter cases— but there have also been many less significant cases hinging on Charter questions, as well as many significant non-Charter cases. How might we reassure ourselves that the simple counting in the earlier sections of this chapter has not missed the significance boat?

Consider this: some Supreme Court decisions, even reserved judgements, are short, deploying 2,000 to 3,000 words (which is to say, half a dozen printed pages) to resolve a specific focused point. Other Supreme Court decisions use the immediate case to resolve major issues that will shape future decisions of the Court for decades to come, and doing so with the discursive rigour one would expect from a landmark decision. *Gosselin v. Quebec*, for example, has the distinction of being the longest decision ever delivered by the Supreme Court of Canada (more than 65,000 words—which is to say, almost as long as this book); the case dealt with a Charter challenge of Quebec's social assistance legislation on the grounds that it violated either or both the right to security of the person and equality rights.[22]

My suggestion is that to some extent, these two paragraphs are making the same point, with the obvious advantage that the second one can be objectively measured. I propose to treat word count as a surrogate measure for the importance of a case—or, more precisely, for the Supreme Court's anticipation of the importance of a case, a judgement that may not be perfect but is certainly a selector of some utility.[23] It seems reasonable to suggest that if the judges of the Court spend 20,000 words explaining the law and the logic of the decision in one case, and only 3,000 words doing so for another case, this is usually because the first case is more important and the Court's reasons are likely to have a greater impact. The greater length allows the Court to better contain and direct this impact, to anticipate and resolve ancillary issues. Indeed, I cannot imagine what we might be saying about the Supreme Court, and the time allocation skills of its members, if we did not accept this suggestion.

To be sure, for any single case there may be countervailing factors. Some cases (insurance cases are a typical example) may present unusual fact situations that require detailed exposition. Some judges may tend to the laconic while others are more expansive (obvious examples would be

---

22 Although admittedly 80 per cent of these words were in minority reasons, and the decision itself was a relatively modest 13,500 words. The longest judgement ever delivered by the Supreme Court was Lamer's reasons in *Reference re Remuneration of Provincial Court Judges of P.E.I.*, [1997] 3 S.C.R. 3, which was just over 43,000 words. Since this too was a Charter case, redefining and regrounding judicial independence, it makes the point equally well.

23 At one time, of course, we would have counted pages, but given the ubiquity of the Internet (where any document, however long, is a "single page"), and given the usefulness of word processors (for which counting words quickly and accurately is merest routine), I use wordcount instead.

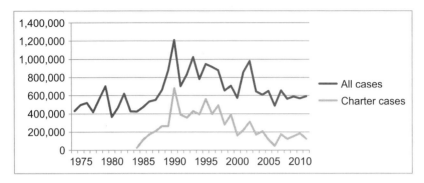

FIGURE 6.7 Total wordcount, Charter and all cases, by year

Major and L'Heureux-Dubé, respectively); and some of the most por-
tentous decisions may limit themselves to a general sketch of a new solution to a major problem, leaving the details for future elaboration. Fair
enough; but for any reasonably large sample of cases, over any reasonable
period of time, wordcount—a proxy for the deployment of the scarce
resources of research time and writing time—is a reasonable guide to the
perceived relative importance of different sets of cases. This allows us to
ask, therefore, how important Charter cases have been within the broader
set of Supreme Court decisions.

Figure 6.7 looks at the total words in all reserved judgements, and
the total words in all reserved Charter cases, for each calendar year. The
overall wordcount tells its own rather impressive story, as wordcounts
rocketed upward during the early Charter period to hit an all-time high
of just over 1.2 million words in the amazing year of 1990; there has only
been one other year (1993) when this count surpassed one million words,
and a second (2002) when it came close. During the decade of the Lamer
Chief Justiceship, the Court's average annual output was over 850,000
words; for the first dozen years of the McLachlin Chief Justiceship, the
corresponding number was just under 650,000 words. Of this total, the
wordcount for Charter decisions also started out low and shot upwards,
topping 600,000 only once—and that, again, was in 1990. The wordcount
exceeded half a million on one other occasion in 1995 and came close in
1997, and since then, it has fallen steadily. The count has not been over
350,000 words since 1999, not over 300,000 words since 2002, not over
200,000 words since 2004, and was below 50,000 words in 2006.

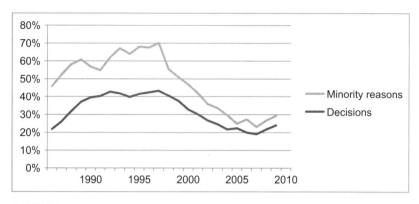

FIGURE 6.8 Charter case wordcounts, as per cent of all case wordcounts

The basic message, and its relevance to my thesis, is obvious: fewer words in Charter cases means a reduced likelihood that these cases contain a large number of major Charter decisions of the sort that rocked the legal foundations and the political community through the 1990s. But since both lines are trending downwards at the same time, they obscure rather than illuminate the major conclusion of the earlier sections, which is not just that the Charter case wordcounts are declining in *absolute* terms (which seems inevitable since most of the total counts are declining as well) but also that they are declining proportionately faster and further than the other elements of the Supreme Court caseload. To make this point, I wish to consider the percentage of this total wordcount that is devoted to Charter cases, and this is shown in Figure 6.8.

The lower line in Figure 6.8 tracks the proportion of this fluctuating and evolving word production that was devoted to Charter cases, focusing first on the decisions (the unanimous or majority or plurality reasons for judgement). Again, it clearly shows the same rise and fall as the earlier figures. Again, it suggests that there was a "Charter decade" that ran from the late 1980s to the late 1990s, and since then the focus on Charter issues has declined. During that decade, Charter cases accounted for 40 per cent of the total word output—and therefore, I am suggesting, for about 40 per cent of the time, attention, and effort—of decisions of the Supreme Court. More recently, however, during the last dozen years, this has slid inexorably downwards such that these cases now account for barely 20 per cent of the Court's output, a reduction of roughly one half of the total over a period when the size of that total (in word count as well as in number of cases) has itself fallen by about a quarter. To be sure, these numbers show that Charter cases still loom larger in total word output than they do as a proportion of the reserved caseload; at their peak, the Charter cases accounted for 30 per cent of the caseload but 40 per cent of the output, and over the last few years this 17 per cent of the caseload has accounted for about 22 per cent of the total word output. This suggests that even now the average Charter case is longer—that is to say, each one receives more time and attention—than the average non-Charter case, hardly a surprising suggestion. But my point is that these proportions are tracking steadily downwards, a long-term trend that shows no signs of reversing itself.

The upper line on Figure 6.8 tracks a related measure, namely, the proportion of the total words in minority reasons that have been devoted to new constitutional cases. I will expand upon the role and the significance of minority reasons below, but for now I will simply suggest that in any significant run of cases they help to identify the "edges" of Supreme Court doctrine. Settled matters tend to generate higher levels of unanimity. Conversely, higher levels of disagreement, and higher frequency of extended explanations of that disagreement, attach to issues that are not settled but remain controversial. The disagreement may take the form of a difference as to direction (dissents) or difference as to "spin" (concurrences); together, they identify cases where the Court is laying the foundation for that which will be (more) settled tomorrow, and gradually working towards the smoothing out of the internal differences that are the inevitable concomitant of jurisprudential novelty.

Minority reasons have accounted for something between one-quarter and one-third of all the words produced by the Supreme Court of Canada over the period; they follow the same general track as that described above, except that all the trends are exaggerated. The Dickson Court averaged 175,000 words per year in minority reasons, for the Lamer Court this went up to 300,000 words, and for the McLachlin Court to date it is again back down to 175,000. The upper line on Figure 6.8 identifies the portion of this evolving total that has been devoted to Charter cases, and this shows a slightly more exaggerated version of the same story as total decision words. For a time, Charter cases accounted for an absolute majority of all minority reason wordage, this despite the fact that they made up only about 30 per cent of the caseload. But this figure peaked very early and has tracked steadily downwards, converging with the line for the proportion of all words directed to Charter cases. Again, this means that the average Charter decision draws more and/or longer minority reasons than the average non-Charter decision, but again it also means that they have become a smaller part of the Court's controversial caseload in recent years. The clear message of both is one of decreasing levels of disagreement for a set of cases that is drawing a decreasing proportion of the Court's workload; that is to say, the message is that the period of revolutionary controversy centred on the Charter is drawing to a close.

Let me present yet one more figure to put this decision/minority wordcount matter in a larger context. This figure is particularly relevant because I have been arguing that wordcount is (primarily) a measure of the time and attention that the Court is devoting to anything and therefore (secondarily) a measure of the importance that the Court attaches to it. To the extent that this is a credible measure, it becomes meaningful to ask, over time, how much of the Supreme Court's output—its allocation of its scarce resource of time and attention—takes the form of judgements (unanimous, majority or plurality), and how much takes the form of minority reasons? The answer to this question is shown in Figure 6.9 (once again using multi-year running averages to smooth out the spikiness of year-on-year data so as to show the trends).

The balance between these types of output is rather more consistent than one might have expected: decisions oscillate around just over 70 per cent of the total wordcount, dissents around 20 per cent, and concurrences around 6.5 per cent. This suggests that there is something approaching long-term stability in the relative levels of time and effort put into the three alternative components of judicial decisions: decisions, dissents, and concurrences. Given the consistency, we may have identified a norm of agreement and of appropriate disagreement on the Court, of the sort that has been most extensively explored with respect to the USSC.

But although the fluctuations are more modest than they might have been, they still take on a pattern that supports my thesis. Looking at the decision wordcount line, it would seem that there are three reasonable long-term "plateaus" on the graph. The first is the several years after 1980, when the ratio of decision words to minority words was about (just

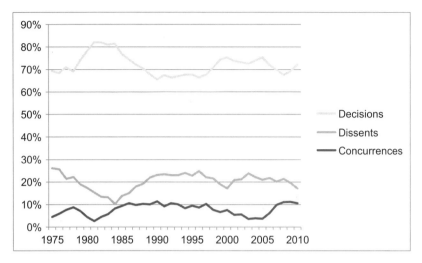

FIGURE 6.9 Decisions and minority reasons as per cent of all words, by year

over) 4:1, the highest point on the table. This represents the "late Laskin Court," when a highly respected Chief Justice pressed consistently for a more unified Court and (when there was disagreement) for a straightforward dichotomous majority/minority presentation of reasons. The second plateau is the low one extending from about 1989 to 1997, when the ratio shifted to a fairly stable 2:1; this period, from the closing years of the Dickson Court to the end of the Lamer "natural court," is the Charter impact period to which we have been directed by figure after figure. The third is the period of 1999 and after, when the ratio shifted upwards to about 3:1 (which is also the long-term average for the entire period).

The last five years seem to put a question mark at the end of this story—the McLachlin plateau has a crumbling edge, which hints at a move towards the decision/minority ratios of the Lamer Court. But even if there was some kind of an adjustment to some locus of uncertainty within the Supreme Court caseload, the earlier figures of this section make it clear that the Charter is no longer providing this locus. Even if there is such a swing, it therefore accentuates rather than attenuates my basic point, which is that the Charter is no longer where significant division and debate within the Court is occurring.

In summary, I have suggested that wordcount is a reasonable proxy for the Supreme Court's time and attention—it spends time on what it thinks is important, and more time on what it thinks is more important. This plays out into those words (and time) devoted to minority reasons. Relatively stable amounts of time are devoted to articulating alternative solutions to those presented in the majority decisions, usually about twice as much to direction-differing dissents as to spin-directing separate concurrences. As I will demonstrate below, these efforts are more potentially fruitful than one might think; there are sometimes returns to these efforts that can be tracked through citation behaviour. That being the case, it is profoundly important to note that the Court is no longer directing as much of its other-than-the-decision writing efforts to Charter cases; to the extent that minority opinions represent "road not (yet) taken" speculation and suggestion, and that this occupies a fairly stable component of the Supreme Court's reasoned product, it is striking that where it once invested twice as much of this effort in Charter cases than in all other legal issues combined, it now spends only one-third as much on Charter issues as on other issues. The Court once devoted more than half of its time and energy (decisions and minorities combined) to Charter issues; it now devotes less than a quarter. The Charter revolution, I would suggest, is over.

4. "SWING" AND "CONTEST" JUDGEMENTS

I have pointed to the dwindling frequency of minority opinions (dissents and separate concurrences)—and then, more precisely, of dissenting and separately concurring behaviour on the part of individual judges—as one sign of the replacement of revolutionary doctrinal ferment with a growing consolidation of judicial opinions. I went on to explore this same question in terms of the amount of work (measured in terms of word counts) that the Court invested in this activity. I will now turn to a very special type of minority opinions, which is in its own right a very strong statement about the play of ideas on the court.

To reprise: when the Court hears an appeal, the judges assigned to that particular panel read the material that both sides (and any interveners) have submitted, they hear oral argument and question the lawyers for both parties, and they then meet in conference to discuss, briefly, their initial impressions. The duty of writing the majority judgement is assigned; and if there are judges who disagree about the outcome, or who prefer alternate argument tracks leading to the majority outcome, they may decide among themselves whether they will collaborate on reasons or each write their own.

But this is by no means the end of it, because the judges who are writing (majority judgement or otherwise) circulate their draft reasons within the panel and invite comment from their colleagues. Appellate decision-making is a collegial process of persuasion and negotiation; judges do not listen, vote and run, but rather they listen, they discuss, they draft and respond to drafts, and they sometimes change their minds or persuade others to change theirs. This may lead to judges changing their initial position presented at conference, deciding either to join a group other than the one they initially supported, or to write their own separate reasons if they are not sufficiently happy about any of the drafts presented by their colleagues. Obviously, sometimes this will result in a larger majority supporting the judgement, if the assigned writer of majority reasons is sufficiently persuasive, or sufficiently accommodating of the focused concerns or objections of his or her colleagues; at the extreme, division may become unanimity. By the same token, judges may also move away from the majority writer, sometimes to such an extent that the majority disappears, and the judgement of the Court is ultimately written by someone who began writing what he or she thought would be minority reasons.

How often does this happen? The Court does not report this directly, but I would suggest that it does in fact tell us about this indirectly, and in a way that allows us to keep count in a thoroughly objective way that is free from guesswork. Over the last quarter-century, the Supreme Court of Canada has evolved a distinctive and unusual format for the presentation of its judgements, a "template" with a standard set of elements that are set out in a standard order.[24] No other comparable court in the world has a strongly similar format and style; each has evolved its own structures and styles and expectations. At the same time, the Supreme Court has evolved an equally distinctive format for minority reasons,

24 For a more expanded version of this argument, see Peter McCormick, "Structures of Judgment: How the Modern Supreme Court of Canada Organizes Its Reasons" *Dalhousie Law Journal* 32 (2009): 35.

which typically includes an acknowledgement of its minority status ("I have read the reasons. ..."), a respect term ("but with respect"), and a focus for their objection ("I cannot agree with respect to [a particular element of the decision]"). This opening style (usually found in the first paragraph, often in the first sentence) is not followed by the same "full format" as the majority reasons, but instead explicitly accepts or simply assumes the basic factual presentation from those reasons (the facts of the case, the actions of the lower courts, the statement of the basic legal issues) and proceeds directly to an analysis of the issues.

Suppose, then, that we find a set of Supreme Court reasons where the judgement of the Court (so labelled in the *Supreme Court Reports*, and carrying the signatures of a majority of the judges on the panel) starts with the triple formula of minority reasons ("I have read the reasons of my colleague but with respect I cannot agree with regard to ... "); and at the same time there is a set of minority reasons, usually much longer, which exhibits the full standard format with no reference at all to the judgement. This has only one credible explanation: the in-the-end minority reasons started as the majority judgement, and therefore were drafted to include the objective elements (facts, lower courts, relevant statutes, immediate issues) that the Court's majority or unanimous reasons always provide, and the in-the-end majority reasons started as minority reasons but won over enough judges to become the judgement of the Court.

The most extreme example, which therefore makes my point in the strongest terms, is *W. v. S.*,[25] where L'Heureux-Dubé has written a separate concurrence of more than 15,000 words displaying the full decision format; but McLachlin has written what is labelled as the judgement of the Court, and which says (I reproduce it in full), "I agree with L'Heureux-Dubé J., subject to my comments in *Gordon v. Goertz*, [1996] 1 S.C.R. 27, on the rights and obligations of custodial parents." It makes no sense to think that McLachlin came away from the conference with the majority assignment and settled for this cryptic sentence; or that L'Heureux-Dubé knew from the start that hers was a minority position but chose to ape the majority style anyway. This is clearly what I will call a "swing" judgement: L'Heureux-Dubé starting with a majority but losing enough of her

---

25 *W. (V.) v. S. (D.)*, [1996] 2 S.C.R. 108.

colleagues' signatures that she lost this status, and McLachlin winning enough support that hers became the judgement. Something of this sort has happened 166 times since Dickson became Chief Justice in 1984. I began my count at that time because that is when the current decision format emerged in a clear enough form to allow me certainty that, in turn, allowed me to include only clear-cut examples of the phenomenon.

There is a second set of decisions that also needs to be considered, which I call "contest" decisions. These cases have two sets of reasons, one labelled a judgement of the Court and the other as dissenting or concurring reasons; both display the full decision format (facts, lower courts, relevant statutes, legal issues, analysis, outcome) and do so without making any direct reference to each other. An excellent example is *Syndicat Northcrest v. Amselem*,[26] the Court's clearest statement about the freedom of religion; Iacobucci's majority reasons and Bastarache's dissent are almost exactly the same length, and the sections into which their reasons are divided and the length of each of those sections mirror each other.

On the face of it, this is perplexing: the doubling of the full format represented wasted effort, and the "dual monologue" denies the collegiality that the Supreme Court's new format has splendidly exemplified. The best explanation is a swing judgement where the lead author of the new majority writes up a new set of the full reasons, just as if he or she had had the majority from the beginning (as McLachlin arguably should have done in *W. v. S.*). These reasons do not refer to the now-minority reasons because (at least until very recently) majority reasons typically do not; and the once-majority-but-now-minority reasons do not refer directly to the new majority reasons because they did not exist when those reasons were initially drafted. There were 89 of these decisions over the same period; combining the two gives me 255 examples of swing and contest judgements, but in case not everyone is persuaded by my explanation of this second set, I will keep and report separate counts of the two.

Figure 6.10 presents the annual count for the "contest" decisions (the lowest of the three lines), the "clear swing" decisions (the middle line), and the sum of the two (the upper line); for all three, I use running

---

26 *Syndicat Northcrest v. Amselem*, 2004 SCC 47.

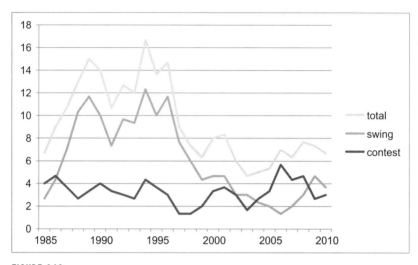

FIGURE 6.10 "Swing" and "contest" judgements, by year

three-year averages to smooth the oscillations and present the trend over time more clearly.

Again, there is a clear temporal dimension to the frequency of this practice. Consider the upper line for "total swings" (combining the two types): it starts very low, but quickly rises to more than a dozen examples per year before dropping sharply after 1996 to bottom out in 2004 and begin a slight recovery (but not one that takes it at all close to the level of the early 1990s). Narrow the attention to the "pure swings" and the picture is even more pronounced, with the frequency topping out above 10 per year in the early 1990s, and falling to below four (and sometimes well below) after 2000; it averages nine per year before 1997, and three per year after it. The "contest" cases actually go against my suggested pattern; they are fairly constant across the board and rise, slightly, after 2005—but I really think that these cases are just a variant of the "swing" judgement such that the upper line is the best representation.

Either way, the pattern fits the idea of a judicial revolution working off a considerable initial uncertainty that gradually fades as that revolution achieves fulfilment and consolidation. At the peak of the revolution, there is enough division within panels and enough lack of confident certainty on the part of the judges within the resulting fragments that initial majorities can be whittled away, and it becomes less unusual for the major statement of judicial doctrine to come from what was initially a minority position. But as the new judicial ideas consolidate, this becomes less likely for two reasons: the panels do not divide as frequently or as badly as they did at the peak, and the judges who find themselves within divided panels are sure enough of their initial position that they are less likely to change their vote. These numbers perhaps do not look very large, but over the whole period they are quite significant: to put them in a slightly different context, they regularly amount to about one-quarter of all non-unanimous reserved judgements, which implies that the lower numbers for the McLachlin Court to some extent simply reflect the declining numbers of non-unanimous decisions. But we cannot attribute this change in performance to the personal style of a new Chief Justice, because it began several years too early for that. It is, I suggest, another footprint, another sign that the change in the Court's performance is driven not by accidents of personnel and personality but rather by a shifting role in relation to a specific transformative event.

5. JUDICIAL CITATIONS, AGE, AND PRECEDENTIAL REPLACEMENT

Persuading you about the fifth of the footprints will appear to involve a bit of a detour, because I need first to establish a basic principle, and then to operationalize it in an unusual and possibly controversial way, and finally to "cash it in" in a way that solidly reinforces my basic argument. I would ask for readers' patience as I follow this somewhat indirect path.

To begin: consider judicial citations, which is to say the practice of providing reasons for the immediate decision by making reference to, or directly quoting, a prior judicial decision. Read any Supreme Court decision, and it will be obvious that the judicial citation is the favourite weapon in the arsenal of judicial explanation. The average Supreme Court decision includes about 20 such citations, and in recent years 60 per cent or more of these are to prior decisions of the Supreme Court itself. Sometimes, the purpose of the citation is essentially to say "We already decided that particular issue" by sending you back to an earlier decision or decisions that dealt with a similar matter. More generally, it serves to locate the reasons for the immediate decision (and it is important to emphasize reasons over outcome in this context) within the context of established law, and this will be particularly important when the immediate reasons involve altering or even partly reversing those earlier statements. Either way, judges do not cite earlier decisions casually, and the choice of which cases to cite is not casual either, because they must include the "obvious" cases that other judges will expect to see.[27] Either way, to cite a previous case is to single it out as something that is both important and specifically relevant to the immediate case. Citation involves selection, and that selection sends a signal, and the changing patterns of those signals convey information.

The first observation is an obvious one: as cases get older, they tend to be cited less often. The major lesson of the broader literature on judicial citation behaviour is that the time variable is a major component. This is not a new idea; Posner and Landes suggested the idea (linked to a "depreciation" metaphor) in 1972.[28] Nor is it an idea that has faded into the background; in a recent study, Black and Spriggs concluded, "A precedent's age is the single most important variable affecting the rate at which a precedent depreciates (i.e., the likelihood that it is cited in subsequent years)."[29]

I want to turn this into a much stronger statement. I want to say that if we calculate the precise length of time between when a case is decided and when it is cited by the Court at a later time, then every increment

---

27 One appeal court judge that I interviewed was baffled that I would be thinking in terms of "choice" at all, as if there was something arbitrary or completely discretionary about the process. She said, "I cite what I need to cite, nothing else." This may be a little bit strong—there is some "flavour" to the citation styles of different judges that you can come to recognize over time—but I think it is closer to the truth than the notion of everything being up for grabs every time, like your choosing which TV programs to watch this week.

28 William M. Landes and Richard A. Posner, "Legal Precedent: A Theoretical and Empirical Analysis," *Journal of Law & Economics* 19 (1976): 249.

29 Ryan C. Black and James F. Spriggs II, "The Depreciation of Precedent on the U.S. Supreme Court" (paper presented at the CELS 2009 4th Annual Conference on Empirical Legal Studies), 4, retrieved September 11, 2011, from http://papers.ssrn.com/sol3/papers.cfm?abstract_id=1421413.

of a year makes cases measurably less likely to be cited. This means that cases will be cited by the Supreme Court more often during the first year after they have been handed down than for any single year that follows, and more often during the second year than for any other year except the first year, and so on. The graph for "age of cited case" will only move downwards; every year of age will mean that cases are cited less often; and citations to new cases will always outnumber citations to old cases. Then I want to push it a step further: I want to suggest that the ratio between the "two-year-old cases" and the "one-year-old cases" will be the same as the ratio between the "three-year-old cases" and the "two-year-old cases," and so on. There is a constant rate at which the citation frequency drops. The graph for age of cited cases mentioned above forms something approaching a smooth line. But it is not a straight line; it is a curve that becomes an asymptote, approaching but never quite reaching the "0" point.

If this is true, then we can calculate the decay rate that is driving this curve—the "percentage decline per year" that takes the general "new cases more, old cases less" and turns it into a specific statement about the persistence of precedent and the rate of replacement of old law with new law. We can then use the idea of "newer more, older less" to test the "end-of-the-revolution" argument—a period of legal revolution is a period when the replacement of old law with new law is happening unusually quickly, and a time of stability and normalcy is one when the replacement of old law with new law happens much more slowly.

For this purpose, I will work from a database accumulated over the last several decades, looking at the citation practices of the Supreme Court of Canada. Narrowing this to look at Supreme Court citations to Supreme Court decisions, and focusing on the period between 1970 (when Bora Laskin was appointed to the Supreme Court of Canada) and the end of December in 2012 (when my data collection concluded), I wound up with a total of 27,240 citations, for each of which I generated the age (date of citation minus date of decision, divided by 365.25). These results are shown in Figure 6.11. For convenience, I end the data presentation at citations that are 30 years old and simply ignore the roughly 3,000 cases that are strung out between 31 years and the maximum citation age of 129 years; there is no further information, and no change to the calculations, in this very long and extended tail.

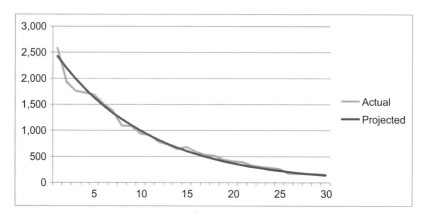

FIGURE 6.11 Number of citations, by age of cite, 1970–2012

The somewhat uneven line is the actual count of citations: of my grand total, 2,581 citations were to decisions that had been handed down within 364 days of the case that was doing the citing, and a further 1,929 were to decisions that had been handed down between 365 and 729 days earlier, and so on. The line is not a perfect curve—sometimes it falls a little more steeply than others, and at a single point around the 15-year mark it actually goes up (slightly) rather than down—but, in general, it clearly shows a steady downwards drift and it looks "curve-like" in the sense that the slope gradually becomes less steep. For what it is worth, the average ratio between adjacent points is 0.91, although this oscillates between the steep .747 of the very first two points, and the 1.06 of the solitary upward spike.

The smooth line is the "projected" set of values, reached by multiplying each number-value on the curve by .906 in order to generate the next number, which in turn is multiplied by .906 to generate the next. This curve value is the best fit to the actual line, as measured by a "sum of squares" method,[30] and the closeness of fit is, considering the phenomenon at issue, surprisingly good. So I will turn this finding into a simple

---

30 For each data point, calculate the difference between the actual value and the projected value; square this difference; and then sum all the squares. For shifting values of the decay rate, the sum-of-the-squares total will change, and these can be graphed as a mathematical curve with a single lowest point. In the immediate example, .0940 is the decay rate that corresponds to that lowest point.

statement that I will pretentiously call "McCormick's Law" to be defined as follows:

> **McCormick's Law**: the frequency with which any set of Supreme Court decisions is subsequently cited by the Supreme Court falls by a constant amount for every additional year of the decisions' age.

This statement is demonstrably true for the last 40 years of Supreme Court citation performance, and the constant amount in question is 9.40 per cent. I do not suggest that it could casually be extended into any earlier period. (I am reasonably sure that my Iron Law would still apply, but I suspect that the decay rate would be considerably lower.) To say "constant decay rate" is to imply "knowable half-life"[31] and this is the most useful application of the law. One meaning of "half-life" is that it represents the time period during which any Supreme Court decision will receive one-half of its total lifetime citations; a second meaning is that it represents the median age of all citations; but the third one, and the one I will emphasize, is that it represents a replacement rate. Assuming a reasonably consistent number of total citations, a particular set of cases can only be cited less often if something else is being cited more often. Given the shape of my graph, this "something else" has to be newer cases—so half-life represents the frequency which new cases, new precedent, new legal interpretations and readings are replacing "old" law. This directly links to the idea of a legal or judicial revolution, which would have to leave unambiguous fingerprints on the replacement rate for the claim to be credible.

For any statement involving every citation for more than four decades, it cannot simply be assumed that a statement that is true about the class as a whole is automatically and equally true of all the subclasses within it—this is the ecological fallacy. Perhaps the attrition rate is different for major ("landmark" or "leading") cases than for lesser cases; perhaps it is lower for the outstanding judges who lead the court for a number of years

---

31 My "decay rate" metaphor conjures up the model of radioactivity, hence "half-life." In the American literature, the metaphor is usually financial, speaking about "depreciation rate" (although I am not aware of any studies that took this metaphor so seriously as to generate a mathematical value for the rate).

TABLE 6.1 Citation "Decay Rates" by Chief Justiceship

CHIEF JUSTICESHIP	DECAY RATE	HALF-LIFE PERIOD
Fauteux 1970–1973	6.45%	10.0 years
Laskin 1973–1984	9.1%	8.3 years
Dickson 1984–1990	16.24%	4.9 years
Lamer 1990–2000	13.5%	5.8 years
McLachlin 2000–2012	6.2%	11.8 years
Total 1970–2012	9.4%	8.0 years

(these two concerns overlapping because the "outstanding" are probably the ones delivering the "leading" case). It turns out that this is not a problem; the attrition rate applies with equal rigour to all cases (even *Oakes* and *Big M Drug Mart* and *BC Motor Vehicle*) and to all judges (even Dickson). But I concede a different dimension of the ecological problem: it varies quite dramatically for the smaller time periods into which these four decades can be divided.

I ran the same calculation as above (a count for citation age, assimilated to a decay curve through a sum-of-squares test) for each of the most recent Chief Justiceships, in which I include the Fauteux Chief Justiceship as a sort of background check. This period is still useful in helping to set the background, even though I do not think it is strictly comparable to the others—first because the Laskin Chief Justiceship marks the transition from the traditional Supreme Court to the modern Supreme Court, which enjoys quite a different role and quite different expectations in quite a different context; second, because it is a much shorter time period than the others; and third because the number of citations per year was so much lower.

Table 6.1 strongly confirms my argument in a double sense. First, it suggests that it really does make strong empirical sense to talk about a legal and judicial revolution occasioned by the Charter, given that the Dickson Court, which coincides with the beginning of Charter cases, exhibited an exceptional focus on the citation of recent cases. The decay rate for this Court is double what it was a dozen of years earlier under Fauteux; and correspondingly the "half-life" has dropped dramatically, with fully half of all citations to judicial authority picking up on

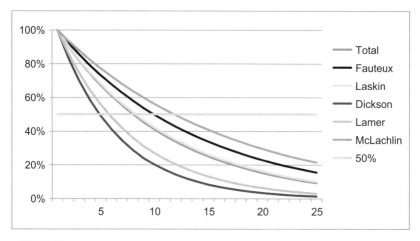

FIGURE 6.12 Decay rates, by Chief justiceship

decisions that were less than five years old. And second, it makes a comparably strong case for the idea that the judicial revolution peaked with Dickson, given that the decay rate steadily dropped (and the half-life replacement period correspondingly rose) during the subsequent Chief Justiceships. This effect is so strong that the McLachlin Court has a lower decay rate (and a longer half-life period) than the Laskin Court or even the Fauteux Court of the early 1970s. This is very much what the end of a judicial revolution and a return to normalcy would look like. Please note that my calculations involve all citations to judicial authority in all decided cases, not simply the Charter cases for which the effect may well be stronger.

The simplest way to use these numbers to address my point is to see where the lines cross the horizontal "50 per cent" line, which reflects the age of the median citation to authority or (putting it slightly differently) the dividing line between "new" and "old" citations. For the overall average line, the slightly lower of the very tight pair in the middle, this happens at the eight year mark, which is to say that a citation from seven years earlier is in the "new half" of all citations, and one from eight years or more earlier is in the "old half." For the Dickson Court, the lowest of the six curved lines, this happens between the four and five year mark—a four-year-old decision is "new" but a five-year-old decision is already "old." For the McLachlin Court, the highest of the six lines, the line is crossed between 11 and 12 years, which means that an 11-year-old decision is still "new."

The decay curve is also a replacement curve, which shows how quickly old law is being replaced by new law. Put this way, those same numbers reflect how long it takes the Court to create a body of new law in the form of decisions that occupy fully one half of its total citation list, replacing older law in the process. This happened at a very rapid rate for the Dickson and Lamer Courts; it is not happening anywhere near as rapidly today. The point is that these citations represent a deliberate selection by the judges themselves for the purpose of communicating with and persuading other judges; they choose from the large universe of possible judicial citations that other judges would expect to see because they are the important and relevant background cases to the immediate decision.

Chief Justiceships are admittedly a rather blunt measure for this phenomenon, the more so because they are not all of equal length— Laskin, Lamer, and McLachlin each represent about a decade, as against six years for Dickson and three for Fauteux. Table 6.2 divides each of the three longer Chief Justiceships into roughly equal halves,[32] giving seven post-Fauteux time periods each of which is five or six years long.

This subdivision strongly reinforces my argument with a clear and dramatic set of upward steps to the dramatic decay and replacement rate of the Dickson Court, and then an equally clear and dramatic set of

---

32 For the Laskin Court, this division is functional rather than arbitrary, because some time in 1979 (arguably, with the appointment of Lamer), it finally became Laskin's Court in the strong sense that he could usually prevail over a Quebec-plus-Diefenbaker bloc of judges centred on Martland. The clearest evidence of this is that Laskin's dissents were frequent before 1979, but vanished afterwards. Similarly, the division between McLachlin A and McLachlin B (in Table 6.2) roughly coincides with the departure of Iacobucci and Arbour and the appointment of Charron and Abella— the moment when a majority of the Court had never known a Chief Justice other than

TABLE 6.2 Citation "Decay Rates" by Split Chief Justiceship

"SPLIT" CHIEF JUSTICESHIP	DECAY RATE	HALF-LIFE PERIOD
Fauteux 1970–1973	7.45%	10.0 years
Laskin "A" 1973–1979	8.05%	9.3 years
Laskin "B" 1980–1984	12.1%	6.4 years
Dickson 1984–1990	16.24%	4.9 years
Lamer "A" 1990–1994	14.8%	5.3 years
Lamer "B" 1995–1999	12.01%	6.4 years
McLachlin "A" 2000–2005	7.73%	9.6 years
McLachlin "B" 2006–2012	4.2%	17.1 years
Total 1970–2012	9.4%	8.0 years

downward steps to the McLachlin Court, which now shows a value for the first half-dozen years that is comparable to the Fauteux Court, but an even lower value for the most recent half-dozen years (by a good margin the lowest on the table). These data are completely consistent with a judicial revolution of sorts that began towards the end of the Laskin Court, peaked under Dickson, and has been steadily heading towards retrenchment ever since. On this evidence, there has been a judicial revolution, but it is now over.

6. CITATIONS OF DISSENTS AND CONCURRENCES

My comments above refer consistently to the citation of judicial *decisions*, a phrasing which I am sure raised no eyebrows and occasioned no concerns. It is a basic principle of judicial authority that it is the *decisions* of the Supreme Court, the reasons for outcomes that have been articulated by unanimous panels or by the majority block within those panels, that constitute precedent. In our current terminology (which does not

---

McLachlin. But dividing the Lamer Court is just an arbitrary halfway mark; if there was a truly distinctive time period on that Court, it was probably the "natural court" from 1992 to 1997.

go back as far as one might think), these are the "judgements" of the Court, as distinct from the "reasons" presented in dissents and separate concurrences.[33]

In its purest form, then, precedent is normally taken to be about citing decisions; minority reasons, whether dissents or separate concurrences, simply vanish, a species of "loser's history" with which we need not concern ourselves. In practice, this is pitching it much too strong, and the doctrine is not (and possibly never was) quite that strong. The Supreme Court has been citing minority reasons reasonably often for several decades; indeed, it did so even before the "modern" Supreme Court that I would date back to Laskin. It is important to note that when minority reasons are cited, it is almost never in order to point them out as clearly established error; instead, they are typically cited, and sometimes quoted, in exactly the same tone and style as the judgements of the Court that make up the bulk of judicial citations. Indeed, you often cannot tell without looking the case up directly that minority reasons are being cited.[34] With very rare exceptions, the Supreme Court does not cite a decision just to say it thinks it is wrong; the ultimate rejection is not to be criticized but to be ignored, which in the case of Supreme Court decisions means not to be cited.

The relevance of the citation of minority reasons to my "judicial revolution" thesis is my suggestion above that the frequency of minority reasons identifies when a Court is managing a variety of alternative suggestions and finding ways to deal with new issues and problems. On the one hand, the judges on a panel generate dissenting and separate concurring reasons because there is no pre-emptive centre of gravity for the Court as new questions arise for the first time; on the other hand, the judges on subsequent panels who continue to have parallel reservations or doubts can draw upon those reasons in later cases and use them to

---

33 In American usage, all sets of reasons are "opinions," one of which is labelled in the syllabus as "the opinion of the Court." In Canadian usage, "the judgement of the Court" indicates a unanimous decision; less-than-unanimous majority or plurality reasons are "the judgement" of the joining judges, while minority judges deliver "reasons."

34 Obviously, then, one hint is the fact that the cited judge is specifically named, as well as the case in which the reasons appear; but only about one-quarter of all "named cites" are to minority reasons, so this is not a particularly good indicator, either.

fashion or modify new and more consensual positions. If a higher number of minority reasons (and a higher number of judges signing on to them) suggests a revolutionary ferment at one point in time, a higher number of subsequent citations to those minority reasons suggests that this is continuing and is being fed by those minority arguments. The polar converse would be a situation where the Court is usually unanimous, and almost never cites any other than earlier judgements.

To step back for a moment: a Supreme Court decision is not a single answer to a single question with judicial citations stacked around it. It is instead a logical progression through a series of steps to a justified conclusion, and the resolution of each step involves the use of citations (which is why major and complex cases can use so many citations). Specific decisions tend to be remembered in terms of a single central question that they resolved (and this is the context within which they will typically be cited in future); this is accurate enough for general use, but the actual reasons are seldom this single-focused. To take an obvious example: *Oakes* is the Supreme Court decision that first laid out a complete test for the application of the "reasonable limits" clause in section 1 of the Canadian Charter of Rights and Freedoms, and this explains most of its (very high) citation count; but it also dealt with the notion of a "reverse onus" clause[35] and is cited (less often) in the (rather uncommon) cases that still raise this issue.[36]

This necessarily means that a judge can cite an earlier set of minority reasons, even a dissent, without declaring or implying "Wait! Stop! We made a horrible mistake!" The Court occasionally does make such a declaration either directly (e.g., *Health Service Workers* vindicated Dickson's

---

35 Reverse onus means that instead of the government having to prove you are guilty, you have to prove you are innocent. In the age of the Charter, there is a very strong presumption against this, but some examples have survived constitutional challenge, and *Oakes* provides part of the rationale.

36 There is an even more striking example in the United States, that being the infamous decision of *Dred Scott v. Sanford*, regarded as one of the two or three worst Supreme Court decisions of all time for its finding that slavery was constitutionally protected, and that an African American could not become a citizen. But the same case also dealt with the question of whether the full rigours of the US constitution and its Bill of Rights applied only within the states, or whether "the constitutional follows the flag" to include non-state territories and holdings as well—and this finding was directly relevant to, and cited in (for example), the recent cases involving Guantanamo detainees.

dissents in the 1987 *Labour Trilogy*) or more coyly (such as saying in *Morin* that the Court "could not understand" how its decision in *Askov* had been so badly understood), but much of the use of ideas from minority reasons is less dramatic, which does not say it is not important. It may be that a separate concurrence took the form of "let me add something" and the evolution of legal issues made that addition more important than the historic centre of the findings; or it may be that a dissent was used by a judge to make wider arguments so that it could be cited as "dissenting (but not on this point)." Judicial decisions might be dichotomous (either you allow the appeal or you do not), but judicial reasons are infinitely more nuanced.

Terrell famously suggested that we should think of judicial decisions as having a notional location on a multi-dimensional grid, and the historic sequence of a string of decisions on related issues creates a notional line that can be projected into the future—this, he suggests, is how precedent really works.[37] By extension, then, I would suggest that minority reasons present different "spins" working on that point, capable of sending the line off in subtly—but, over time, importantly—different directions. For a Court to have these "spin" options available, in the form of minority reasons from past cases, is important; for it to demonstrate a practice of reasonably frequently taking advantage of those options by citing those minority reasons is the other half of that story.

Table 6.3 presents the data that answers the question, "How often does the Supreme Court under each of a series of Chief Justices use citations to minority reasons (dissents or separate concurrences) as part of its mix of citations to earlier cases decided by the Court?" Reaching all the way back to the 1949 court, when the Supreme Court became truly supreme with the abolition of appeals to the Judicial Committee of the Privy Council, it is obvious that the Court has for a long time been willing to cite decisions that were not judgements of the Court.[38] (One might even suggest that the slightly higher figure for the Rinfret Court than for

---

37 Timothy P. Terrell, "Flatlaw: An Essay on the Dimensions of Legal Reasoning and the Development of Fundamental Normative Principles," *California Law Review* 72 (1984): 288.

38 It is also true that the earlier Supreme Court was not always as focused on identifying a specific set of reasons as "the judgement" of the Court—indeed, in the early decades, a good number of decisions were *seriatim* reasons in which every judge or almost every judge on the panel wrote his or her separate reasons, with the "votes"

TABLE 6.3 Frequency of Minority Citations, by Chief Justiceship

CHIEF JUSTICESHIP	ALL CITATIONS OF SCC DECISIONS	CITATIONS OF MINORITY REASONS	MINORITY CITES AS % OF ALL CITES
Rinfret	680	46	6.8%
Kerwin	1,026	46	4.5%
TCF[39]	1,480	81	5.5%
Laskin	3,564	303	8.5%
Dickson	3,298	353	10.7%
Lamer	8,981	753	8.4%
McLachlin	9,345	520	5.3%

the successor Kerwin Court comes from the fact that this new-found post-1949 supremacy already constituted some kind of a judicial revolution of its own, although that is probably pushing a small difference pretty hard.) The Supreme Court has for decades been citing minority reasons as a modest part of its precedential mix, as shown in Table 6.3.[40]

The shape of the numbers in Table 6.3 is the familiar one—a relatively lower frequency for such references before the Laskin watershed, rising frequencies through the Laskin Chief Justiceship into the beginning of the Charter era, and then a decline from a notional high point. If there is anything distinctive about this apparent curve as against the earlier ones, it is that the peak seems to come earlier, during the Dickson Court rather than the Lamer Court.

Implicit within Table 6.3 is another message: within the general category of minority reasons, the balance has been shifting between dissents and concurrences. Before and even during the Laskin Chief Justiceship,

---

being summed to generate the outcome, such that subsequent judges and courts had to determine which parts of which reasons constituted the finding and the precedent.

39 Combining the brief sequential Chief Justiceships of Taschereau, Cartwright, and Fauteux into a single composite Chief Justiceship more directly comparable to the others in terms of length—with some allowance for Rinfret and Dickson—the Chief Justiceships are then very close to decades.

40 This section builds on the argument in Peter McCormick, "Second Thoughts: Supreme Court Citations of Dissents and Separate Concurrences, 1949–1996," *Canadian Bar Review* 81 (2002): 369. Table 6.3 is reproduced from page 375 of that article, with the figures for McLachlin added and the totals revised accordingly.

when minority reasons were cited, these were disproportionately citations to concurring reasons—that is, to the ideas of judges who agreed with the outcome but not (or at least not completely) with the reasons for that outcome. Under Dickson, Lamer, and McLachlin, it is now dissents that are cited about half again as often as separate concurrences.

But the percentage column is not the only one to notice, and the powerful message of the table is perhaps clearer if we look at the second column and run it back against the length of each of the Chief Justiceships. Table 6.3's up-and-down-again curve of the relative frequency of minority reasons is happening against a background of a steadily increasing frequency of judicial citations generally and judicial citations to the Supreme Court's own cases in particular. Perhaps we should think in terms of how the absolute count of such citations works out each year. Before Laskin, minority reasons are cited 10 times per year (or once a month) or less; to find such a citation in the Court's reason is an unusual event, even a slightly surprising one. For Laskin, this frequency goes up to 30 times a year, for Dickson it doubles again to 60 times, and for the Lamer Court it goes up again to 80 times. (In percentage terms, the Lamer Court is down a little, but its judicial citations per year are much higher.) This means that the Lamer Court cites as many minority reasons in a month as the pre-Laskin Courts cited in a year or more. The peak years for the Lamer Court are higher yet: 126 times in 1990, 110 in 1993, and 99 in 1995. At this point, the citation of minority reasons would no longer be a surprising find in the Supreme Court Reports. What was once unusual had become something close to routine.

But no sooner do the frequencies reach this level than they begin to fall. In 1997 the count is down to 60, in 1998 to 40. The McLachlin Court continues this trend, averaging only 40 citations to minority reasons per year. To divide this into an "early McLachlin" and a "later McLachlin" period, with December 2005 as the dividing point, reinforces the implication of a downward trend: the count falls from just over 50 per year for the first six years to barely 30 per year for the second. This is still on absolute count rather more than the pre-Laskin courts experienced, but it is quite different from what was happening under Dickson and Lamer.

Echoing the argument of the previous section that a Chief Justiceship is a rather blunt period of time to be working on, Figure 6.13 runs annual counts of the percentage of all Dickson-and-after citations to Supreme

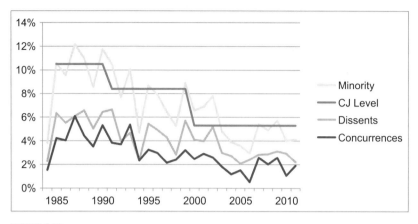

FIGURE 6.13 Frequency of citations of minority reasons, by year

Court cases that are made to separate concurrences (the bottom line) or to dissents (the middle of the three oscillating lines), with the higher oscillating line summing the two. (The picture is clear enough that I have not aggregated the figures into multi-year running averages to smooth the curves.) The set of downward plateaus shows the average level for each of the three Chief Justiceships—just above 10 per cent for Dickson, just above 8 per cent for Lamer, and just below 6 per cent for McLachlin. The trend would be even more pronounced had minority reason citations not rebounded after hitting a 30-year low in 2006—but they have still just rebounded to the McLachlin Court plateau, which is already well below that of the two previous Chief Justiceships.

To be sure, 11 per cent or so does not seem like a really large number, so let me pause to expand upon what this means. Under the Dickson Court, one judicial citation in every nine (one in every eight in the single peak year) was to the ideas contained in a set of judicial reasons that at the time of writing had not gained the support of a majority of the panel, and therefore had not provided a judgement of the Court. Since none of these were, on the strictest reading of *stare decisis*, normally expected to be sufficiently authoritative to guide future decisions, this must mean that things were unusually unsettled, that yesterday's majority decisions were not as definitive and conclusive as they would normally be, and that as a result the minority reasons that are usually just pushed off to the side remained to an unusual extent "on the table" and available to the judges deciding later cases. Under Lamer, this fell a little, but we are still talking about one citation in every 12 drawing on sets of ideas that had not drawn the support of—given the way that panels deliberate, we can make that stronger and say "had explicitly and consciously not been approved by"—the majority. For the McLachlin Court, as it was for the pre-Laskin Courts, this same figure is now one in 20, which I would suggest demonstrates a resumption of normalcy.

The picture, then, is of a period of judicial uncertainty, which included not only unusual high levels of disagreement as expressed in dissents and separate concurrences but also an unusual readiness on the part of the judges to cite those dissents and separate concurrences. This double presentation of uncertainty has been replaced by a double layer of increasing certainty: much lower levels of dissent and separate concurrence, and a much reduced willingness to cite them, to incorporate their "spin" in the increasing certainty of the law. All these things, of course, are relative—even at the high end, citations of minority reasons never rose above one-eighth of the total, while at the low end they still account for 1 in 20—but the swing from the high to the low is pronounced enough to support the notion of a judicial revolution that has since been normalized.

7. "FOREIGN" CITATIONS

The entrenchment of a Charter of rights was a new adventure for Canada, but it is not unique in the world. Most obviously (and something that was often noted with some concern) the United States has had an entrenched Bill of Rights for 200 years, and a Supreme Court that has (at least sometimes, and rather more recently than many think) enforced it vigorously; but it is also a staple of the recent literature that the move towards a stronger judicial role in the protection of human rights, with or without prior constitutional entrenchment, has in recent decades become pervasive. With a paucity of relevant domestic jurisprudence on which to draw (other than that the Court was generating itself), it would be entirely logical to think that the Canadian Court might draw on the experience of other countries to help fill the void. It might even be suggested that this reliance on the ideas of other countries and other countries' courts might continue to be part of the process, reflecting the emergence of a global judicial community whose interactions very much centre on notions of constitutional rights—a suggestion that was all the more plausible given that some academics such as Patrick Glenn have long spoken of Canada's openness to a wide range of jurisprudential influences from around the world.[41]

To be sure, the notion of citing the decisions of other countries' courts is not without its controversies. In some countries—most notably in the United States—this practice has aroused vigorous debate in the academic journals,[42] and the justices on the United States Supreme Court have demonstrated the same division both within their reasons and in more public debates (Scalia in particular championing the opposition to the practice, Breyer defending it).[43] In rather less dramatic terms, the same debate has been carried on in Australia. No such controversy currently rages in Canada, although (as I will discuss below) the individual judges on our Supreme Court vary dramatically in their willingness to use such sources.

If the hypothesis is that the Supreme Court has been drawing on foreign judicial citations considerably more often in the age of the Charter, then this is to a large extent an empirical question that has an objective empirical answer—all we have to do is look at the full range of Supreme Court citations over the last few decades, and see how many of them have been to foreign courts. Table 6.4 takes a first look at this question.

---

41 Patrick Glenn, "Persuasive Authority," *McGill Law Journal* 32 (1987): 261.

42 For example, Richard Posner warns against "judicial cosmopolitanism" in his "A Political Court," *Harvard Law Review* 119 (2005): 31 at 84; while Mark Tushnet pithily poses the opposed point of view in his transparently titled "When Is Knowing Less Better Than Knowing More? Unpacking the Controversy over Supreme Court Reference to Non-U.S. Law," *Minnesota Law Review* 90 (2005–06): 1276; and Austen Parrish dismisses the whole debate in his "A Storm in a Teacup: The U.S. Supreme Court's Use of Foreign Law," *University of Illinois Law Review* (2007): 637.

43 For the "conversation" between Justice Scalia and Justice Breyer on the validity of using foreign law in US cases, see Norman Dorsen, "A Conversation between U.S. Supreme Court Justices—The Relevance of Foreign Legal Materials in U.S. Constitutional Cases: A Conversation between Justice Antonin Scalia and Justice Stephen Breyer," *International Journal of Constitutional Law* 3 (2005): 519.

TABLE 6.4 Frequency of Non-Canadian Citations, by Chief Justiceship

CHIEF JUSTICESHIP	CANADIAN CITATIONS	NON-CANADIAN CITATIONS
Rinfret	38.4%	61.6%
Kerwin	50.1%	49.9%
TCF	63.0%	37.0%
Laskin	67.8%	32.2%
Dickson	74.2%	25.8%
Lamer	85.0%	15.0%
McLachlin	88.8%	11.2%

I am sure that every reader's reaction is that there seems to be something very wrong with this table, something quite inconsistent with a modern trend towards globalization—the foreign numbers start high, but then decline steadily. But I present this data only to make the point that although the domestic/foreign dichotomy may usefully frame the debate in the United States, it is not useful for the consideration of Canadian practices. And the reason for this is the fact that most of the non-Canadian citations are to various English courts, which have such a special status in Canadian law as to require the bracketing of the notion of "foreign" courts.

What is special about citations to English courts? For one thing, an English quasi-court, the Judicial Committee of the Privy Council, served as Canada's highest court of appeal until 1949—not a Supreme Court "of" Canada, to be sure, but effectively a Supreme Court "for" Canada (and for other territories in the British Empire and Commonwealth). Decisions of the Supreme Court could be, and not infrequently were, appealed to the JCPC, which was not at all reticent about overturning them. These decisions constituted the original core of precedent on questions of Canadian constitutional interpretation, and at one time they could account for up to one-tenth of the total citation count. They still show up in this capacity on the Supreme Court's citation lists today, especially in cases involving the federal/provincial division of legislature jurisdiction, although for a much lower citation count.

Further, the English high courts held (and to a lesser extent still hold) a special status and authority within the common law. Canadian

TABLE 6.5 Frequency of English, American, and "Other" Citations

CHIEF JUSTICESHIP	SCC	OTHER CDN	ENGLISH	US	OTHER
Rinfret	21.7%	16.7%	59.8%	0.8%	1.0%
Kerwin	28.7%	21.4%	46.9%	1.5%	1.5%
TCF	38.8%	24.3%	32.8%	3.1%	1.1%
Laskin	38.4%	29.4%	27.0%	3.3%	1.9%
Dickson	38.9%	35.3%	16.6%	7.2%	2.0%
Lamer	55.8%	27.5%	9.4%	5.6%	1.8%
McLachlin	58.7%	30.1%	6.1%	3.5%	1.6%

common law did not replace English common law, but rather located itself within English law while fully accepting the authority of its venerable English roots. For some time even after 1949 the House of Lords was still arguably the "highest court" for the English common law (even if Canadian cases could never be appealed to it). Ian Bushnell describes Canadian common law as being dominated at least until the 1960s by an implicit "law of Canada = law of England" equation that effectively made the House of Lords "the ultimate court."[44] But this too has been a declining feature of Canadian judicial citation; if I have been treating the Charter as part of a "big story" in the operations of the Supreme Court of Canada, there is no question that another comparably big story was the steady waning of English influence, and the rise of Canadian judicial self-reference, during the whole period since World War II. Fifty years ago, then professor Laskin complained bitterly about the "English captivity" of the Supreme Court; those days are well and truly over.

So, for present purposes, it is more useful to shift the focus from "non-Canadian" judicial citation to "foreign" judicial citation, using this last term in such a way as to exclude English judicial authority. Table 6.5 above facilitates this refinement: the "other" category is a complete residual for non-Canadian, non-English, and non-US citations, but miscellaneous collections of this sort are not inappropriate so long as they make up only a very modest part of the total count—and these definitely do.

---

44 Ian Bushnell, "The Use of American Cases," *University of New Brunswick Law Journal* 35 (1986): 157 at 164–65.

The most obvious message from Table 6.5, and the logical converse of the relentless erosion of the direct influence of English courts, is the equally relentless rise of citations to the Supreme Court's own prior decisions. These became the largest single bloc of citations in the 1960s, but they have gone on to become an absolute and still-growing majority of all judicial citations for the Lamer Court and after. It is increasingly the case that even the more significant recent Charter decisions will cite nothing other than Supreme Court cases in both majority and minority reasons. To be sure, this is neither unexpected nor inappropriate, and the USSC demonstrates an even more self-citation-centred style of jurisprudence, but it is worth noting how recently our Supreme Court has developed a focus that is even vaguely comparable.

To support my argument, the figures for both elements of non-Canadian and non-English citation should exhibit two features: first, a noticeable increase around the time of the entrenchment of the Charter, and second, a steady decline from that initial jump. This double pattern reflects an initial judicial revolution that was unusually open to the exploration of alternative ideas or formulations, but this proved to be a window that gradually closed as domestic sources, and especially domestic judicial decisions, became available in sufficient numbers. Table 6.5 hints at this in that the Dickson Court shows the highest relative frequency for both categories, although the modest increase in American citations starts earlier than might have been expected, in the 1960s, and the increase in "other" citations is so modest as to be almost invisible. Let me unfold the data from the Chief Justiceships into a year-by-year pattern in one of my by-now-familiar graphs. Figure 6.14 gives a calendar-year count of the total number of judicial citations to each of these two sources, answering the implicit question: "If I were to read through the *Supreme Court Reports* month by month, how often could I expect to come across a citation to an American or a foreign (non-English) court?"

The picture for the citation frequency of American cases is quite spectacular. The pre-1980 figures reflect a long-standing practice for Canadian courts not to cite American authority outside of a few very specific areas of law (such as insurance law or—La Forest's example—riparian water rights law), a practice so pronounced that some scholars have spoken of an actual Canadian antipathy to the work of the American courts, although others have pointed to such factors as poor library resources

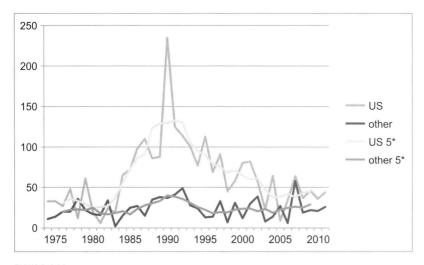

FIGURE 6.14 Frequency of US and "other" citations, by year

* Five-year running average.

that made access to current American decisions difficult. But the upwards trend is strong, with 1979 being the first time that the single-year count went above 50, and 1987 the first time that it went above 100. The count for 1990 almost makes my argument in itself—as in many other respects identified in previous figures, 1990 is really the *annus mirabilis* of the Charter, but less as a new beginning than as a unique high-water mark—although I could excise that single point from the calculations and what remained would still make the same point. The smoother curve within these dramatic fluctuations is the five-year running average for American citations. Having trended strongly upwards through the Dickson years, and holding steady over the early part of the Lamer Chief Justiceship, the count then moves relentlessly down: 1995 is the last calendar year for which the American citation count for the full year is over 100, and 2005 is the first time since 1981 that it fell to single figures, although it has rebounded somewhat since. The Dickson Court averaged 87 American citations per calendar year; the Lamer Court averaged 103 (although, more realistically, only 88 without the surge in 1990); and the McLachlin Court has averaged a much more modest 48.

When citations to American cases began to increase, it was not quite clear where this might be taking us. The first possibility we might call the "open–the-floodgates" theory, suggesting that although the novelty of the entrenched Charter was the reason for the initial surge in American citations, this would simply broaden out as these cases became embedded in the relevant jurisprudence and a growing familiarity with American cases led to more use of the case law in other areas as well; this is what La Forest suggested could happen. He noted "our modern and expanding reliance on foreign materials," and he expected that "the use of American, international, and foreign materials will continue to grow."[45] The second we might call the "temporary void" theory, which saw our Supreme Court initially drawing more heavily on American cases because there was an immediate dearth of domestic case law bearing on an entrenched Charter, but this would be short-lived as domestic case law would rapidly grow to displace the foreign cases. This was suggested by Shannon Smithey, trying to generalize from the experiences of Canada and South Africa.[46]

Figure 6.14 strongly suggests that the Smithey thesis was the correct one for Canada. There was an initial surge in American citations, somewhat focused on Charter cases, but it did not last. As an initial movement into something of a doctrinal vacuum, American cases may have helped to frame the debate in the first decade, although even here direct influence was very limited,[47] just as there was a temporary bulge in citations to the provincial courts of appeal around the same time, but both have been overwhelmed by an increasing emphasis by the Supreme Court on its own prior cases and this, rather than either Americanization or globalization, has been the major trend in the use of precedent.

The trajectory of American citation frequency echoes once again the pattern that I have been suggesting as proof of a judicial and constitutional revolution that has given way to its own process of consolidation

---

45 Gérald V. La Forest, "The Use of American Precedents in Canadian Courts," *Maine Law Review* 46 (1994): 211 at 212, 217.

46 Shannon Ishiyama Smithey, "A Tool, Not a Master: The Use of Foreign Case Law in Canada and South Africa," *Comparative Political Studies* 34 (2001): 1188 at 1192–99.

47 See Peter McCormick, "American Citations and the McLachlin Court: An Empirical Study," *Osgoode Hall Law Journal* 47 (2009): 83, for a closer look at the way that American citations have been used. Surprisingly often, this involves a careful survey of the American cases concludes with a declaration of "our constitutional framework is different" or "the Canadian practices point us in a different direction" as a way of simply brushing the US ideas to one side.

and normalization, of an initial surge of a certain kind of behaviour that has not been sustained over time. The new constitutional realities and the judicial response therefore represent simply an interruption to a longer-term status quo, and it is that status quo rather than the interruption that should shape our expectations for the decades to come.

It remains to discuss "other" judicial authority—that is to say, everything other than Canadian or English or American citations—and the numbers here are much more modest. Only once (2007) has the single year count exceeded 50,[48] and on only one other occasion (1992) did it approach this level. The line on the figure for this "other citation" fluctuates considerably from year to year, and it is squeezed to the bottom of the graph by the much more impressive numbers for American citations; I have therefore added a third line that reflects the five-year running averages for other citations. Expressed this way, there is a (modest) surge for these citations, a bulge that peaks in 1990 with a couple of lower "waves" since. It would be a little strong to say that this pattern significantly confirms my thesis, but it would, I think, be reasonable to say that it does nothing to undermine its credibility. Even at this, many of the citations can be explained without making any use of such grand labels as "judicial globalization"[49] and without talking about legal and constitutional reasoning "going global."[50] It is instead a reflection of the common law that Canada shares with a number of other countries, such as Australia (and, more recently, New Zealand), which lead this "other" category by a good margin. In terms of judicial citations, we are indeed still "waiting for globalization."[51]

There was some thought at the time of entrenchment that the citation of American case law would become a strong component at least of our

---

48 The single case that drove this uniquely high count was *Bruker v. Markovitz*, 2007 SCC 54, dealing with a Jewish divorce and featuring a lengthy decision (by Abella) matched by a comparably lengthy dissent (by Deschamps), both citing an unusual range of authority, including (nor surprisingly) an unusual number of Israeli decisions. This was a Charter case.

49 Anne-Marie Slaughter, "Judicial Globalization," *Virginia Journal of International Law* 40 (2003): 1103.

50 Ken Kersch, "The 'Globalizing Judiciary' and the Role of Law," *The Good Society* 13 (2004): 17, at 17.

51 See Peter McCormick, "Waiting for Globalization: An Empirical Study of the McLachlin Court's Foreign Judicial Citations," *Ottawa Law Review* 41 (2010): 209.

Charter jurisprudence, and possibly (with this as the beachhead) gradually of other areas of law instead. This has not happened. After an initial surge of interest in American cases, coinciding with the entrenchment of the Charter and building to a peak in the single year of 1990, which stands out in so many other graphs as well, this has steadily declined, and now seems to have levelled out at something close to the numbers for the Laskin Court. We no longer measure this in the hundreds but rather in the dozens, and a single year for the McLachlin Court (2005) is only the second year in the last 40 (1981 was the other) when the US citation count fell into single digits.

Similarly, the more recent academic literature has reverberated with the idea of a global community of judges, organized primarily around human rights law and especially entrenched human rights law, and driven by the unprecedentedly high levels of interaction between national high court judges. If the United States Supreme Court in recent decades is no longer an "exporter" of groundbreaking ideas about entrenched rights (Canada probably has a better claim), then there are certainly new ideas to be found in countries like Israel and South Africa. There is no sign in the citation patterns of this having happened either. The count for "other" citations (not Canadian, not English, not American) has remained modest, only once rising above 50 in a single calendar year. It may be true that the swing to entrenched human rights is a major development in recent global constitutionalism, but in terms of the Supreme Court's handling of the meaning of the Charter, an initial brief openness to some wider set of ideas has been replaced by an interpretation that is increasingly focused on Canadian precedents and Canadian judicial ideas.

8. ACADEMIC CITATIONS

I have spent some time looking at the way that the Supreme Court works with judicial citations, and exploring how it might cast some light upon the idea of a "spent" Charter revolution. However, the Canadian Supreme Court also cites other sources—specifically, it sometimes cites academic sources. To the extent that this, like foreign citations, is also a slightly unusual source of ideas it might also be thought of as providing a different stream of ideas to help fill the void as the Supreme Court rises to the challenge of generating an entirely new body of law. As an empirical test, then, I am once again looking for the double marker of my theory: *first*, a strong surge in the practice in the early years of the entrenched Charter, this followed by *second*, a pronounced and steady decline that appears sometime in the 1990s.

When I say that the Supreme Court sometimes cites academic material as well as prior judicial decisions, I am actually describing a development that is more recent and that was initially more controversial than one might assume. As recently as the 1950s, our Supreme Court had a firm practice of not allowing academic books or journals to be cited in arguments presented to the Court. Only in 1985 did the new Chief Justice Dickson change the reporting format of Supreme Court decisions to include a listing of "authors noted" to parallel the long-standing list of "cases noted," and my firm data and year-by-year counts therefore date from that period.

Why would academic citations matter? Citations to academic material are a way of expanding the universe from which judges draw the cues and their information and their theoretical orientation, and a way of involving a broader set of legal and academic professionals in the development of those ideas. Given that the books are often legal textbooks, the academic journal articles are a particular important dimension of this nexus, in that the turnaround time for submitted journal manuscripts (although much more leisurely than most academics would like) is considerably quicker than that for a book; and articles have the advantage that they are more focused than books and sketched on a smaller canvas. If members of the academic community want to contribute to the ideas that are being considered by the judges and incorporated in their judgement, they no longer need to wait to be invited by litigants to submit expert reports that will be incorporated in their litigation; instead, they can present their ideas through articles in law journals or through scholarly books, with some assurance that the judges are reading these sources and are willing to draw ideas from them.[52] Presumably the novelty of the Charter, and the

---

52 On the basis of the ongoing work of a graduate student working under my supervision, for example, it would seem that there is not a single article on federalism that has been published in a Canadian law journal that has not been cited by the Supreme Court of Canada at least once, clearly implying that the judges do read the journals.

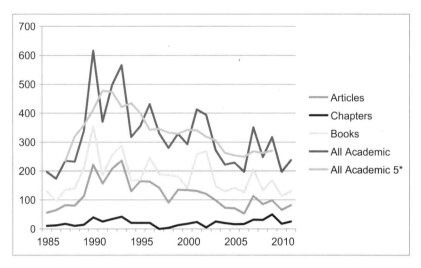

FIGURE 6.15 Count of "academic" citations, by year
* Five-year running average.

doctrinal void it created, would make this source of ideas more attractive than it had been before. This tendency is perhaps enhanced by the fact that judges over the last few decades are much more likely to have been drawn from the ranks of those lawyers who taught full- or part-time in law faculties. By a parallel logic, as the void is filled by new judicial decisions, the academic material would be squeezed out.

Since there are several possibly confusing lines in the graph in Figure 6.15, I should explain each in turn. The second-from-the-bottom line represents articles in legal journals (this being the only type of academic articles that the court ever cites), and the third-from-the-bottom line represents citations to books (almost always legal texts, and typically the long-standing law school reference texts that have gone through a steady string of revised editions). The bottom line is labelled "chapters" and the reference is to articles in edited collections of some kind, sometimes the result of a specific conference, and including published proceedings of conferences. The oscillating line of the top pair is the year-by-year total of the three lower lines; and the smoother line that runs through its oscillations is the five-year running average of the total count.

This figure, too, follows the usual shape, both overall and for books and articles (although not for the smaller count of chapters). There is a sharp rise through the late 1980s, peaking some time during the 1990s (although this peak is much earlier than the others), and then a slow slide back to the initial levels from which the jump began. I made a distinction above between the quicker turnaround time and closer focus of articles as compared with books. However, in terms of the figure, this argument need not be pressed: the retreat from books is just as pronounced and just as consistent as the retreat from legal journal articles. Both reflect a judiciary that no longer needs the up-to-date input and the quick turnaround time from the academic profession to fuel quickly developing judicial doctrine, and is increasingly content to work off the more traditional source of judicial citation, especially its own.

CONCLUSION

Some of these signals are stronger and clearer than others, like a trail of footprints where some stand clear and sharp and others are obscured or partially obliterated. Perhaps not one of them is completely convincing on its own, but it seems to me that they reinforce each other by following a similar pattern and that they all point to the same story: something very significant and destabilizing happened to the Supreme Court of Canada in the late 1980s and the early 1990s. If we didn't already know about the entrenchment of the Canadian Charter of Rights and Freedoms, these patterns would send us looking for something of the sort, just to explain this major (and ultimately containable) disruption of normal patterns of behaviour.

To summarize my string of footprints:

- During the "new Charter period," Charter cases made up more than a third of the caseload; today, they account for about half as large a proportion, even though the Court's total caseload has been declining steadily. In two years out of the past 10, the number of Charter cases decided has been in single digits.
- During the "new Charter period," non-unanimous decisions were twice as frequent for Charter cases as for non-Charter cases; today, non-Charter non-unanimity rates are unchanged, but Charter rates have fallen to join them.
- During the "new Charter period," judges wrote or joined minority reasons in 40 per cent of their Charter case panel

appearances, more than double the rate for non-Charter panel appearances; today, non-Charter minority participation rates are slightly lower, and Charter rates have fallen to roughly the same level.

- During the "new Charter period," more than half of all the words in Supreme Court cases were devoted to Charter cases, this being even more pronounced for minority rates (over two-thirds) than for decisions (over two-fifths); the same figures today are 20 per cent for decisions, 25 per cent for minority reasons.
- During the "new Charter period," the initial writer of majority reasons "lost the majority" more than a dozen times a year; now, the rate is less than half as high.
- During the "new Charter period," the Supreme Court made one half of all of its citations to judicial authority to cases that had been decided within the previous five years; today, it makes one half of all such citations to cases decided within the previous 12 years, signalling a much slower rate of replacement of "old" law with "new" law.
- During the "new Charter period," more than 10 per cent of all Supreme Court citations to its own prior cases was to minority reasons; today, they do so only half as often, suggesting that there is a diminished interest in alternative tracks to the main line of majority decisions.
- During the "new Charter period," there was a pronounced increase in the citation of American cases (cited 110 times per year) and "other" cases[53] (cited 30 times per year); today, American cases are cited less than 40 times a year, and other cases less than 20 times per year.
- During the "new Charter period," the Supreme Court cited academic sources—not even accepted by the Court 20 years earlier—more than 400 times per year; today, these have declined by almost half, and the decline has been more pronounced for academic journal articles than for references to the standard legal textbooks.

---

53 That is to say: not Canadian, not English, and not American.

It always was possible, of course, that any or all of these changes would be permanent in the sense of marking a new plateau, a "new normal" marking a permanent revolution. When I first discovered the big jump in the frequency of American citations in the late 1980s and early 1990s,[54] I was convinced that this was the new normal—not that "US citations per year" would continue their dramatic upward climb, but that they would stabilize at something like the much higher level I was finding for a string of years. This did not happen; instead, having ratcheted up to quite impressive temporary highs, they promptly slid back down again, and by the time of the McLachlin Court, they were back to the same levels as the 1950s and 1960s. Again and again, across these various empirical markers, I kept finding that these dramatic changes in behaviour did not indicate a new plateau but rather a high point followed by a drop-off, not the creation of a "new" normal but a return to an old one.

To put the point differently: in a real sense, this book has been "written backwards" in that I did not come up with the "end of revolution argument" and then go looking for data to support it. Had I done that, you would be right to be sceptical: as I warn my students all the time, let me pick the examples and I will win every argument. Here, the examples came first, in the form of two decades of ongoing empirically based research, and the argument gradually developed as the only way I could explain the parallel patterns of rise and fall, of destabilizing and restabilizing. If a whole string of practices characterized the Court for a while, but don't characterize it any more, then there must be some underlying phenomenon driving all these changes. The broader the range of don't-do-that-any-more practices, the greater the need for a deeper explanation. Again to cite Henderson: these things don't "just happen" and they are not simply reducible to personnel and personalities and leadership, they are driven by some major change to role or external circumstances.[55] Form follows function; performance responds to mission, context and challenge; significant change is always for a reason. So "the end of the Charter revolution" was not my premise, it was my conclusion, the only

---

54 Peter McCormick, "The Supreme Court of Canada and American Citations 1949–1994: A Statistical Overview," *Supreme Court Law Review* (2nd Series) 8 (1997): 499.

55 Henderson, "From *Seriatim* to Consensus and Back Again."

thing I could think of that would explain why all those interesting things that had emerged just recently were now disappearing.

My basic message is that the new constitutional revolution (a slightly broader concept than the Charter revolution that it includes) is over. The groundbreaking mission of the Supreme Court is largely accomplished because the ground has been broken, and the trails have not been blazed so much as paved. Interesting things will continue to happen from time to time, and there may be the occasional surprise, but basically the Court from now on will be working within the framework that it has spent the last 25 years constructing. Dealing with legal disputes against the background of settled law is what courts do all the time; in this sense, the Charter has become business as usual.

This really should not be a surprise; we should all have known that this would happen at some point, and two dozen years is ample time. What I have added to the argument is the demonstration that there are solid and objective statistical measures, as drawn from the Supreme Court's own performance and behaviour and utterances, which demonstrate the various stages of the evolution through which the Court has gone. In a variety of ways—caseload, length of reasons, frequency of minority reasons, citation patterns—the Court has been signalling the changes in its role, in transparent and understandable ways.

The patterns reinforce the general point we would always have made about the various Chief Justiceships. After the watershed period of the Laskin Court, the Dickson Court assumed the role of cautiously but firmly laying the basic framework for attaching specific meaning to the broad new constitutional structures; the Lamer Court aggressively pushed out the frontiers of the new doctrine; and the McLachlin Court has played a more modest and less confrontational consolidationist role. But this book represents a caution against turning these general descriptions into suggestions about character traits or personality features of the successive Chief Justices, grounding the performance instead in an evolution of that role that is the perfectly logical, even predictable, consequence of major constitutional change. To make the point by pushing it perhaps one small step too far: shuffle the three Chief Justices around within this sequence and they would have behaved differently, they would have been products of the period more than the periods were products of them. The strongest argument against attributing too much of the difference to the character and personality of the Chief Justice emerges from figure after figure—the measurable changes in the performance of the Court that I have been describing do not date from 2000, when the new Chief Justice took her place, but rather from some time closer to the middle of the 1990s. To the extent that there has been a consolidationist phase, it did not begin with McLachlin but earlier—even the temptation to identify it with the end of the "natural court" that was centred in the 1990s (i.e., with the departure of La Forest and Sopinka) errs by linking the shift to changes in personnel rather than to deeper changes in the role of the Court.

For years, I have introduced students to my constitutional law course by enthusing about the fact that the course is not only about dusty history but also about current events; I have told them to anticipate new Supreme Court decisions through the semester that the course outline would be adjusted to accommodate, and urged them to stay up with the national news so as to be ready to discuss them. It has been several years since the Court has really delivered on my promises; this chapter has explained why this has happened, and demonstrated why I should entertain more modest expectations for the future. For political scientists, it has been an exciting period as the Supreme Court has come to terms with its new role and turned the open poetic language of the new constitution into familiar and settled doctrine; what we now need to do is adjust our descriptions and our expectations to a quieter period as the Court's role shifts again, not to a pre-revolutionary quietism, but to post-revolutionary consolidation. To the extent that the Court's decisions continue to make it interesting and exciting, these are more likely to involve other issues—the indications from a combination of the current caseload and the headline-generating decisions would highlight both "new" areas like Aboriginal rights and more longstanding areas like federalism.

CONCLUSION

The Charter revolution is (largely) concluded and accomplished. The flow of blockbuster decisions that ambushed and often surprised provincial and federal governments and left them scrambling to salvage something from the wreckage, to fill unanticipated gaps in legislation or policy, has effectively come to an end. To be sure, from time to time there will still be Charter decisions that claim the news headlines, but these will be occasional rather that frequent—when they arise, they will, in the Chief Justice's own words, be something of a "surprise" to the Court itself. There will still be Supreme Court decisions that require us to adjust our thinking about particular tests or definitions or applications. There will be litigants who identify useful lacunae on the edges of the established doctrines, but these will tend to occasion fine-tuning rather than bold novelty—again to use the Chief Justice's own words, these will be "subtle interpretations" rather than bold transformative innovations. They will be border skirmishes on limited fronts, not the opening of some major new beachhead, and this because there are no longer any major beachheads left to open.

Why has this happened? Who is to blame? (Or, of course, if some readers were Charter sceptics, reluctant rather than enthusiastic followers of these transformations, not particularly happy to be tugged down the paths of enlightenment by our new judicial masters, this should perhaps be worded: Who deserves the credit?) Either way, and more neutrally, why has the mighty Charter river run dry?

At the risk of sounding anticlimactic, the answer is—nobody is to blame. What we have observed is the normal cycle for the judicial assimilation of policy or legislative or constitutional novelty, a cycle that plays itself out over and over again, although seldom on such a spectacular scale. (Of course, it can sometimes be the Court itself that introduces some destabilizing novelty that provokes a similar cycle—for example, the rethinking of federal and provincial responsibilities regarding the criminal law, triggered by the surprising decision in *Hauser*[1] in 1976, clarified and consolidated after some initial confusion in *Canadian National*[2] and *Wetmore*[3] in 1983. My point is the cycle of judicial accommodation to novelty, the relentless drive towards routinization and normalization, regardless of the source of the disruption.) New legal measures mean new questions without clear answers, and the proposed answers that are competing for judicial approval will advantage or disadvantage different sets of actors, will connect in different ways to the legal and policy past, will emphasize different values and different frames for assessing the alternatives and their consequences. This is one of the faces of litigation, as perfectly predictable a response to legal novelty as the snowplows are to a snowstorm; chasing legal uncertainty in the interests of clients is part of what good lawyers do, just as reducing that uncertainty by giving clear answers is part of what courts (and especially appellate courts, and double-especially national high courts) do. But every question answered clearly and definitively is a question that does not need to be asked again (or a question, if asked again, that requires a much stronger case to be made to justify a different or a significantly modified answer than it might have required to prevail in the first place). The big waves gradually become smaller waves, and they gradually become ripples.

D'Amato[4] usefully explores this from the other side—his point is that a legal/judicial system can never entirely eliminate uncertainty because

---

1 *R. v. Hauser*, [1979] 1 S.C.R. 984.

2 *A.G. (Can.) v. Can. Nat. Transportation, Ltd.*, [1983] 2 S.C.R. 206.

3 *R. v. Wetmore*, [1983] 2 S.C.R. 284.

4 Anthony D'Amato, "Legal Uncertainty," *California Law Review* 71 (1983): 1. For a rather more elaborate discussion, arguing for an equilibrium between legal certainty

litigants will chase, and seek to expand and to exploit, whatever uncertainties remain; and then, when a certain answer is given, they will once again pursue the possibly smaller elements of uncertainty that remain around the edges, or possibly back up and find a new and different angle and try to come at the same basic issue again from this new side. He presents the intellectually delightful picture of a constant tension between the two sides of the process, with uncertainty-generating lawyers on the one side and uncertainty-reducing judges on the other. Like the old argument that jailbreaks are the natural outcome of the endless tournament between prisoners and guards (because there are more prisoners, and because they work full time trying to get out), so uncertainty is the natural outcome of the interaction between lawyers and judges, since there are more lawyers and they are working full time to maximize and exploit the uncertainty. But my suggestion is not that the uncertainty ever disappears entirely, just that the tendency in any given sector of importance is for the uncertainty to be steadily reduced, for the temporary upward blips to be methodically reduced. Since it is only the initial huge surge of uncertainty, and the initial big steps towards creating predictability in its midst, that attract attention and excitement, this is enough to make my case.

I should stop to deal with lacunae of my own. Readers may think that I am straining mightily to avoid the obvious, constructing an elaborate narrative frame when there is in fact an elephant in the centre of the room, which is itself a powerful reason for at least part of the trends. That elephant is the fact that prime ministers appoint Supreme Court justices, and although that appointment process has undergone a somewhat bewildering string of minor configurations and reconfigurations in recent years, none of them have seriously reduced the prime minister's considerable discretionary capacity to appoint judges who are (let me word this carefully) facing the right direction on the major issues that are likely to come before the Court. Since there are some reasons to think that Canada's current prime minister may be less enthusiastic about the Charter project than some of the prime ministers who preceded him, and since that prime minister has been more lucky that many in terms of Supreme Court

---

and uncertainty, see Giuseppe Dari-Mattiacci and Bruno Deffains, "Uncertainty of Law and the Legal Process," *Journal of Institutional and Theoretical Economics* 163 (2007): 627.

vacancies to be filled in fairly short order, one might wonder if this is not part—and perhaps a large part—of any change in style or direction.

The notion that prime ministers—if they serve long enough, if they have enough vacancies to fill—can shape the Supreme Court is not something that we in Canada have talked about until very recently, although it has for some time been a staple of American political contestation. I do not wish to imply that the justices in any sense take instructions from the prime minister who appointed them (and in any event they regularly outlast their appointer); nor (again unlike the United States) can we even use "party of appointing prime minister" as a major cleavage in the Court's voting behaviour. But it is absolutely clear that one recent prime minister—namely, Trudeau—used the appointment power for a major restructuring of the Supreme Court starting in the late 1960s, a process which clearly gave us a "modern Supreme Court" that was distinctly different from its predecessors in many ways.

Perhaps, then, the changes that I am describing in the style and direction are best discussed not in terms of "the Dickson Court" (or whatever), but in terms of the prime ministers whose appointees dominate the seats on the Court. Maybe we should not be labelling courts by using the name of the Chief Justice but rather the prime minister who did most of the appointing. For example, in the 1970s, it could have been called the Trudeau Court, which had replaced the Diefenbaker Court, and (more recently) the Harper Court has replaced the Chrétien/Martin Court. This suggestion is all the more credible in light of that fact that several of our prime ministers—Trudeau and Mulroney in particular—appointed high numbers of judges (see Table 7.1).

Trudeau clearly stands out, appointing no fewer than 10 justices to the Supreme Court, including three (Laskin, Dickson, and Lamer) who became Chief Justices and whose Chief Justiceships spanned a quarter century.[5] He also appointed two Chief Justices (Laskin and Dickson)— although, with the extremely important but very lonely exception of Laskin, it is seniority (length of service on the Supreme Court) that is

---

5 There was never a time during this period when all nine justices on the Court had been appointed by the same prime minister—the Diefenbaker-appointed Ritchie was the only exception to an "all-Trudeau" Court, and Lamer was the only justice who prevented an all-Mulroney Court.

TABLE 7.1 Appointment of Judges by Prime Minister, 1977–2012

PRIME MINISTER	TOTAL APPOINTED	FIFTH APPOINTMENT	DATE
Trudeau	10	W.Z. Estey	1977
Mulroney	8	Gonthier	1989
Chrétien	5	Fish	2003
Harper	5[6]	Wagner	2012

clearly the major factor in the selection of a Chief Justice, so there is perhaps not a great deal to be read into that. Although there is a clear case to be made for the idea that Trudeau used his appointments to transform the Court, none of the other dates in the final column point to anything particularly useful.[7] The one "fifth Justice appointment" date that seems at first glance to mean anything is Chrétien's appointment of Fish in 2003, the moment when the balance on the Court tipped from Mulroney appointments to Chrétien appointments; this is very close to the Charter decisions in 2005 that I have suggested make that date a reasonable candidate for "Charter high point." This is the emergence not of "Harper's Court" but rather of Chrétien's; and the first Harper appointment does not happen until Rothstein in 2006.[8] If Harper's first appointment[9] was not until the year after the most credible turning point in the Court's behaviour, then clearly there is something going on that is driven by something other than the appointment dynamic. Trying to find a direct political electoral driver for the Supreme Court's shift in behaviour does

---

6 Depending, of course, what happens with the Nadon appointment as of 2014, and with two Quebec vacancies that will push the number to seven.

7 Although 1977 seems a little too early for the purpose; it is more plausible to see Lamer's appointment in 1979 as the one that gave Laskin a reliable if narrow Trudeau-appointed majority.

8 An even weaker argument would be to suggest that the justices saw the writing on the wall when Harper became prime minister, and began to shift their behaviour accordingly—but if the Supreme Court is going to be this responsive to the election returns, the whole Charter project of entrenching rights to put them beyond the reach of transient majorities is completely pointless, and I make no such suggestion.

9 That from a short list that had been drawn up by the previous Liberal government, with the appointment process caught in mid-step by the election that made Harper prime minister.

not take us anywhere, which is perhaps reassuring; on the other hand, if there is going to be some jurisprudential consequences of Harper's selection preferences, there has not yet been time for this to emerge.

But if the electoral connection does not explain the phenomenon I have been describing, then what does? It may be that court-carried rights dynamics have a natural life cycle to them, and that life cycle is something between two and three decades long. For example, consider the United States. From the celebratory rhetoric in that country, one would think that the entrenchment of the Bill of Rights for 200 plus years, combined with a robustly independent Supreme Court, has given them 200 years of rights-driven judicial activity. With the exception of sporadic episodes around freedom of expression, this is not at all the case; the Supreme Court's reputation as rights-driven really dates back only to the Warren Court, which completely transformed the way that people think about national high courts and their political potential.[10] Magliocca would put this initiating date a bit earlier; he suggests that it was in the 1930s that the first 10 amendments began to be (in his term) "canonized" by being lumped together as "The Bill of Rights" and celebrated as an American constitutional accomplishment that contrasted starkly with the less happy constitutional adventures of other countries.[11] At this, he is pointing to the politicians (specifically President Franklin Delano Roosevelt) rather than to the courts; the first judicial invocation of that Bill of Rights as something pre-emptively important or special was not until *West Virginia v. Barnette*[12] in 1943, at the very earliest. What both suggest, however, is that the judicially daring high profile "Bill of Rights" period has a clear starting point, and that starting point is not the eighteenth century and arguably not the nineteenth century—and quite possibly not the first half of the twentieth century, either.

But by the 1990s, that impetus had completely dried up; when we talk about a constitutional rights revolution in that country, that picture

---

10 See, for example, Lucas A. Powe, *The Warren Court and American Politics* (Boston: Harvard University Press, 2002).

11 See Gerard Magliocca, "Becoming the Bill of Rights," Indiana University Robert H. McKinney School of Law Research Paper No. 2013–16 (March 20, 2013), retrieved June 16, 2014 from http://papers.ssrn.com/sol3/papers.cfm?abstract_id=2236457.

12 *West Virginia State Board of Education v. Barnette*, 319 U.S. 624 (1943).

is built around the admittedly spectacular actions of the Warren Court (1953–69) (and some incremental changes that the Warren Court judges were still able to rack up through the early years of the Burger Court [1969–86]). If you want to talk about constitutional rights-driven judicial activism today, it is not the United States Supreme Court you would be studying;[13] for a while (but no longer), it would have been ours; I am not sure who it would be today. The spotlight on judicial power focused on entrenched rights that has been so pronounced a feature of politics for decades seems to have swung on to something else; I will discuss later in this chapter whether it has swung away from courts or just away from the rights-promoting activities of courts. To suggest that Charter revolutions or their like have a self-limiting period of high-profile prominence, followed by stasis or decline, is therefore not without precedent.

Of course, even if there was some political or public pushback, this would itself be part of the accommodation cycle. Courts enjoy considerable autonomy, and they exercise the measured professionalism that earns and deserves that autonomy, but they do not reside on some other planet and hand down decisions in pure Olympian detachment, nor would we want them to. As the recent American literature on judicial behaviour frames it, courts (and especially appellate courts whose small numbers and physical proximity facilitate such discussions) are to some extent consciously and deliberately strategic—they are fully aware that they operate in an environment that includes many other actors, and they are most effective when they anticipate the reactions of those other actors and respond accordingly. There may be times when justice must be done, and done immediately, but there are other times when the destabilizing confrontation can be postponed for a later and more fortuitous occasion—perhaps by denying leave to appeal, or by deciding narrowly rather than by engaging the broader issues, or by engaging in what the American literature calls "issue fluidity" whereby the Court broadens or narrows or otherwise alters the question that the litigants thought they

---

13 This is a common observation among comparative law scholars in recent years; see, for example, David Law, "The Declining Influence of the United States Constitution," *New York University Law Review* 87 (2012): 762.

were asking.[14] It is not fanciful to think that judges at the conference table argue about whether or not now is the time to move from the immediate case to deal with some much broader issue of which it is only a subset; these disagreements sometimes show up in minority reasons.

But this is secondary to my central thesis, which would operate regardless of whether or not there was a public or political pushback of any significance, or whether the judges were docile or defiant in the face of such a pushback. Rather, I am simply invoking the most banal of observations: judges in the courts seek to be predictable. This is why they follow precedent, carefully linking as many elements as possible to the reasons contained in a string of earlier (although these days not *that* much earlier) decisions of their own and other courts. The implicit message, which any justice would cheerfully make explicit if you asked them is this: "Almost everything I am saying has been said before, and had you done your research my conclusions would have been completely predictable." This may sometimes be a little disingenuous, because the issues can be very complex and there may have been other approaches and other lines of precedent that were not transparently wrong (and that have in fact been picked up by a minority of judges on the immediate panel), but this mode of decisional presentation is both serious and functional. Judges in the courts, and especially appeal courts, strive to be predictable.

Novelty happens, to be sure. New governments may use their mandate to challenge the status quo with policy innovations; constitutions may be amended in major or minor ways; the Court may from time to time be persuaded to revisit long-standing but dated doctrines; social changes may result in long-standing rules being applied to rather different circumstances and assumptions. But the Court's reaction is always the same; it may or may not resist the changes (Magliocca presents American history of a cycle of pre-emption, confrontation, and accommodative surrender) but always it will work over time to contain novelty, to routinize it, to make it not novel any more. This may take some time, and it may

---

14 See, for example, Kevin T. McGuire and Barbara Palmer, "Issue Fluidity on the United States Supreme Court," *American Political Science Review* 89 (1995): 691; Barbara Palmer, "Issue Fluidity and Agenda Setting on the Warren Court," *Political Research Quarterly* 52 (1999): 39.

be interrupted by divisions in the Court or new appointments that shift the voting balance, but it always moves steadily and relentlessly in that direction.

Many Supreme Court decisions perform this function consciously and directly, as the wording of decisions reveals—the Court presents itself as clearing up possible misunderstandings from earlier decisions, as clarifying tests or procedures, as striving to reconcile apparent divergent trends emerging in the caselaw, as considering scenarios that allow it to address various fact permutations and combinations.[15] Supreme Court decisions seldom simply resolve the dispute in the immediate case; typically, decisions are framed as answering more basic and more general questions so that these questions do not have to be asked again. And then the Court deals with ancillary questions in the same spirit, with firm statements and clarifications that hopefully mean that those questions as well do not need to be relitigated. Years ago, Posner and Landes wrote about the concept of the "superprecedent"—that is to say, a decision that was "so effective in defining the requirements of the law that it prevents legal disputes from arising in the first place, or, if they do arise, induces them to be settled without litigation."[16] Put so baldly, of course, such a decision is probably not even possible; it presents such a counsel of perfection that not even Dworkin's Justice Hercules could hope to achieve it save on the rarest of occasions.[17] But although it cannot be accomplished, it can be approximated; good judicial decisions are the ones that come as close as possible to achieving this, and the progressive accomplishment of judicial decisions from an effective and coherent bench is to lay down a string

---

15 Often in the form of "companion cases" that raise related issues and are considered together, the decisions all being handed down on the same day and systematically referring to each other.

16 William M. Landes and Richard A. Posner, "Legal Precedent: A Theoretical and Empirical Analysis," *Journal of Law & Economics* 19 (1976): 249, at 251.

17 More recently, American usage has considered an alternative definition of a superprecedent—"cases that are so firmly entrenched that they ought not to be overturned despite being in error." Daniel Solove, "The Problem with Superprecedents," Concurring Opinions Weblog, retrieved October 30, 2005, from http://www .concurringopinions.com. There is considerable academic scepticism as to whether there are indeed such things, but in any case my own usage draws on the earlier Landes and Posner usage.

of such decisions that progressively reduce uncertainty and constantly amplify predictability on a steadily expanding number of issues.

In this context, it is the paradoxical mission of lawyers to *maximize* uncertainty by finding, and seeking to exploit to the benefit of their clients, whatever cracks and crannies of uncertainty remain in the emerging doctrines. However, to the extent that these are successful, the lacunae they identify are dealt with in precisely the same way—through decisions that answer questions in such a way as to provide precedents that make it unnecessary to ask the same (or too closely similar) questions again, because the Court's answer will have become predictable. By definition, the predictable Court does not generate surprises for the thoughtful watcher; and even if the Court cannot possibly render itself perfectly predictable, it is continually working towards being as predictable as reasonably possible, under the circumstances.

To concede the obvious: this is a book that has been written in the passive voice—it has all been about how the Charter has been interpreted by the Supreme Court. But this sentence really must be turned around, at least briefly, to deal with the flip side of this particular coin: what is it that judges do, and how do they do it, and why do they do it that way and not some other way? What are the motives or the forces or the rules that guide them in their decisions, that direct them towards one set of decisions and one line of judicial doctrine rather than another, that sometimes lead them to change their minds dramatically and other times to regard themselves as bound by precedent, which is to say by the decisions and the interpretations of their predecessors? What is the guiding theory of judicial interpretation that has lain behind my narrative?

This is not an easy question to answer, because the study of judicial behaviour has continuously shifted in terms of the current idea of the best way of understanding what judges do. My description will therefore tend to the eclectic rather than the narrowly focused, and some of the elements will be rather obvious.

The first element of judicial decision-making is of course the words of the relevant document, which are never enough in themselves to settle the big questions but that create parameters beyond which judges cannot go. I take it that the first rule of interpretation is the "plain meaning" rule, and it is only when the words have created ambiguities, or when different sets of words point different directions, or the words as written don't seem to deal directly with the immediate issue that a more complex search for meaning takes over. Push "the words" too far, and you wind up with literalism or formalism, with a mechanical and replicable objective process that generates a single outcome. The Supreme Court has explicitly repudiated formalism (or, in Dickson's phrase from *Southam*,[18] "the austerity of tabulated legalism") in favour of an approach that it has constantly identified (in some 400 decisions) as "contextualism."[19] But the first step towards understanding why the Court is saying what it is saying is to read the words it is talking about. Carefully.

Second, the judges take very seriously the need to fit what they are saying in with what the Court itself (and lower Canadian courts and to some limited extent the courts of other countries) has done with these and similar issues in the light of these and similar texts. The citation of judicial authority is a major component in the explanation of why a particular set of judges has gone a particular direction (and this is not a matter of "pick your outcome and then just choose the caselaw to justify it" because the explanatory centre of judicial citation is very much common to all Supreme Court judges). It is not that these earlier precedents cannot be modified over time, because they definitely can be; indeed, they can be directly and explicitly repudiated (*Health Service Workers* at para. 22 is the paradigmatic example), although this is rare. Rather, they are usually changed gradually, and reversed only reluctantly—but the gradual incremental change is relentless and constant. The earlier caselaw is a "rut in the road" that is hard, but not impossible, to climb out of.

This must sound more than a little naive, as if I were trying to return to an earlier view of there being a sharp separation between law and politics, such that the two could operate independently of each other. This view, of course, was thoroughly discredited by the legal realists about a century ago, with their firm insistence that judges and courts were very

---

18 *Hunter et al. v. Southam Inc.*, [1984] 2 S.C.R. 145.

19 As the Supreme Court described it on one occasion, this approach emphasizes the importance of the "historical, social and economic context" in which the legislation was created and/or the Charter claim presented. *R. v. Laba*, [1994] 3 S.C.R. 965. For a fuller discussion, see Shalin M. Sugunasiri, "Contextualism: The Supreme Court's New Standard of Judicial Analysis and Accountability," *Dalhousie Law Journal* 22 (1999): 126.

deeply embedded in the political, social, and economic realities of their time, such that the idea of strict separation could only be a fiction. But if there is an emerging trend in the academic literature today, it is a growing sense that the more formal legal elements of judicial decision-making have to be taken more seriously, as constraints on the way judges see their available alternatives and as strong influences in their own right.[20] Judges are neither totally free to decide as they please (as distinct from how they think they should) nor are they (usually) totally constrained.

Third, judges have their own professional values and priorities, developed over years of legal and judicial practice; this is what they bring to the bench with them, and this is the standard against which they measure their own behaviour. This will be subtly different for any pair of judges, and more significantly different for some of them, so these individual professional commitments will play out differently, depending on where they locate themselves within the Supreme Court at any given time and, to some extent, within the broader judiciary. The slightly misleading term in the literature for this is attitudinalism,[21] which the judges themselves tend to resent because it makes them sound as if they were pre-programmed to find quasi-reflexively in favour of particular types of litigant on particular sorts of issues. But find a term for personal variability that is less visceral and more reflective, more professional, more principled, and more nuanced, and it approaches common sense, and it explains why even the most conscientious and rigorous of judges can sometimes disagree quite vehemently with each other (as, for example, Laskin and Dickson clearly did on federalism issues).

Push the point a bit further, and it starts to become possible to predict what different judges on the court are probably going to do, at least

---

20 See, for example, Michael A. Baily and Forrest Maltzman, *The Constrained Court: Law, Politics and the Decisions Justices Make* (Princeton University Press, 2013); and Pamela Corley, Amy Steigerwalt and Artemus Ward, *The Puzzle of Unanimity: Consensus on the United States Supreme Court* (Stanford, CA: Stanford Law Books, 2013).

21 Ostberg and Wetstein tried to apply an attitudinal analysis to the Supreme Court of Canada, but had to admit that, although their model worked reasonably well in some areas of law, it was not at all useful for others. See C.L. Ostberg and Matthew E. Wetstein, *Attitudinal Decision Making in the Supreme Court of Canada* (Vancouver: UBC Press, 2007).

in general terms and over some reasonable run of cases.[22] If the decision-supporting tendencies of individual judges are generally predictable—to some limited but not negligible extent and possibly in some types of issues more than others—then this is one sense in which over the long run and in very general terms the Court can be "steered." It is the government of the day that makes, in a very modestly constrained way, the choice of which new judges will fill the vacancies on the Court; and a string of such choices has the potential for changing the tone and even the direction of the Court. Whether this is a good thing—because it prevents the Court and the government from being perpetually at loggerheads—or a bad thing—because it undermines the desired degree of separation between law and politics—I will leave to the judgement of others, but it is a factor that must be acknowledged.

Fourth, judges respond to effective arguments based on relevant legal material. They are attached to, and rely heavily on, argument, both in the sense that two parties and a range of interveners have been arguing to persuade the judges, and in the sense that the Supreme Court itself has only the persuasive argumentative powers of its own reasons to direct behaviour and command respect. One indication of this attachment to specific ideas and the power of specific nuanced arguments is the fact that judges clearly focus on reasons as well as on outcome—hence the significant number of "separate concurrences" which agree with the majority on appropriate outcome but differ, sometimes very significantly, on the reasoning that leads to that outcome.[23] (The fact that dissenting judges often write their own solo dissents rather than always signing on to a single minority position is

---

22 I hasten to add that such predictions are much harder to make than most people think. South of the border, the website Fantasy SCOTUS (http://www.fantasyscotus .net) allows individuals, usually organized in terms of "teams" within "leagues" of various sorts—such as Faculties of Law at various universities—to predict what the USSC will decide in upcoming cases. The overall success rates of these predictions are not impressive, even in terms of outcome rather than actual vote, running just under 60 per cent in 2011 and just over 60 per cent in 2012—tossing a coin would, over any long run, probably give you 50 per cent. Ratchet up your measure of success—what was the vote? who was on each side?—and the success rate falls even further, even for the highly polarized USSC.

23 See Peter McCormick, "Standing Apart: Separate Concurrence and the Supreme Court of Canada, 1984–2006," *McGill Law Journal* 53 (2008): 137.

a similar indication.) Another is the fact that judges clearly change their minds with reasonable frequency during the write-and-circulate process that follows the post-hearing judicial conference, sometimes changing the precedential set of explanatory reasons carries the majority of the panel and sometimes changing the outcome as well; on some indications, this happens in fully one-quarter of all the non-unanimous decisions of the Supreme Court.[24] A third is what has recently been referred to as "the puzzle of unanimity"—the fact that these disparate individuals with their disparate attitudinal tendencies still manage to reach complete agreement on a surprisingly large number of the cases that are brought before them.[25] Reasons matter, and arguments matter, and therefore persuasion before the court and within the court has some real traction.

Fifth, judges respond to the expectations that are placed upon them by the society of the day—in terms of the relevant publics (a weasel phrase, I admit, to be understood as neither reducing to nor completely ignoring "the public" in its broadest sense), and in terms of the anticipated reactions of political authorities. As James Kelly so cogently pointed out: in the early decades of the Charter, it was entirely mistaken to think of the expansion of Charter doctrine in terms of "governments versus the courts" because the governments were by and large dominated by the people who had put the Charter in place, such that both the courts and the governments were essentially "pro-Charter."[26] This is not to deny that some decisions were unexpected or inconvenient from time to time, just to suggest that both were in a real sense facing much the same direction on Charter issues. Things are different today. At the very least, we can point

---

24 See Peter McCormick "'Was It Something I Said?' Losing the Majority on the Modern Supreme Court of Canada, 1984–2011," *Osgoode Hall Law Journal* 50 (2012): 93.

25 Pamela Corley, Amy Steigerwalt, and Artemus Ward, *The Puzzle of Unanimity: Consensus on the United States Supreme Court* (Stanford, CA: Stanford Law Books, 2013). The unanimity rates for the Supreme Court of Canada have long been considerably higher.

26 See James Kelly, *Governing with the Charter: Legislative and Judicial Activism and Framers' Intent* (Vancouver: UBC Press, 2005). Kelly's major argument was that the net effect of the Charter was to sideline elected legislatures as the experts in the government and the experts on the courts got on with business, but this is another matter altogether.

out that that generation of politicians has passed from the scene, and (a separate point, which is equally important) a number of governments are rather less Charter friendly, one might even say some are Charter-hostile. This makes a considerable difference—courts do not just want to proclaim truth, but to contribute to a movement of the law in a desirable direction, and this calls for a strategic calculation of the reactions of other actors. Even the same set of judges would behave differently in a different political environment; when the weather turns colder, the judges wear sweaters, too. I have pointed out that the shifts in the style of Charter decisions do not coincide at all with personnel changes on the Court; but it is beyond argument that they coincide with major personnel changes in political office. I pointed out earlier that the Court's "Charter-expanding" decisions seem largely to have ended in 2007, and their much more Charter-constraining judgements seem to have started in 2008. It cannot be entirely coincidence that there was a major change in government and in political style in Canada in 2006. It is also undeniable that personnel changes on the Court will, over time, have their own contributing effect; what is perhaps surprising is how much change preceded this shift in membership.

Sixth, the Supreme Court can only answer the questions that it is asked, and to some extent it can only deal with them if they have been asked (researched, grounded, and presented) in a thorough way with a comparably thorough response. Again to draw on Epp's analysis: a Court can only undertake a rights revolution if the groundwork has been prepared, if civil society has generated the rights-promoting and rights-supporting organizations that will flesh out the apparent but misleading simplicity of a Charter claim.[27] These organizations as well have to respond to changes in public and governmental mood. A victory on a Charter claim is only a first step, because the fruits of that victory have to be organizationally and procedurally incorporated by a variety of actors in a variety of ways.[28] This may explain the shifting caseload of the Court, and the smaller number of Charter cases—both in absolute numbers and as a proportion of

---

27 Charles R. Epp, *The Rights Revolution: Lawyers, Activists and Supreme Courts in Comparative Perspective* (Chicago: University of Chicago Press, 1998).

28 In a sense, this is the point of Epp's second book, *Making Rights Real: Activists, Bureaucrats and the Creation of the Legalistic State* (Chicago: University of Chicago Press, 2009).

a generally smaller caseload—which is not to deny that the Court's own opaque procedures for deciding when to grant applications for leave to appeal may also play a role.

The Canadian Charter of Rights and Freedoms represented the grandest imaginable collection of brand-new constitutional questions that came with no clearly established answers; indeed, it even contained some lapidary-sounding phrases ("the principles of fundamental justice") that came with no judicial history whatsoever attached to them. For an extended period, this meant that many questions raised by Charter cases had no precedentially predictable answers, which in turn meant decisions in those cases were always something of a surprise. But every answer crossed something off the list of questions that had no clear binding precedential history, every decision narrowed the set of cases for which there was no strongly relevant precedent, and after a while the list became short and the significance of each of the remaining questions became smaller. To use McLachlin's metaphor at the beginning of her Chief Justiceship: after a while, the heavy lifting has been done and only the smaller and lighter stuff remains. "Smaller and lighter" does not always or necessarily mean "trivial and uninteresting," but it does mean that the day of the blockbusters is over.

But if the Charter revolution is over, does this mean that the judicial power revolution is over? It was certainly the Charter, and the Patriation controversy that preceded it, that propelled the Supreme Court of Canada to a visible central role on the Canadian political stage in a way and to an extent that had never been seen before. Vacancies on the Supreme Court fuel public speculation about possible candidates for appointment; this, to put it mildly, never used to happen. An incoming Chief Justice today, on the rare occasion that there is such a vacancy, does the rounds of the major news media in a way that has no earlier counterpart. If the Charter has been their spotlight, does the end of the Charter revolution imply a return to relative obscurity for judges?

Personally, I very much doubt it. We as a people are now accustomed to a Supreme Court that plays a prominent and visible role in political controversies. That wording may be jarring, so let me rephrase: many political actors are now aware that many political controversies (and by no means only those raising Charter issues) have important legal and constitutional aspects on which the Supreme Court can be invited to pronounce. Lacking an American-style "political-questions" doctrine,[29] our Court has a limited capacity for evading this recruitment into controversy. A recent string of interesting cases (most particularly the *Securities Reference*) suggests that the new centre of the spotlight may be federalism issues. Or, in the aftermath of the Idle No More protests, as the more established First Nations leaders struggle to regain their point positions, perhaps it will be issues of Aboriginal rights and governance. Nor should we ignore the potential of apparently dustier and less exciting angles such as administrative law—as cases like *Trinity Western* and *St.-Jérôme* showed, these provide alternate and less immediately provocative ways of dealing with what could have been major Charter issues.

It has been obvious for some time that there is a shift in style and direction going on within the Supreme Court. This shows up in my empirical data— there are not just more non-unanimous cases, but also non-unanimous cases involving either more fragmentation of the panels or larger blocs of minority-reason judges rather than solo efforts. As I have already suggested, cases like *Fraser* display disagreements that spill over the Court's usual practices of polite courtesy. I have suggested above that to date this is not primarily attributable to the growing ranks of Harper judges confronting the shrinking ranks of Chrétien/Martin judges; this is a further element of change that will work itself into the jurisprudence in the coming years.

I have spoken only of "the end of the Charter revolution" and described this in terms of consolidation; to revert to a military metaphor, the Charter troops are no longer pushing forward but digging in, and sometimes pulling back to more defensible territory first. It is not beyond the realm of possibility that I have caught the Court at a moment of change and mistaken it for a new consolidation. Perhaps a decade from now we will be talking about a major rollback and someone will write about this current decade in more dramatic terms: a "Charter rollback" or even "the Charter counter-revolution" as major doctrines are watered down or solid Charter precedents are reversed in the same way that the McLachlin Court (temporarily) reversed the *Labour Trilogy* (or at least tried to). For the present, however, the "end of the revolution" will do. Let's wait and see what happens next.

---

29 This is part of the legacy of the *Operation Dismantle* case, and a reason for taking its contribution to constitutional law seriously.

CASES CITED

Alberta v. Hutterian Brethren of Wilson Colony, 2009 SCC 37
Andrews v. Law Society of British Columbia, [1989] 1 S.C.R. 143
A.G. (Can.) v. Can. Nat. Transportation, Ltd., [1983] 2 S.C.R. 206
Attorney General of Canada v. Lavell, [1974] S.C.R. 1349
Attorney General of Quebec v. Grondin, [1983] 2 S.C.R. 364
Attorney General (Que.) v. Kellogg's Co. of Canada et al., [1978] 2 S.C.R. 211
Birks v. City of Montreal, [1955] S.C.R. 799
Bliss v. Attorney General of Canada, [1979] 1 S.C.R. 183
Boucher v. The King, [1951] S.C.R. 265
Bruker v. Markovitz, 2007 SCC 54
Canada (Attorney General) v. Bedford, 2013 SCC 72
Canada (Attorney General) v. Hislop, [2007] 1 S.C.R. 429, 2007 SCC 10
Canada (Attorney General) v. PHS Community Services Society, 2011 SCC 44, [2011] 3 S.C.R. 134
Canada (Human Rights Commission) v. Taylor, [1990] 3 S.C.R. 892
Canada (Prime Minister) v. Khadr, [2010] 1 S.C.R. 44, 2010 SCC 3
Central Hudson Gas and Electric Corp. v. Public Service Commission, 447 U.S. 557 (1980)
Chaoulli v. Quebec (Attorney General), [2005] 1 S.C.R. 791, 2005 SCC 35
Chromiak v. The Queen, [1980] 1 S.C.R. 471
Citizens United v. Federal Election Commission, 558 U.S. 310 (2010)
Congrégation des témoins de Jéhovah de St.-Jérôme-Lafontaine v. Lafontaine (Village), [2004] S.C.R. 650, 2004 SCC 48
Corbiere v. Canada (Minister of Indian and Northern Affairs), [1999] 2 S.C.R. 203
Doucet-Boudreau v. Nova Scotia (Minister of Education), [2003] 3 S.C.R. 3
Dred Scott v. Sandford, 60 U.S. 393 (1857)
Dunmore v. Ontario (Attorney General), [2001] 3 S.C.R. 1016, 2001 SCC 94

R. v. Great West News Ltd., [1970] 4 C.C.C. 307
R. v. Hauser, [1979] 1 S.C.R. 984
R. v. Kapp, [2008] 2 S.C.R. 483, 2008 SCC 41
R. v. Keegstra, [1990] 3 S.C.R. 892
R. v. Laba, [1994] 3 S.C.R. 965
R. v. Latimer, 2001 SCC 1, [2001] 1 S.C.R. 3
R. v. Malmo-Levine; R. v. Caine, [2003] 3 S.C.R. 571, 2003 SCC 74
R. v. Mills, [1999] 3 S.C.R. 668
R. v. Morgentaler, [1988] 1 S.C.R. 301
R. v. N.S., 2012 SCC 72
R. v. O'Connor, [1995] 4 S.C.R. 411
R. v. Oakes, [1986] 1 S.C.R. 103
R. v. Rose, [1998] 3 S.C.R. 262
R. v. Sawyer, [1992] 3 S.C.R. 809
R. v. Seaboyer; R. v. Gayme, [1991] 2 S.C.R. 577
R. v. Sharpe, [2001] 1 S.C.R. 45; 2001 SCC 2
R. v. Shelley, [1981] 2 S.C.R. 196
R. v. Sparrow, [1990] 1 S.C.R. 1075
R. v. Therens, [1985] 1 S.C.R. 613
R. v. Wetmore, [1983] 2 S.C.R. 284
R. v. Zundel, [1992] 2 S.C.R. 731
Re: Agricultural Marketing Act, [1978] 2 S.C.R. 1198
Re: Board of Commerce, [1922] 1 A.C. 191
Re: B.C. Motor Vehicle Act, [1985] 2 S.C.R. 486
Re: Manitoba Language Rights, [1985] 1 S.C.R. 721
Re: Objection by Quebec to a Resolution to amend the Constitution, [1982] 2 S.C.R. 793
Re: Public Service Employee Relations Act (Alta.), [1987] 1 S.C.R. 313
Re: Remuneration of Judges of the Prov. Court of P.E.I., [1997] 3 S.C.R. 3
Re: Residential Tenancies Act, 1979, [1981] 1 S.C.R. 714
Re: Resolution to amend the Constitution (Patriation Reference), [1981] 1 S.C.R. 753
Re: Validity of Section 5 (a) Dairy Industry Act (Margarine Reference), [1949] S.C.R. 1
Reference re Public Service Employee Relations Act (Alta.), [1987] 1 S.C.R. 313
Reference re Remuneration of Judges of the Prov. Court of P.E.I., [1997] 3 S.C.R. 3
Reference re Secession of Quebec, [1998] 2 S.C.R. 217
Reference re Securities Act 2011 SCC 66
Reference re Senate Reform 2014 SCC 32
Robertson and Rosetanni v. The Queen, [1963] S.C.R. 651
Rodriguez v. British Columbia (Attorney General), [1993] 3 S.C.R. 519
Roncarelli v. Duplessis, [1959] S.C.R. 121
Ross v. New Brunswick School District No. 15, [1996] 1 S.C.R. 825
Russell v. The Queen, (1882) 7App Cas 829
RWDSU v. Saskatchewan, [1987] 1 S.C.R. 460
Saskatchewan Human Rights Commission v. Whatcott, 2013 SCC 1
Saumur v. City of Quebec, [1953] 2 S.C.R. 299
Saumur et al. v. Procureur général du Québec, [1964] S.C.R. 252
Sauvé v. Canada (Attorney General), [1993] 2 S.C.R. 438
Sauvé v. Canada (Chief Electoral Officer), [2002] 3 S.C.R. 519, 2002 SCC 68
Schachter v. Canada, [1992] 2 S.C.R. 679
Seneca College v. Bhadauria, [1981] 2 S.C.R. 181
Singh v. Minister of Employment and Immigration, [1985] 1 S.C.R. 177

Smith v. California, 361 U.S. 147 (1959)
Sobeys Stores Ltd. v. Yeomans and Labour Standards Tribunal (N.S.), [1989] 1 S.C.R. 238
Somerville v. Canada (Attorney General), (1996), 184 A.R. 241 (C.A.)
Switzman v. Elbing, [1957] S.C.R. 285
Syndicat Northcrest v. Amselem, 2004 SCC 47
Thibaudeau v. Canada, [1995] 2 S.C.R. 627
Trinity Western University v. College of Teachers, [2001] 1 S.C.R. 772, 2001 SCC 31
United States v. Burns, [2001] 1 S.C.R. 283, 2001 SCC 7
United States v. Carolene Products Co., 304 U.S. 144 [1938]
Valente v. The Queen, [1985] 2 S.C.R. 673
Vancouver (City) v. Ward, 2010 SCC 27
Virginia State Board of Pharmacy v. Virginia Citizens Consumer Council, 425 U.S. 748 (1976)
Vriend v. Alberta, [1998] 1 S.C.R. 493
W. (V.) v. S. (D.), [1996] 2 S.C.R. 108
West Virginia State Board of Education v. Barnette, 319 U.S. 624 (1943)
Westendorp v. The Queen, [1983] 1 S.C.R. 43
Withler v. Canada (Attorney General), 2011 SCC 12

BIBLIOGRAPHY

"10 Years as CJ for McLachlin." *Globe and Mail*, January 7, 2010, A1.

Baily, Michael A., and Forrest Maltzman. *The Constrained Court: Law, Politics and the Decisions Justices Make*. Princeton: Princeton University Press, 2013.

Baker, Dennis, and Rainer Knopff. "Minority Retort: A Parliamentary Power to Resolve Judicial Disagreement in Close Cases." *Windsor Yearbook of Access to Justice* 21 (2002): 347.

Balkin, Jack. "'Wrong the Day It Was Decided': *Lochner* and Constitutional Historicism." *Boston University Law Review. Boston University School of Law* 85 (2005): 677.

Barak, Aharon. *Purposive Interpretation in Law*. Princeton: Princeton University Press, 2005.

Bastien, Fréderic. *La Bataille de Londres: Dessous, secrets, et coulisses du repatriement constitutionnel*. Montreal: Les Éditions du Boréal, 2013.

Bergman, Matthew P. "Dissent in the Judicial Process: Discord in the Service of Harmony." *Denver University Law Review* 68 (1991): 79.

Black, Ryan C., and James F. Spriggs II. "The Depreciation of Precedent on the U.S. Supreme Court." Paper presented at the CELS 2009 4th Annual Conference on Empirical Legal Studies. Retrieved September 11, 2011, from http://papers.ssrn.com/sol3/papers.cfm?abstract_id=1421413.

Bobbitt, Philip. *Constitutional Fate: Theory of the Constitution*. New York: Oxford University Press, 1984.

Bushnell, Ian. "The Use of American Cases." *University of New Brunswick Law Journal* 35 (1986): 157.

———. *The Captive Court: A Study of the Supreme Court of Canada*. Kingston: McGill-Queen's University Press, 1992.

Bzdera, Andre. "Comparative Analysis of Federal High Courts: A Political Theory of Judicial Review." *Canadian Journal of Political Science* 26 (1993): 3. http://dx.doi.org/10.1017/S0008423900002420.

Cheffins, Ronald I. "The Supreme Court of Canada: The Quiet Court in an Unquiet Country." *Osgoode Hall Law Journal* 4 (1966): 259.

Choudhry, Sujit, and Kent Roach. "Putting the Past behind Us? Prospective Judicial and Legislative Remedies." *Supreme Court Law Review* 21 (2003): 205.

Cohen-Eliya, Moshe, and Iddo Porat. *Proportionality and Constitutional Culture.* Cambridge: Cambridge University Press, 2013.

Corley, Pamela, Amy Steigerwalt, and Artemus Ward. *The Puzzle of Unanimity: Consensus on the United States Supreme Court.* Stanford, CA: Stanford Law Books, 2013. http://dx.doi.org/10.11126/stanford/9780804784726.001.0001.

Coughlan, Steve. "The End of Constitutional Exemptions." *Criminal Reports* 54 (2008): 220.

D'Amato, Anthony. "Legal Uncertainty." *California Law Review* 71 (1983): 1.

Dari-Mattiacci, Giuseppe, and Bruno Deffains. "Uncertainty of Law and the Legal Process." *Journal of Institutional and Theoretical Economics* 163 (2007): 627. http://dx.doi.org/10.1628/093245607783242990.

Dorsen, Norman. "A Conversation between U.S. Supreme Court Justices— The Relevance of Foreign Legal Materials in U.S. Constitutional Cases: A Conversation between Justice Antonin Scalia and Justice Stephen Breyer." *International Journal of Constitutional Law* 3 (2005): 519.

Dyzenhaus, David. *Judging the Judges, Judging Ourselves: Truth, Reconciliation and the Apartheid Legal Order.* Oxford: Hart Publishing, 1998.

Epp, Charles R. *The Rights Revolution: Lawyers, Activists, and Supreme Courts in Comparative Perspective.* Chicago: University of Chicago Press, 1998.

———. *Making Rights Real: Activists, Bureaucrats and the Creation of the Legalistic State.* Chicago: University of Chicago Press, 2009. http://dx.doi.org/10.7208/chicago/9780226211664.001.0001.

Epstein, Lee, William M. Landes, and Richard A. Posner. "Why (and When) Judges Dissent: A Theoretical and Empirical Analysis." John M. Olin Law and Economics Working Paper No. 510 (January 2010). http://dx.doi.org/10.2139/ssrn.1542834.

Eskridge, William N., Jr., and John Ferejohn. "Super Statutes: The New American Constitution." In Richard W. Bauman and Tsvi Kahana, eds., *The Least Examined Branch: The Role of Legislatures in the Constitutional State.* New York: Cambridge University Press, 2006. http://dx.doi.org/10.1017/CBO9780511511035.017.

———. *A Republic of Statutes: The New American Constitution.* New Haven, CT: Yale University Press, 2010.

———. "Superstatutes." *Duke Law Journal* 50 (2011): 1215. http://dx.doi.org/10.2307/1373022.

Feeley, Malcolm M., and Edward L. Rubin. *Judicial Policy Making and the Modern State: How the Courts Reformed America's Prisons.* New York: Cambridge University Press, 1998.

Fried, Charles. "Balls and Strikes." *Emory Law Journal* 61 (2012): 641.

Gardbaum, Stephen. *The New Commonwealth Model of Constitutionalism.* New York: Cambridge University Press, 2013.

Gibson, James L., Gregory Caldeira, and Vanessa Baird. "On the Legitimacy of National High Courts." *American Political Science Review* 86 (1997): 343.

Girard, Philip. "A Tempest in a Transatlantic Teapot." *Osgoode Hall Law Journal* 51 (forthcoming 2014).

Glenn, Patrick. "Persuasive Authority." *McGill Law Journal* 32 (1987): 261.

Goldsworthy, Jeffrey. "The Preamble, Judicial Independence and Judicial Integrity." *Constitutional Forum* 11 (2000): 60.

Graber, Mark A. *Dred Scott and the Problem of Constitutional Evil*. New York: Cambridge University Press, 2006. http://dx.doi.org/10.1017/CBO9780511805370.

Guttman, Daniel. "*Hislop v. Canada:* A Retroactive Look." *Supreme Court Law Review* 42 (2008): 547.

Hellman, Arthur D. "The Shrunken Docket of the Rehnquist Court." *Supreme Court Review* (1996): 403.

Henderson, M. Todd. "From *Seriatim* to Consensus and Back Again: A Theory of Dissent." *Supreme Court Review* 1 (2007): 283.

Hogg, Peter. *Constitutional Law of Canada. 2012 Student Edition*. Toronto: Carswell, 2012.

———, and Alison Bushell. "The Charter Dialogue between Courts and Legislatures (Or Perhaps the Charter Isn't Such a Bad Thing After All)." *Osgoode Hall Law Journal* 35 (1997): 75.

Huscroft, Grant. "'Thank God We're Here': Judicial Exclusivity in Charter Interpretation and Its Consequences." *Supreme Court Law Review* 25 (2nd series) (2004): 243.

———. "Rationalizing Judicial Power: The Mischief of Dialogue Theory." In James B. Kelly and Christopher Manfredi, eds., *Contested Constitutionalism: Reflections on the Canadian Charter of Rights and Freedoms*. Vancouver: UBC Press, 2009.

Idleman, Scott. "A Prudential Theory of Judicial Candor." *Texas Law Review* 73 (1995): 307.

Issacharoff, Samuel. "The Elusive Search for Constitutional Integrity." *Stanford Law Review* 57 (2004): 727.

Kahana, Tsvi. "The Constitution as a Collective Agreement: Remuneration of Provincial Court Judges in Canada." *Queen's Law Journal* 29 (2004): 487.

Kelly, James. *Governing with the Charter: Legislative and Judicial Activism and Framers' Intent*. Vancouver: UBC Press, 2005.

Kersch, Ken. "The 'Globalizing Judiciary' and the Role of Law." *The Good Society* 13 (2004): 17.

Knopff, Rainer. "Charter Reconsiderations." *National Magazine* 21 (2012): 38.

———, Dennis Baker, and Sylvia LeRoy. "Courting Controversy: Strategic Judicial Decision Making." In James B. Kelly and Christopher Manfredi, eds., *Contested Constitutionalism: Reflections on the Canadian Charter of Rights and Freedoms*. Vancouver: UBC Press, 2009.

Krishnakumar, Anita S. "On the Evolution of the Canonical Dissent." *Rutgers Law Review* 52 (2000): 781.

La Forest, Gérald V. "The Use of American Precedents in Canadian Courts." *Maine Law Review* 64 (1994): 211.

L'Heureux-Dubé, Claire. "The Length and Plurality of Supreme Court of Canada Decisions." *Alberta Law Review* 28 (1989–90): 581.

Landes, William M., and Richard A. Posner. "Legal Precedent: A Theoretical and Empirical Analysis." *Journal of Law & Economics* 19 (1976): 249. http://dx.doi.org/10.1086/466868.

LaRue, L.H. *Constitutional Law as Fiction: Narrative in the Rhetoric of Authority.* University Park: Pennsylvania State University Press, 1995.

Laskin, Bora. "The Supreme Court of Canada: A Final Court of and for Canadians." *Canadian Bar Review* 29 (1951): 1038.

Law, David. "The Declining Influence of the United States Constitution." *New York University Law Review* 87 (2012): 762.

Lederman, W.R. "Judicial Independence." *Canadian Bar Review* 34 (1956): 1139.

Macdonald, Roderick. "The Fridge-Door Statute." *McGill Law Journal/Revue de Droit de McGill* 47 (2002): 11.

Macfarlane, Emmett. "Supreme Court Splits in Messy Decision on Face Veils." *Maclean's*, December 20, 2012. Retrieved February 13, 2013, from http://www.macleans.ca/news/canada/supreme-court-splits-in-messy-decision-on-face-veils.

MacIvor, Heather. "Judicial Review and Electoral Democracy: The Contested Status of Political Parties under the Charter." *Windsor Yearbook of Access to Justice* 21 (2002): 479.

Maclennan, Christopher. *Toward the Charter: Canadians and the Demand for a National Bill of Rights 1929–1960.* Kingston: McGill-Queen's University Press, 2004.

Magliocca, Gerard. "Becoming the Bill of Rights." Indiana University Robert H. McKinney School of Law Research Paper No. 2013–16 (March 20, 2013). Retrieved June 16, 2014, from http://papers.ssrn.com/sol3/papers.cfm?abstract_id=2236457.

Makin, Kirk. "Ruling Ensures Death Penalty Won't Return, Conference Told." *Globe & Mail*, April 13, 2007. Retrieved June 16, 2014, from http://www.theglobeandmail.com/news/national/ruling-ensures-death-penalty-wont-return-conference-told/article4259388.

Mandel, Michael. *The Charter of Rights and the Legalization of Politics in Canada.* Revised edition. Toronto: Thomson Educational Publishing, 1994.

Manfredi, Christopher. "Strategic Behaviour and the Canadian Charter of Rights and Freedoms." In Patrick James, Donald E. Abelson, and Michael Lusztig, eds., *The Myth of the Sacred: The Charter, the Courts and the Politics of the Constitution in Canada.* Kingston: McGill-Queen's University Press, 2002.

———, and James B. Kelly. "Misrepresenting the Supreme Court's Record?" *McGill Law Journal* 49 (2004): 741.

McCormick, Peter. "Judicial Councils for Provincial Judges in Canada." *Windsor Yearbook of Access to Justice* 6 (1986): 160.

———. "The Supreme Court of Canada and American Citations 1949–1994: A Statistical Overview." *Supreme Court Law Review* (2nd Series) 8 (1997): 499.

———. *Supreme at Last: The Evolution of the Supreme Court of Canada.* Toronto: Lorimer Press, 2000.

———. "Compulsory Audience: Appeals by Right and the Lamer Court 1990–1999." Paper presented at CPSA Annual General Meeting, Congress of the Social Sciences and Humanities, Toronto, ON, June 2002.

———. "Second Thoughts: Supreme Court Citations of Dissents and Separate Concurrences, 1949–1996." *Canadian Bar Review* 81 (2002): 369.

———. "New Questions about an Old Concept: The Supreme Court of Canada's Judicial Independence Decisions." *Canadian Journal of Political Science* 37 (2004): 839. http://dx.doi.org/10.1017/S0008423904030951.

———. "The Choral Court: Separate Concurrences on the McLachlin Court 2000–2004." *Ottawa Law Review* 37 (2005–06): 1.

———. "Standing Apart: Separate Concurrence and the Supreme Court of Canada, 1984—2006." *McGill Law Journal* 53 (2008): 137.

———. "Structures of Judgment: How the Modern Supreme Court of Canada Organizes its Reasons." *Dalhousie Law Journal* 32 (2009): 35.

———. "American Citations and the McLachlin Court: An Empirical Study." *Osgoode Hall Law Journal* 47 (2009): 83.

———. "Waiting for Globalization: An Empirical Study of the McLachlin Court's Foreign Judicial Citations." *Ottawa Law Review* 41 (2010): 209.

———. "Sharing the Spotlight: Co-Authored Reasons on the Modern Supreme Court of Canada." *Dalhousie Law Journal* 34 (2011): 165.

———. "'Was It Something I Said?' Losing the Majority on the Modern Supreme Court of Canada, 1984–2011." *Osgoode Hall Law Journal* 50 (2012): 93.

———. "Precedent by the Numbers: The Laskin Court." Paper presented at Midwest Political Science Association Annual Meeting, Chicago, IL, April 2012.

McGuire, Kevin T., and Barbara Palmer. "Issue Fluidity on the United States Supreme Court." *American Political Science Review* 89 (1995): 691. http://dx.doi.org/10.2307/2082983.

McLachlin, Beverley. "The First Decade of the 21st Century: The Supreme Court of Canada in Context." Foreword in Adam Dodek and David A. Wright, eds., *Public Law at the McLachlin Court: The First Decade.* Toronto: Irwin Law, 2011.

Minor, Janet E., and James S.F. Wilson. "Reflections of a Supervisory Order Sceptic: Ten Years after *Doucet-Boudreau*." In Kent Roach and Robert A. Sharpe, eds., *Taking Remedies Seriously.* Ottawa: Canadian Institute for the Administration of Justice, 2009.

Newman, Peter C. *Renegade in Power: The Diefenbaker Years.* Toronto: McClelland and Stewart, 1963.

Note: "From Consensus to Collegiality: The Origins of the 'Respectful' Consent." *Harvard Law Review* 124 (2011): 1305.

O'Brien, David. "A Diminished Plenary Docket." *Judicature* 89 (2005): 134.

Ogilvie, Margaret H. "And Then There Was One: Freedom of Religion in Canada—the Incredible Shrinking Concept." *Ecclesiastical Law Journal* 10 (2008): 197. http://dx.doi.org/10.1017/S0956618X08001191.

Ostberg, C.L., and Matthew E. Wetstein. *Attitudinal Decision Making in the Supreme Court of Canada.* Vancouver: UBC Press, 2007.

Palmer, Barbara. "Issue Fluidity and Agenda Setting on the Warren Court." *Political Research Quarterly* 52 (1999): 39.

Parrish, Austen. "A Storm in a Teacup: The U.S. Supreme Court's Use of Foreign Law." *University of Illinois Law Review* (2007): 637.

Petter, Andrew. "Twenty Years of Charter Justification: From Liberal Legalism to Dubious Dialogue." *University of New Brunswick Law Journal* 52 (2003): 187.

———. "Charter Legitimacy on Trial: The Resistible Rise of Substantive Due Process." In *The Politics of the Charter: The Illusive Promise of Constitutional Rights.* Toronto: University of Toronto Press, 2010. Originally published in *Supreme Court Law Review* 9 (1987).

Pinard, Danielle. "A Plea for Conceptual Consistency in Constitutional Remedies." *National Journal of Constitutional Law* 18 (2006): 105.

Posner, Richard. "A Political Court." *Harvard Law Review* 119 (2005): 31.

Powe, Lucas A. *The Warren Court and American Politics*. Boston: Harvard University Press, 2002.

Primus, Richard A. "Canon, Anti-Canon and Judicial Dissent." *Duke Law Journal* 48 (1998): 243. http://dx.doi.org/10.2307/1373107.

Renke, W.N. *Invoking Independence: Judicial Independence as a No-Cut Wage Guarantee*. Edmonton: Centre for Constitutional Studies, University of Alberta, 1994.

Robertson, David. *The Judge as Political Theorist: Contemporary Constitutional Review*. Princeton: Princeton University Press, 2010.

Rosenberg, Morris, and Stephan Perreault. "Ifs and Buts in Charter Adjudication: The Unruly Emergence of Constitutional Exemptions in Canada." *Supreme Court Law Review* 16 (2002): 375.

Ryder, Bruce. "Suspending the Charter." *Supreme Court Law Review* 21 (2003): 289.

Scalia, Antonin. "The Dissenting Opinion." *Journal of Supreme Court History* 19 (1994): 33.

Schauer, Frederick. "Easy Cases." *Southern California Law Review* 58 (1985): 399.

Shapiro, Martin. *Courts: A Comparative and Political Analysis*. Chicago: University of Chicago Press, 1986.

Siegel, Neil. "Umpires at Bat: On Interpreters and Legitimation." *Constitutional Commentary* 24 (2007): 701.

Slaughter, Anne-Marie. "Judicial Globalization." *Virginia Journal of International Law* 40 (2003): 1103.

Slayton, Philip. *Mighty Judgment: How the Supreme Court of Canada Runs Your Life*. Toronto: Penguin Group, 2011.

Smithey, Shannon Ishiyama. "A Tool, Not a Master: The Use of Foreign Case Law in Canada and South Africa." *Comparative Political Studies* 34 (2001): 1188. http://dx.doi.org/10.1177/0010414001034010004.

Snell, James G., and Frederick Vaughan. *The Supreme Court of Canada: History of the Institution*. Toronto: University of Toronto Press, 1985.

Solove, Daniel. "The Problem with Superprecedents." Concurring Opinions Weblog. Retrieved October 30, 2005, from http://www.concurringopinions.com.

Starr, Kenneth. "The Supreme Court and Its Shrinking Docket." *Minnesota Law Review* 90 (2006): 1363.

Stratas, David. "Damages as a Remedy against Administrative Authorities: An Area Needing Clarification." In Robert J. Sharpe and Kent Roach, eds., *Taking Remedies Seriously*. Ottawa: Canadian Institute for the Administration of Justice, 2009.

Stribopolous, James. "Has Everything Been Decided? Certainty, the Charter and Criminal Justice." *Supreme Court Law Review* 34 (2nd series) (2006): 381.

Sugunasiri, Shalin M. "Contextualism: The Supreme Court's New Standard of Judicial Analysis and Accountability." *Dalhousie Law Journal* 22 (1999): 126.

Sunstein, Cass R. *One Case at a Time: Judicial Minimalism on the Supreme Court*. Boston: Harvard University Press, 2001.

Terrell, Timothy P. "Flatlaw: An Essay on the Dimensions of Legal Reasoning and the Development of Fundamental Normative Principles." *California Law Review* 72 (1984): 288. http://dx.doi.org/10.2307/3480480.

Tibbetts, Janice. "Politicians Duck Divisive Issues, Chief Justice Says." *National Post*, July 12, 1999, A4.

Tushnet, Mark. "'Shut Up' He Explained." *Northwestern University Law Review* 95 (2001): 907.

———. "When Is Knowing Less Better Than Knowing More? Unpacking the Controversy over Supreme Court Reference to Non-U.S. Law." *Minnesota Law Review* 90 (2005–06): 1276.

———. *Weak Courts, Strong Rights: Judicial Review and Social Welfare Rights in Comparative Constitutional Law*. Princeton: Princeton University Press, 2009.

Walker, Vaughn R. "Moving the Strike Zone: How Judges Sometimes Make Law." *University of Illinois Law Review* (2012): 1207.

INDEX

Page numbers in italics refer to figures and tables.